Understanding Business

Accounting and Decision Making

Third Edition

D. R. Myddelton and Peter Corbett

Longman

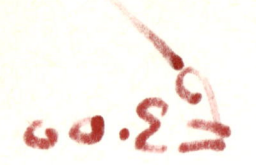

LONGMAN GROUP UK LIMITED
Longman House
Burnt Mill, Harlow, Essex CM20 2JE *England*
and Associated Companies throughout the World

© Cambridge Business Studies Project Trust 1977, 1978, 1984

All rights reserved. No part of this publication
may be reproduced, stored in a retrieval system,
or transmitted in any form or by any means, electronic,
mechanical, photocopying, recording or otherwise,
without the prior permission of the copyright owner.

First published 1977
Second edition 1978
Third edition 1984
Third impression 1986

ISBN 0 582 35476 5

Set in 10/12 pt Plantin, Linotron 202

Printed in Great Britain
by Bell and Bain Ltd., Glasgow

Contents

Acknowledgements   iv
Introduction to the Series   v
Preface to Third Edition   vii

PART I   Background
 1 Accounting   1

PART II   Financial Accounting
 2 The Financial Statements   9
 3 Foundations of Accounting   21
 4 The Balance Sheet   36
 5 The Profit and Loss Account   59
 6 Depreciation of Fixed Assets   80
 7 Valuing Stock   96
 8 Accounting for Inflation   116
 9 Analysing Accounts   138

PART III   Management Accounting
 10 Costs and Budgets   163
 11 Budgeting in Action   186

APPENDICES:
 1 Retail Price Index since 1970   204
 2 Professional bodies and qualifications   204
 3 Accounting abbreviations and acronyms   205

Glossary   206

Index   219

Acknowledgements

We are grateful to the following companies for permission to use statistics from their annual accounts: Beecham Group, BOC International, Courtaulds, and The Rank Organisation; and to The Controller of Her Majesty's Stationery Office for permission to use the Retail Price Index statistics from the Employment Gazette, in Appendix 1 and in Figures 8.1 and 8.2.

Introduction to the Series

This series produces a new approach to the teaching of business. It is suitable for young managers, students and academic sixth-formers. It has been developed over the last decade to give understanding of the nature and purpose of business activity, whilst also stimulating the minds of the more academically gifted members of society.

The material provides for an analytical understanding of people's problems and behaviour within organisations. The texts discuss the nature of problems, and explore concepts and principles which may be employed to aid their solution. Test materials have been selected from industrial and commercial organisations; from the private and public sector; from non-profit-making institutions. The material is as much to provide general understanding about industrial society and the workings of organisations, as it is to help those who are already engaged in their business or professional career.

The approach of decision-making has been used to draw together ideas, and produce significant elements of reality; the approach gives purpose and challenge to the reader. Any organisation is striving towards more or less closely defined objectives by deciding how to carry out, and control, its activities within constantly changing conditions. The programme looks carefully at these processes of decision-making; it provides the student with an understanding of their overall nature. Ideas from the four functional areas of human behaviour, quantitative data, accounting and the economic environment are drawn together within a decision-making framework; the approach is then applied to different areas of business activity, particularly to those of finance, marketing and production.

This series of eight books has been designed to meet the needs of students (and their lecturers/teachers) studying the business world. The up-to-date materials within each book provide many ideas and activities from which the teacher can choose. Lecturers on management courses may use the books to introduce analytical concepts to practitioners; tertiary management courses may use them as a first text and as a source of well-tried and up-to-date cases; BEC and 'A' Level students may use the books as complete courses.

To meet these different needs, each book in the series has been designed to stand either as a part of the whole, or complete in its own right.

All books have the same chapter format:
a chapter objective and synopsis so that the purpose and pattern are clear;
a factual/explanatory text with case examples where applicable;
a participative work section to provide materials for learning, application and discussion.

The participative sections are an integral part of the whole text and allow students to gain understanding by doing. They are usually divided into three parts. Firstly, some simple revision questions to enable the students to check their own basic understanding. Secondly, a series of exercises and case problems to test their application and to increase their knowledge of the area. Thirdly, a set of essay questions.

There is a teachers' booklet accompanying each student text which introduces the topic area, clarifies possible objectives, suggests approaches to the selected materials and adds additional ideas. The teachers' booklets also provide solutions, where appropriate, to the participative work sections.

The philosophy, approach and materials have been forged in discussion with businessmen, lecturers and teachers. Trial and error has refined much of the text and most of the participative work. The whole venture has been co-ordinated by the Cambridge Business Studies Project Trust. Initial work developed from a link between the Wolfson Foundation, Marlborough College and Shell International Ltd. Trustees for the Project include Professor John Dancy, Sir Michael Clapham and Sir Nicholas Goodison; much early guidance was also given by Professor Sir Austin Robinson.

The series can be used as the basis for an 'A' Level examination run by the Cambridge Local Examinations Syndicate and established in 1967. The examination syllabus and objectives are in line with the materials in these texts.

Richard Barker
Series Editor

Preface

This book is for people who are studying business decisions. It is intended to introduce the concepts, language, and methods of accounting in the context of business decision-making. It covers external financial accounting and (more briefly) internal management accounting.

The scope of the book is wide. It should be useful for people in business, as well as for students in business schools, polytechnics and colleges of further education, and for sixth-formers on business studies courses. Most of the essential assumptions and related problems in modern accounting are touched on, and there is plenty of participative material to assist and challenge a student.

Part I consists of a single background chapter describing and contrasting the scope of financial accounting and management accounting. Part II contains eight chapters dealing with financial accounting. Finally, in Part III, there are two chapters on management accounting.

This third edition is based firmly on the previous editions by Peter Corbett, though in preparing it I have worked independently of Peter Corbett, who is abroad. Apart from Chapter 8, on Accounting for Inflation, which is substantially revised, and Chapter 10, on Costs and Budgets, which is new, the remaining chapters follow the framework of the earlier editions fairly closely. Chapters 3 and 4 of the earlier editions have now been combined in Chapter 3, Chapters 5 and 6 in Chapter 4, Chapters 8 and 9 in Chapter 6, and Chapters 13 and 14 in Chapter 9. These are changes of form rather than of substance.

At the start of each chapter there is a detailed list of contents together with a brief synopsis. The entire text has been completely revised and updated. In particular the vertical (columnar) form of balance sheet has generally been substituted for the horizontal format, which is now becoming outdated.

The book, like others in this series, contains at the end of each chapter many revision questions, exercises and case studies, and essay questions.

The A Revision Questions, averaging about 35 per chapter, are related to the text material, and set out in the same order. They are meant to be helpful as 'instant revision' after reading a chapter or part of one. Between them the A questions cover nearly all the points made in the text.

Apart from Chapter 1, most of the chapters contain 10 to 15 B Exercises and Case Studies. Nearly all the B questions from the previous editions have been retained, but the total number of questions has been more than doubled. In accounting, perhaps more than many subjects, it is essential for students to have the opportunity to work on a number of detailed problems to give them practice and confidence.

The number of C Essay Questions has been increased to 10 per chapter. Clearly there are many more B and C questions than any one person is likely to want, so there is a need to be highly selective in their use.

A feature of this book, as of others in the series, is the Glossary at the end, which has also been significantly extended. It contains definitions and descriptions of about 220 common words or expressions used in accounting. These are shown in **bold letters** the first time they appear in the text.

I have tried to avoid unnecessary jargon; but accounting has its own technical language, with which students need to be familiar. Whenever you come across a word or phrase you don't understand, it is good practice to look it up *at once* in the Glossary. Otherwise you may believe that you understand the text when you don't. Common abbreviations and acronyms are listed in Appendix 2 (p. 204).

Finally there is an extensive index. The letter G as the first item after the index entry means that the word or phrase is shown in the Glossary.

The book is intended for readers working on their own, as well as for students enrolled on courses. For teachers there is an extensive Teacher's Guide available from the publishers. It contains worked answers to all the B questions, as well as detailed summaries of key points in each chapter, suggestions about alternative ways of using the text, and an analysis of B questions by chapter section and by 'difficulty' grading.

I would like to acknowledge helpful comments from Marek Kwiatkowski, John Powell, and Ron Stevens at Marlborough College, and from Richard Barker, Headmaster of Sevenoaks School, the series editor. I should also acknowledge that I may have gained some knowledge of accounting (and of text-book writing) from Professor Walter Reid of the London Business School.

D. R. Myddelton

Part I Background

1 Accounting

1.1 Users of Accounts
1.1.1 Types of Users
1.1.2 Needs of External Users

1.2. Purpose of Accounting
1.2.1 Financial Accounting
1.2.2 Management Accounting
1.2.3 Differences between Financial and Management Accounting

1.3. Accounting as a Profession
1.3.1 The Different Professional Bodies
1.3.2 Characteristics of Accountants

Objective: *To explain who uses accounts, the differences between financial and management accounting, and some characteristics of accountants.*

Synopsis: *'Outsiders' (mainly shareholders and lenders) use financial accounts, while 'insiders' use management accounts.*

Financial accounting, originally based on 'stewardship', tells owners and others at regular intervals about a business's financial performance and position. Its basic aim is to present a 'true and fair view' of past results for the whole business. Management accounting is more concerned with the future: it helps managers to plan and control, and often deals with only parts of a business.

Qualified accountants may work in public practice as professional accountants and auditors, in industry (either as financial or as management accountants), or in the public sector.

1.1 Users of Accounts

1.1.1 Types of Users
Accounts provide financial facts about a business. Who needs them, and why? We can show the role of accounting in business decisions by asking some

hypothetical questions. They are of two kinds: those asked by 'outsiders' (people external to the firm), and those asked by 'insiders' (managers working in the firm).

'Outsider' questions
* *As a shop steward representing the production workers, you have been chosen to ask the management of your firm for a wage increase. How can you find out if the managers are right to say: 'No; we can't afford it.'?*
* *A golfing friend who runs a local furniture business walks into the branch bank of which you are manager. He asks for a bank loan to tide his firm over a sticky patch. How will you decide what to do?*

'Insider' questions
* *As managing director of a large firm with branches all over the country, how can you control the performance of each branch? How can you measure your firm's success or failure? What can you do to improve matters?*
* *After several years of making a good profit, your company suddenly finds itself making a loss. How will you set about finding out why?*

To answer any of the above questions, you need financial information. This is what accounts aim to provide. There are many different potential users of accounting information, as set out in Fig. 1.1.

	Shareholders	Lenders	
Suppliers			Customers
	Managers		
Workers			Competitiors
	National Government	Local Community	

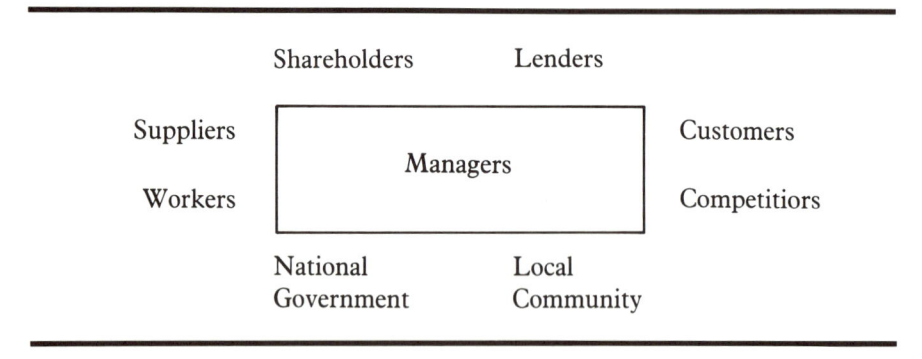

Fig. 1.1: Potential users of accounting information

1.1.2 Needs of External Users
Not all external users have the same needs for accounting information. Moreover their desire to receive it must be set against the cost of producing it, as well as the occasional need to maintain commercial secrecy. In publishing accounts, company directors must comply with legal requirements and with statements of standard accounting practice (see **3**.1.3). But they still have some discretion over how much accounting information to publish, and in what form.

Shareholders are legal owners of shares in a company. They are entitled to know how well the managers are running their business.

Accounting 3

Bankers and others will not lend money without being satisfied about a borrower's ability to pay regular interest and to repay the loan in due course.

Customers may require information about a supplying company, to ensure continuity of supply, to be assured that spares and replacements will be available if needed for products with a long life, and to be confident that a firm is financially sound if they make deposits or payments in advance.

Competitors will be interrested in comparing their own financial performance with that of other companies in the same industry. They may also wish to participate in formal schemes of interfirm comparison (see Ch. 11).

The local community will be interested in prospects for local employment, and also in any plans to increase production capacity. Companies' annual reports and accounts represent one potential source of such information.

The national government needs to know how a company is doing, for purposes of taxation, as well as to collect and publish a variety of aggregate statistics.

Workers may want to know both about profits, as an indication of the possibility of wage increases, and about long-term prospects for secure employment.

Suppliers will want to be sure that buying firms are well able to pay, where goods and services are supplied on credit.

1.2 Purpose of Accounting

1.2.1 Financial Accounting

This book deals mainly with **financial accounting***, which provides financial information for external users. At the end of the book, Chapters 10 and 11 discuss **management accounting**, which is used by business managers to run their firms. This section discusses some differences between the two.

For generations, households themselves could provide for people's needs. But as the population expanded, from about 1750, the numbers living in towns grew. As a result, the amount of trading by means of market exchanges greatly increased.

There were business firms before the Industrial Revolution, but their accounting needs were not complex. The village cobbler was clearly doing well if, after buying his leather, he earned enough surplus cash to feed, clothe, and house his family properly.

The last 200 years have brought a vast expansion in the need for accounting information. The evolution of **limited companies** began to separate the ownership of a firm from its day-to-day management, as the size of firms increased. Hence some way was needed for the managers to report regularly to the owners on their **stewardship**.

Early accounting was often 'venture accounting'. A ship set sail from Plymouth for the Indies, laden with supplies. When it reappeared two years

---

* Words and phrases shown in **bold letters** are explained in the Glossary (pp 206–218)

later, the value of the treasure on board, less the value of the supplies taken at the start, showed what **profit** or loss the venture had made.

Modern business firms are intended to last for decades, not to be **wound up** at the end of a specific venture. (Indeed, some people seem to think survival itself is now a major corporate objective.) Moreover, the use of long-lasting capital equipment makes more difficult the provision of annual accounting information. Figure 1.2. shows how the need for regular accounting statements in effect requires the continuing flow of a modern enterprise's operations to be 'chopped up' into artificial short periods. We shall see in later chapters how this gives rise to important problems of valuation of assets and measurement of profits.

...Ongoing stream of business events...

Regular accounting statements

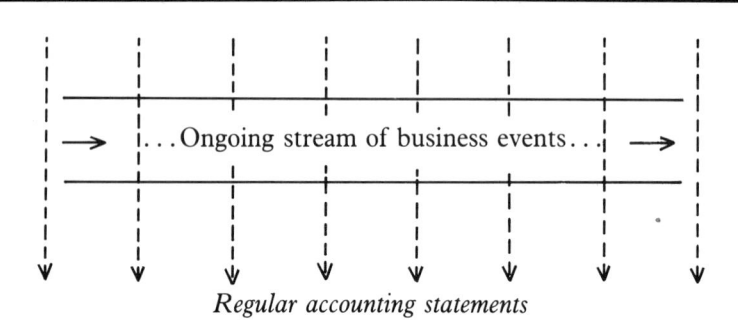

Fig. 1.2: 'Chopping up' business operations into short time periods

1.2.2 Management Accounting

Management accounting aims to help business managers to run their firms. Of course accounting *alone* is not nearly enough. Managers also need technical production data, about technology and raw materials, market research about customers' wishes and competitors' actions, and much else. But a great deal of accounting information is essential to run a modern business of any size.

Management accounting is based on two different disciplines:
1. Economics, dealing with the use of scarce resources.
2. Behavioural science, dealing with how individuals and groups behave in organisations.

Management accounting has four main purposes, covering different time periods:

1. Score-keeping   PAST
2. Problem-solving   PRESENT
3. Controlling   PRESENT
4. Planning   FUTURE

The score-keeping function is much like that required for external accounting. The sorts of problems that management accounting may be able to

Accounting 5

help solve are: (a) should a firm accept a special low price for a bulk order, if a factory is running well below capacity? (b) is it worth installing a new cost-saving machine? (c) would it be a good idea to change the basis on which sales commissions are paid? (d) why is the Newcastle office so much more expensive than the larger Birmingham one?

Two other major aspects are planning and control. **Planning** involves co-ordinating the activities of different parts of a business, gaining the agreement of various responsible managers to their part in the plan, and projecting possible outcomes of future events. **Control** involves monitoring the actual outcome against the agreed budget, and where necessary taking corrective action. Chapter 10 describes the budget process in more detail.

1.2.3 Differences between Financial and Management Accounting

Figure 1.3. outlines several differences between financial accounting and management accounting.

	Financial accounting	*Management accounting*
1. Use	External	Internal
2. Time direction	The past	The future
3. Coverage	Whole company	Divisions and sub-groups
4. Nature of data	Somewhat technical	For use by non-accountants
5. Emphasis	Accuracy	Speed
6. Accounting unit	Money*	Money* or physical units
7. Governed by	Company law, SSAPs	Managers' needs
8. Ideally	Objective, verifiable	Relevant, useful

* But see Chapter 8 on inflation accounting

Fig. 1.3: Differences between financial and management accounting

1.3 Accounting as a Profession

1.3.1 The Different Professional Bodies

There are nearly 150,000 **qualified** accountants in the British Isles, belonging to one of six different professional bodies. The six bodies act together in certain matters, for example in agreeing **Statements of Standard Accounting Practice**

(SSAPs). For this purpose there is a single body, called the Consultative Committee of Accountancy Bodies (CCAB). In general, qualified accountants work either in professional accountancy firms ('in practice'), in industry and commerce, or in various government organisations. Figure 1.4 lists the membership of each body of accountants.

	('000 members)	
Chartered Accountants		
England and Wales (ICAEW)	76	
Scotland (ICAS)	11	
Ireland (ICAI)	5	
	—	92
Certified Accountants (ACCA)		25
Cost and Management Accountants (ICMA)		22
Public Sector Accountants (CIPFA)		9
		148

Fig. 1.4: Membership of professional accountancy bodies

Only **chartered accountants** and **certified accountants** are allowed to act as **auditors** of limited companies under the Companies Acts (see 2.4.6). Many of them work 'in the profession', either as partners or as employees in firms of professional accountants. But many chartered accountants, who have to be trained in the offices of such firms, move into industrial jobs after they have qualified. (They do so by completing their period of training, and passing the necessary examinations.) Thereafter they may be involved in financial accounting work for companies, in management accounting work, or in other work (often of a financial nature).

Cost and management accountants, as the name implies, tend to work in management accounting. Their examinations emphasise that aspect of accounting work; and they are not permitted to act as auditors. Nevertheless a fair number become financial accountants in industry.

CIPFA stands for the Chartered Institute of Public Finance and Accountancy; and its members work as financial or management accountants in the public sector, mostly employed either by local authorities or by one of the nationalised industries.

In general chartered and certified accountants tend towards financial accounting, and cost and management accountants towards management accounting. But members of any of the professional bodies may work in either

Accounting

area – or in others (such as teaching). The examinations of all the professional bodies cover both financial and management accounting, though in different proportions. Other subjects include: company law, taxation, and economics.

Many new accountants now (though by no means all) are university graduates. But they certainly need not have studied accountancy at university. An accounting degree incorporates no practical training, which is regarded as essential for professional qualification.

1.3.2 Characteristics of Accountants

Financial accountants in industry supervise the **book-keeping** records, and generally scrutinise all financial aspects of running a firm. Once a year they summarise all these activities in the company's **published accounts**. (Larger companies also publish **interim accounts** during the year.) Acting as independent professional external auditors, they check that a company's **accounts** give a **true and fair view** of its affairs.

Management accountants in industry obtain and present information to managers, for the purpose of planning and controlling the business. They provide data for specific decisions, as well as preparing routine monthly reports of operations. Larger firms employ management accountants as **internal auditors** to review their management information systems.

Figure 1.5 lists some of the main qualities required of financial and management accountants in industry. Clearly there is much common ground.

Financial accountant
a. Knowledge of:
　(i) accounting techniques for all likely situations;
　(ii) company law and auditing requirements;
　(iii) taxation law, especially as it affects companies.
b. Ability to:
　(i) work to schedule under severe time pressure;
　(ii) control office staff of all ages;
　(iii) deal with people at all levels in a firm, from store-keepers to top management and auditors.
c. Numeracy and a liking for precision.

Management accountant
a. Knowledge of:
　(i) financial accounting concepts and methods;
　(ii) data processing methods and equipment;
　(iii) economics and modern management methods.
b. Ability to:
　(i) present relevant information clearly;
　(ii) grasp the inter-relationships of different parts of a business;
　(iii) work with employees at all levels.
c. Imagination and a persistent nature.

Fig. 1.5: Qualities needed by financial and by management accountants

Work Section

A. Revision Questions

A1 What two kinds of user may require accounting information?
A2 How might their needs differ?
A3 Name three different external users of accounts.
A4 How might their needs differ?
A5 For whom are internal accounts prepared?
A6 Name two modern developments which have affected accounting.
A7 Name aspects of management accounting dealing with:
    (a) the past;   (b) the present;   (c) the future.
A8 What do you understand by   (a) planning?   (b) control?
A9 Into which categories can professional accountancy bodies be split?
A10 What is the role of the financial accountant in industry?
A11 What is the role of the management accountant?
A12 Name four differences between financial and management accounting.
    Identify as many qualities as you can which are needed by:
A13   financial accountants
A14   management accountants
A15   *both* financial and management accountants.

C. Essay Questions

C1 'A company with no accounts would be a ship without a rudder.' Discuss.
C2 Explain why and how the financial accountant and management accountant should co-operate with each other.
C3 Write a memo to the managing director of your company explaining why you think he should create a department of management accounting.
C4 As personnel officer, design a questionnaire to be filled in by a prospective applicant for the post of management accountant.
C5 As personnel officer, design a questionnaire to be filled in by a prospective applicant for the post of financial accountant.
C6 Is there good reason for several separate professional accountancy bodies?
C7 In what respects may different external users of accounts require different sorts of financial information?
C8 How are internal management needs for accounting information likely to differ from the needs of external users of accounts?
C9 Might you be suited to a career in accounting? Why or why not?
C10 Explain why management accounting depends both on economics and on behavioural science.

Part II Financial Accounting

2 The Financial Statements

2.1 Introduction

2.2 A Personal Example

2.3. Company Accounts
2.3.1 The Balance Sheet
2.3.2 The Profit and Loss Account

2.4 Additional Statements
2.4.1 Notes to the Accounts
2.4.2 The Directors' Report
2.4.3 The Chairman's Statement
2.4.4 Statistical Tables
2.4.5 The Funds Flow Statement
2.4.6 The Auditors' Report

Objective: *To outline the purpose of the two main accounting statements, the balance sheet and profit and loss account; and to describe the other statements comprising a company's 'accounts'.*

Synopsis: *The balance sheet shows the financial position of a business at a point in time, while the profit and loss account shows how much profit or loss has been made in a period (usually one year).*

The balance sheet lists assets (what a business owns) and liabilities (what it owes to others), and the difference represents the owners' equity in the business. The profit and loss account for a period deducts expenses from sales revenue to determine profit or loss.

The other component parts of a company's 'accounts' are: notes to the accounts, the directors' report, the report of the auditors, and (for larger companies) a funds flow statement. Other statements, not part of the accounts, may be useful; such as the chairman's statement and tables of statistics covering a number of past years.

2.1 Introduction

Business accounts try to answer two different questions:
1. What is the financial position at a particular point of time?
2. What profit or loss has the business made during a given period?

A simple analogy can illustrate the difference between them:

Imagine that you set out to record on video tape a day in the life of a local market trader. During the day many people visit his stall: some buy fruit, while others just look and then move on. Those who buy hand money to the trader, who puts it in a cash drawer behind the stall.

When you get home that evening, you want to find out what the position was at 12 noon. So you run the tape through, and freeze it when you get to that moment. You can see how many apples, bananas, and so on the trader had left on his stall, and the amount of cash in the drawer. A complete list of these things would be a 'stock' of his possessions: it would describe the state of affairs of the business at the instant at which the film was frozen.

You may then want to know what the trader sold between 12 noon and 4 p.m. You re-start the film; and as it runs through, you note down what fruit is handed to customers, and how much money they pay the trader. If you summarised all these transactions, you would have a measure of the 'flow' of events for the four-hour period.

When the film is again frozen, you can make a second list of the trader's stock of possessions at 4 p.m.

A company regularly buys and sells goods and services during its life. It needs to summarise its position from time to time, and its transactions in between. In this way accounts can provide both 'stock' and 'flow' information.

Of course the transactions and position of a business cannot be summarised by purely physical descriptions. The various kinds of possessions and activities are too different for that. Instead *money* is the 'common denominator' in accounts, used to allow different objects and events to be added or compared. So a company translates all physical amounts into terms of money, in order to express the measures of 'stocks' and 'flows' in a single **unit of account**.

2.2 A Personal Example

To illustrate these principles, we can look at a year in a person's life, before going on to consider the more complex affairs of a company in business.

Example: On 1 January, Alison Robbins sits at her desk and lists her possessions. Next to each she writes an estimate of its money value. Then she calculates a total from the individual values, as shown in Fig. 2.1.

It might seem that Alison's 'wealth' amounts to £25,900; but she almost forgot that she owes the building society £12,000, which she borrowed four years ago to buy her house. So her net wealth is not £25,900 but only £13,900.

Exactly one year later, Alison sits down again, and summarises her financial

The Financial Statements

	(£)
One semi-detached house	20,000
Furniture and household goods	4,000
One three-year-old car	1,800
Current account at the bank	100
Total	25,900

Fig. 2.1: Alison's possessions at start of year

transactions during the past year (Fig. 2.2). She gets this information from the records she has kept. Her pay slips tell her how much she has earned in her job, and her cheque book counterfoils show how much she has spent, and on what. She lists separately her receipts and her payments; and then subtracts the total of the payments from the total receipts.

	(£)
Receipts	
Monthly wages (*less* PAYE tax deductions)	5,000
Payments	
To building society (of which £700 interest)	1,500
Rates, light and heat, etc.	900
Housekeeping	1,200
Motor car running expenses	500
Clothing, holiday, etc.	600
	4,700
Surplus of receipts over payments:	£ 300

Fig. 2.2: Alison's receipts and payments during the year

During the year Alison has received £300 more than she paid out. But does this mean her 'wealth' is now exactly £300 more than it was at the start of the year?

When she lists her possessions again (Fig. 2.3), she finds, of course, that she has £300 more cash in her current account with the bank than she had a year earlier. But she owes less to the building society, since £800 of the £1,500 paid during the year was to reduce the loan outstanding (the rest being interest). She also recognises that not all the values shown a year ago still apply. The car and the household furniture have partly worn out during the year, and are now worth somewhat less than before (Ch. 6 discusses such 'depreciation'). On the other hand, she believes the house has actually risen in value. Alison identifies all these changes in Fig. 2.3, and compares her list of possessions at the beginning of the year (shown in Column A) with those at the end of the year (Column B).

	A Start of year	B End of year
	(£)	(£)
One semi-detached house	20,000	21,500
Furniture and household goods	4,000	3,600
One four-year-old car	1,800	1,400
Current account at the bank	100	400
	25,900	26,900
less: Owing to building society	12,000	11,200
Net 'wealth':	13,900	15,700

Fig. 2.3: Alison's 'wealth' at the start and end of the year

Alison's net 'wealth' appears to have increased by £1,800 during the year, which is much more than the £300 increase in her bank balance. In the light of the adjustments she made to the valuations of her various possessions, Alison is able to prepare a statement (Fig. 2.4) showing the sources of her increase in wealth during the year.

	(£)
Increase in value of house	+1,500
Fall in value of car, furniture, etc.	− 800
Surplus of income over living expenses★	+1,100★
Net increase in wealth during the year:	+1,800

★ £5,000 income less £3,900 expenses (= £4,700 less £800 mortgage repaid).

Fig. 2.4: Alison's increase in wealth during the year

The Financial Statements 13

2.3 Company Accounts

In the last section we saw how an individual might work out how much her possessions and liabilities amount to in money terms at a particular date. (Don't worry if you found it hard to see exactly where all the numbers came from: at this stage it's the general idea that matters.)

A company produces each year a document called a **balance sheet** which is broadly similar to Alison's statement of 'wealth' in Fig. 2.3. A company also produces a statement called a **profit and loss account**, which describes the result of a year's trading, in much the same way that Alison did in Fig. 2.4.

The accounting ideas involved in a domestic example also largely apply to limited companies. The main changes are in terminology and degree of complexity. A company's 'accounts' consist of these two statements, the balance sheet and the profit and loss account, together with certain other documents to be described later in this chapter. Together they summarise the results of a year's trading. Here we merely outline these statements: we discuss them in much more detail in Chapters 4 and 5.

2.3.1 The Balance Sheet

The balance sheet of a company shows the equivalent of the 'wealth' of an individual – with one important exception. Companies usually value their possessions (called **assets**) at their *original cost* (**historical cost**), not – as Alison did – at their current market values. The traditional balance sheet format (Fig. 2.5) sets out assets on the right-hand side, and **liabilities** (what is owed to others) on the left. The difference between the two is written in on the left-hand side to make the two totals equal (hence the name 'balance sheet'). This 'difference' is called **owners' equity** (or **shareholders' funds**).

Shareholders' funds	Assets
Liabilities	

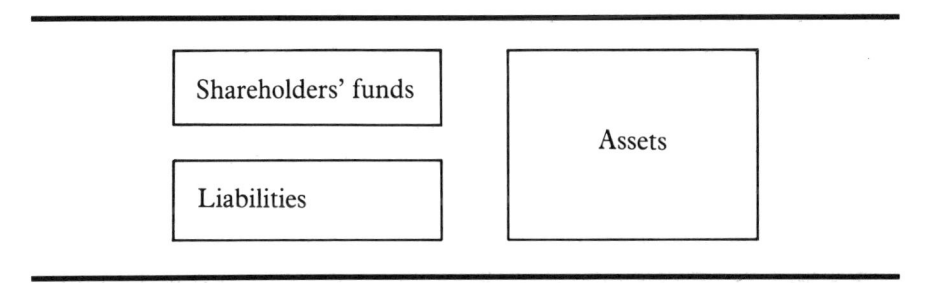

Fig. 2.5: Traditional balance sheet format

Companies must produce balance sheets at yearly intervals, but they can choose when to end their **financial years**. Some companies choose the calendar year, ending on 31 December; others choose the tax year, ending on 5 April. (The British tax year used to end on 25 March, a quarter day, until eleven days were 'lost' in September 1752 on the change to the Gregorian calendar!) Other companies choose year ends which suit the nature of their business: for example, many department stores end their year on 31 January, after the end of the post-Christmas sales; and many schools on 31 August, at the end of the academic year.

Chapter 4 discusses the balance sheet in more detail. Meanwhile, Fig. 2.6 shows a 'balance sheet' for Alison's financial position at the end of her year.

	£		£
Owner's equity		*Assets*	
Alison's 'wealth'	15,700	House	21,500
		Furniture and household	
		goods	3,600
Liability		Car	1,400
To building society	11,200	Cash at bank	400
	26,900		26,900

Fig. 2.6: Net 'Wealth' of Alison Robbins at end of year

2.3.2 The Profit and Loss Account

The profit and loss account summarises changes in shareholders' funds due to trading and other operations. Chapter 5 discusses in detail how **sales revenues** are determined for a period, and how the amount of expenses is estimated. The surplus is the profit for the period (or any deficit is called a *loss*, if total expenses exceed sales revenue).

Figure 2.7 outlines the relationship between the profit and loss account for a year and the beginning and ending balance sheets. We already know that the amount of profit may not be reflected in an identical increase in the asset *cash*; so the profit for the year is simply added to total assets, without being specified as any particular assets.

2.4 Additional Statements

2.4.1 Notes to the Accounts

The main 'accounts' are the profit and loss account for a period, and the balance sheet at the end of the period. But for various reasons some detailed information is shown, not on the face of the accounts, but instead in separate **notes to the accounts**. For example, the notes will contain details of fixed assets, of changes in shareholders' funds due to capital transactions, and of long-term liabilities. The modern practice of simplifying the basic accounts means that the notes

The Financial Statements 15

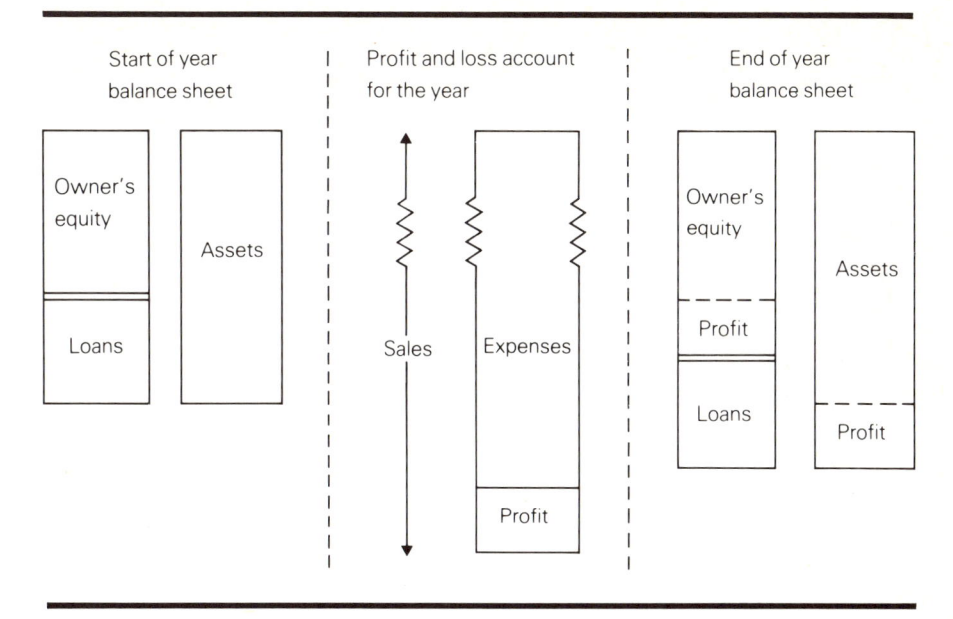

Fig. 2.7: Relationship between profit and loss account for a year and beginning and ending balance sheets.

contain important information. They should strictly be regarded as a *part* of 'the accounts', not merely as an optional extra.

2.4.2 The Directors' Report
Company law requires a **directors' report** with the financial statements. It contains certain details, if not mentioned elsewhere, such as the number of employees and their total wages; changes in the board of directors during the year; and an analysis of trading results by product and by geographical area.

2.4.3 The Chairman's Statement
Although not required to do so, the chairmen of most public companies publish a statement with the annual accounts. This is broader in scope than the directors' report; it comments on figures for the past period, and may indicate prospects for the future. It can discuss factors which are not easily quantifiable, such as political events. Although it is not strictly a part of the accounts, the chairman's statement should be read carefully by anyone trying to analyse company accounts.

2.4.4 Statistical Tables
In addition to all the financial statements mentioned so far (including the notes to the accounts), most public companies also publish a table of financial statistics at the end of their annual reports. These summarise the main

accounting information over the past five or ten years. They are not subject to audit, as a rule, and need to be interpreted with some care. In particular, comparing **trends** over many years is difficult without proper allowance for inflation (see Ch. 8).

2.4.5 The Funds Flow Statement

In addition to the balance sheet and profit and loss account, in recent years a third financial statement has been required for larger companies. This reflects the increased emphasis placed on *cash* in times of rapid inflation. As we have seen, the balance sheet sets out a company's financial position as at a particular point in time, listing its assets, liabilities and shareholders' funds. The profit and loss account shows sales revenue and expenses for a period, and the resulting profit or loss.

The **funds flow statement** shows a company's new sources and new uses of funds for a period. In its simplest form it may be regarded as a statement showing balance sheet *changes* between the beginning and end of a period. (In contrast, a balance sheet may be regarded as showing the *cumulative* sources and uses of funds of the business ever since it was started.) Funds flow statements are discussed in more detail in **9**.4.

2.4.6 The Auditors' Report

Under the Companies Acts, a company's *directors* are responsible for its published accounts. But limited companies must also have their accounts 'audited'. An **audit** is an examination of accounts by professional accountants who are independent of the company's management, in order to determine whether they present a true and fair view of the state of the company's affairs.

A standard form of auditors' report to a set of company accounts might read as follows:

We have audited the financial statements in accordance with approved auditing standards. In our opinion the financial statements give a true and fair view of the company's state of affairs as at the (end of the financial year) and of the profit (or loss) for the year then ended, and comply with the Companies Acts 1948 to 1981.

The auditors are acting on behalf of a company's owners – its shareholders. They do not assert that the accounts are 'correct'; as we shall see later, preparing company accounts involves many subjective estimates and judgements. Nor do auditors *guarantee* to discover any fraud that may have occurred. (A famous legal judgment called the auditor 'a watchdog not a bloodhound'.)

Where the auditors are *unable* to report that in their opinion the accounts give a true and fair view, then they must say so in their report. They must **qualify** their report, and give reasons for doing so. Where there is substantial *uncertainty*, the auditors may *disclaim* any opinion. (They would say: 'We are unable to express an opinion.') Where there is *disagreement*, the auditors may express an *adverse* opinion. (They would say: 'In our opinion the accounts do *not* give a true and fair view...')

The Financial Statements

Examples of uncertainty might include:
 (i) lack of proper accounting records;
 (ii) doubts about the company's ability to continue as a going concern (such as those expressed in British Steel's 1982 accounts);
 (iii) inherent uncertainties in relation to major litigation or long-term contracts (such as those expressed in Vosper's 1982 accounts in relation to the company's large claim for compensation in respect of nationalised interests).

Examples of disagreement might include:
 (i) failure to follow Statements of Standard Accounting Practice;
 (ii) disagreement as to facts or amounts included in the accounts;
 (iii) disagreement as to the manner or extent of disclosure in the accounts.

Where the auditors disagree with the directors' proposed treatment of certain accounting items, there is likely to be pressure on the directors to change their treatment, and on the auditors not to 'qualify' their report. Often one side or the other gives way, and the fact of the disagreement never becomes public knowledge.

Work Section

A. Revision Questions

A1 What two questions do business accounts try to answer?
A2 How can diverse business activities be summarised?
A3 Why did Alison Robbins need to deduct her building society mortgage in estimating her 'wealth'?
A4 Why did Alison's wealth change by a different amount than the change in her bank balance?
A5 What are the two main documents contained in a set of company accounts?
A6 What does a company 'balance sheet' show?
A7 What are three main headings in a balance sheet?
A8 How often must companies publish balance sheets?
A9 What does a company 'profit and loss account' show?
A10 What are three main items in a profit and loss account?
A11 What does the chairman's statement contain?
A12 What does the funds flow statement show?
A13 How does the funds flow statement differ from the balance sheet?
A14 What are the notes to the accounts?
A15 When may auditors 'qualify' their report on a company's accounts?

B. Exercises and Case Studies

B1 a. Make a list of all your personal possessions and liabilities as of three months ago, and value them to estimate your 'wealth'. Do the same as of now. Try to construct a statement which will show how the difference in your 'wealth' came about.

b. Write down any problems you came across in giving values to any of your possessions or transactions. How did you resolve these problems? Do you think your solutions are completely satisfactory? If not, why not?

B2 A further year has passed for Alison Robbins (see **2.2**). At the end of it, she reckons her house's value is unchanged, while the value of her furniture and household goods, and of her car, have each declined by a further £400. Her receipts and payments for the year are listed below:

The Financial Statements 19

	(£)
Receipts	
Monthly wages (*less* PAYE tax deductions)	5,400
Payments	
To building society (of which £600 interest)	1,300
Rates, light, heat, etc.	1,000
Housekeeping	1,300
Motor-car running expenses	700
Clothing, holiday, etc.	500
	5,200
Surplus of receipts over payments:	£ 200

a. Draw up a list of Alison's 'wealth' as at end of second year.
b. Prepare a statement accounting for the change in Alison's wealth during second year.

B3 Your local village grocer, knowing you are studying accounting, asks for your help. He wants to know how his company stands at the year end, and what sort of year it had. He provides you with the following information about the company, which is called Village Traders Ltd. All the figures refer either to the year ended 31 March, or to that date itself.

	(£)
Paid wages to Mrs Molloy	1,248
Value of delivery van at end of year	1,600
Cost of goods sold to customers	23,480
Salary paid to self	5,200
Sales of goods to customers	36,940
Value of shop building and land as at end of year	20,000
Cash in the till and at bank	700
Sundry expenses paid (e.g. rates, telephone, etc.)	3,500
Amounts owing to suppliers at end of year	1,200

You are also told that during the year property values in the area have risen, but because the general state of repair of the shop has deteriorated, its value has, on balance, stayed the same as a year ago. The van, on the other hand, was worth £2,000 a year ago, but is now a year older, and hence has been valued at a lower figure.

B4 John Clippitt is a barber. In the year which has just ended, his records disclose the following transactions. Draw up a profit and loss account for the year ended 31 March.

	(£)
Wages to John Clippitt	3,600
Wages to apprentice	1,000
Cash received for haircuts	10,000
Lease of premises for year	1,200

Cost of electricity and telephone	500
Sundry small expenses	300
New chair bought and installed on 30 March	600
Income from sub-lease of a surplus room	300
Tax paid on profits	1,700

N.B. The value of the equipment has not changed much during the year.

C. Essay Questions

C1   A close friend of yours has decided to set up in business as a butcher. What sorts of information would you advise him to collect in order to prepare accounts? How might he record this information?

C2   How would you work out whether you are living within your current income? (How *do* you work it out?)

C3   You are the accountant for a small business which has recently been inherited by the son of the founder. He knows nothing of accounting, and asks you to write him a brief memo explaining what the financial accounts are intended to show him.

C4   What are the advantages and disadvantages of using money as a common denominator in accounting?

C5   The chairman of a medium-sized company is wondering whether for the first time to publish a separate statement with the company's annual report, which will be distributed to the company's 500 shareholders. As the company secretary, write him a brief memo arguing either for or against this proposal.

C6   What does the funds flow statement show that the profit and loss account and balance sheet between them do not?

C7   Why should company accounts be audited, even if company law did not require it?

C8   If auditors do not guarantee either that published accounts are correct, or to discover any fraud which may have been perpetrated, how can they justify their fees?

C9   Explain why additional documents are needed in a set of accounts, besides the balance sheet and profit and loss account.

C10 Explain to someone who knows nothing about accounting what is meant by a 'true and fair view'.

3 Foundations of Accounting

3.1 Accounting Guidelines
3.1.1 Fundamental Concepts
3.1.2 Accounting Conventions
3.1.3 Legal and Other Requirements

3.2 Double-entry Accounting
3.2.1 Exchanging Assets and Liabilities
3.2.2 Changes in Shareholders' Funds
3.2.3 Recording Business Transactions

Objective: *To identify the fundamental concepts and conventions which underlie financial accounts, and to illustrate the essence of the double-entry approach in accounting.*

Synopsis: *Four fundamental concepts in accounting are: going concern, accruals, consistency, and prudence. Four conventions are: separate entity, double entry, money terms, and historical cost. Conventions may change if they cease to be useful. Statements of Standard Accounting Practice (SSAPs) based on these guidelines aim to narrow differences of approach in preparing accounts without suppressing independent judgement of complex businesses. In addition, there are certain legal and other requirements, but these too mostly focus on the need for accounts above all to present a 'true and fair view'.*

Each transaction has two aspects in double-entry accounting, and affects a balance sheet in one of only four possible ways:

1. Asset   +   2. Liability   +
   Asset   −   Liability   −
3. Asset   +   4. Asset   −
   Liability +   Liability   −

The profit and loss account summarises for a period all the trading transactions which affect shareholders' funds. A simple example illustrates how the balance sheet shows the cumulative *results of business transactions to date.*

3.1 Accounting Guidelines

The basic purpose of financial accounts is to show a 'true and fair view' of a business's financial position and profit or loss for a period. There are two sets of guidelines which help accountants to prepare accounts which will give a true and fair view: fundamental concepts, and accounting conventions. In addition, there are certain legal and other requirements which must be followed.

Ideally any accountant should follow the guidelines sufficiently closely to produce a similar picture from the same underlying data. But as we shall see in more detail later, *judgement* is also important in preparing accounts. In complex businesses, competent accountants can honestly exercise their independent judgement quite differently. Thus often there is not *only one* 'true and fair view' that could be derived from a specific set of events and transactions.

Figure 3.1 summarises the main fundamental concepts, conventions, and legal and other requirements affecting financial accounts.

Legal and other requirements
a. Companies Acts
b. Statements of Standard Accounting Practice
c. Stock Exchange requirements

Fundamental concepts
a. Going concern
b. Accruals
c. Consistency
d. Prudence

Conventions
a. Separate entity
b. Double entry
c. Money terms
d. Historical cost

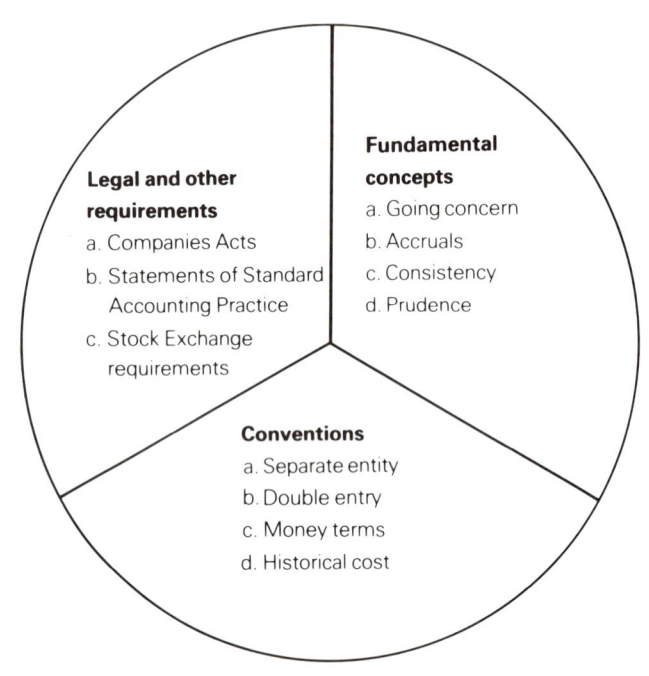

Fig. 3.1: Accounting guidelines

3.1.1 Fundamental Concepts

Four fundamental accounting concepts underlie the figures in any set of accounts:

a. Going concern
b. Accruals
c. Consistency
d. Prudence.

Foundations of Accounting 23

a. The **going concern** concept assumes that an enterprise will continue in business in the foreseeable future. This normally means valuing assets *at cost*, on the assumption that they are worth at least this much. An alternative might be to assume that the business was soon going to be wound up (liquidated). It might then be prudent to value assets at the amount they would realise on immediate sale (which might be less than cost).
b. The **accruals** concept tries to match expenses against revenues. It recognises revenues as they are earned and expenses as they are incurred. In general the timing coincides with the delivery of goods or the performance of services. An alternative approach would be to recognise transactions only when *cash* was received or paid; but this would be less realistic in a credit economy. (But some non-commercial activities, such as government operations, still use cash accounting.)
c. The **consistency** concept requires the same treatment for similar items. Otherwise comparing accounting results between periods and between businesses would be meaningless. (The same concept applies to all statistics.)
d. The **prudence** concept means that accounts include revenues (and profits) only when they are 'realised', either in cash or in the form of assets whose ultimate cash proceeds are reasonably certain. In contrast, full provision is made at once for all known losses and expenses, even where their amount has to be estimated. This concept is sometimes called 'conservatism'.

Do not worry if the full implications of these concepts are not immediately obvious. Later chapters will spell them out in much more detail. For example, the 'matching' principle is discussed in Chapters 5 and 6, and the 'prudence' concept in connection with valuing stocks in Chapter 7. You may find it useful to refer back to the four concepts listed in this sub-section from time to time as you go through the book.

As a rule the fundamental concepts and accounting conventions also apply to management accounting, though *not* the legal and other requirements.

3.1.2 Accounting Conventions

As accounting has developed over the centuries, certain procedures (known as **conventions**) have become generally accepted, and are now taken for granted everywhere. They have been adopted because they have been found useful; but if conditions were to change in future, they might need to be modified or even abandoned. Four of the most basic conventions are:

a. Separate entity
b. Double entry
c. Money terms
d. Historical cost.

(a) Separate entity
A company is a legal 'person' in its own right, completely separate from its managers, owners, and employees. The accounts of a company therefore deal only with the affairs of the company. This is obvious with large companies:

Unilever's balance sheet does not include the personal possessions of its directors! But with small companies, where the owners are also the managers, care may be needed to separate the personal affairs of the owners from those of the business.

(b) Double entry
Section 3.2 discusses **double-entry accounting**, which Goethe called 'the finest invention of the human mind'. It means that any transaction can be looked at from two points of view. Any funds *used* by a company (e.g. to buy equipment) have to be obtained *from* somewhere (e.g. from a bank loan). Similarly, any funds that *have* been obtained from somewhere (e.g. share capital from the owners) must be *used* somehow (even if only to place on deposit with a bank).

(c) Money terms
Traditionally the accounting 'unit of measurement' is money, which is often regarded as the 'language' of business. Many diverse business activities can be expressed in terms of money and added together, or subtracted from one another. But only those matters which are capable of being expressed in money are included in financial statements. (Thus the state of the managing director's liver cannot be allowed for – even though it may be an important business fact!) Another disadvantage of using money as the unit of account has become apparent in recent years, with soaring rates of inflation. Chapter 8 discusses how accounts can try to cope with inflation.

(d) Historical cost
Another accounting convention is to use original cost to value assets, rather than current value. This may seem odd at first sight. (For instance, Alison Robbins naturally tried to estimate the current value of her various possessions in 2.2.) As a rule, though, accountants have preferred to use definite known historical cost figures which can be independently verified, rather than current values which can only be estimated with a very wide margin of error. In times of inflation, however, historical cost figures can become far removed from current values; which is why one of the proposals for 'inflation accounting' (discussed in Ch. 8) involves the use of current values in accounts in place of historical costs.

3.1.3 Legal and Other Requirements

(a) Companies Acts
The legal requirements with respect to company accounts are laid down in various Companies Acts. The main requirement is that accounts should show a 'true and fair view' of the state of a company's affairs and of the profit or loss for the year. It is also the Companies Acts that require accounts to be audited.

In general the British Companies Acts have tended not to be too specific in laying down precise rules, for example about the format to be adopted in accounts. But more recently, since the UK's entry into the European Economic Community, some more detailed regulations have started to apply. (They are imposed by UK Companies Acts as a result of European agreement.)

(b) Statements of Standard Accounting Practice
Since the early 1970s a series of Statements of Standard Accounting Practice (SSAPs) have been issued by the accountancy bodies. They are issued in two stages: first an **Exposure draft** (ED), indicating what is proposed; then, following comments and arguments, an SSAP – which may represent a major change from the exposure draft if necessary.

SSAPs are mandatory, in that companies are supposed to follow them; though they do not carry the force of law. In practice some companies sometimes fail to abide by an SSAP. If they have good reasons, their auditors will agree with their failure; if not, not. It is widely recognised both that there are advantages in having uniform methods for dealing with particular accounting problems, and that there are dangers in trying to force very different kinds of business into following a single set of rules.

SSAPs have dealt with many of the major accounting problem areas: inflation accounting, depreciation, stock valuation, tax, foreign currencies, and so on. From time to time an SSAP may be revised in the light of new conditions, or changes in professional views.

(c) Stock Exchange Requirements
Listed companies, whose shares are quoted on the **Stock Exchange**, are subject to stock exchange regulations. (One of them is that SSAPs must be followed.) These tend to be more detailed than the Companies Acts, and tend to require more disclosure. The penalty for failing to follow the stock exchange's requirements, in theory, would be for the company's 'quotation' to be suspended. But in practice there would be a good deal of debate before such a drastic step was taken for a major company.

The over-riding tenor of British rules about accounting is to insist on extensive disclosure of what has been done. There is much less keenness for official bodies to prescribe exact accounting treatment in any particular case; but external parties are thought entitled to know how a company has seen fit to treat transactions.

3.2 Double-entry Accounting

3.2.1 Exchanging Assets and Liabilities
We have already mentioned the double-entry principle in accounting. It is the reason why the balance sheet always 'balances'; and why, in total, the sources of funds on the left-hand side of the balance sheet always equal the uses of funds on

the right-hand side. Figure 3.2 repeats Fig. 2.5 in showing the basic layout of the balance sheet.

Sources of Funds   *Uses of funds*

Shareholders' Funds	
Liabilities	Assets

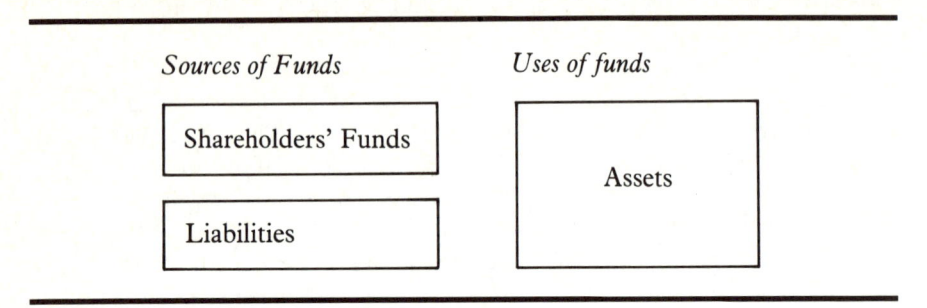

Fig. 3.2: Traditional balance sheet format

Each transaction has two aspects. For example, when a company buys goods on credit, it obtains the goods (an asset), but at the same time it incurs an obligation to pay for them later (a liability). Double-entry accounting records *both*. Any transaction must affect the balance sheet in one of the four ways shown in Fig. 3.3 In each case, the two aspects exactly offset each other, so the balance sheet will continue to balance.

a.		Asset + Asset −
b.	Liability + Liability −	
c.	Liability +	Asset +
d.	Liability −	Asset −

Fig. 3.3: The four effects of transactions on a balance sheet

Let us now look at a simple example of each kind of transaction, and the resulting changes to the balance sheet.

Foundations of Accounting

(a) *Asset + / Asset –*
A company buys stock for £100 cash.

	Stocks	+ £100
	Cash	– £100

(b) *Liability + / Liability –*
A company increases its bank overdraft by £500 to pay a supplier (trade creditor) who is pressing for settlement of his account. The company still owes the same total amount, but to different people. £500 more is now owed to the bank, £500 less to trade creditors.

Bank overdraft	+ £500	
Trade creditors	– £500	

(c) *Liability + / Asset +*
A motor vehicle is purchased, on credit, for £4,000. So an asset has been acquired in return for an obligation to pay later (a liability).

Creditor	+ £4,000	Motor vehicle	+ £4,000

(d) *Liability – / Asset –*
A company draws a cheque for £300 to pay trade creditors who supplied goods some months earlier.

Trade creditors	– £300	Cash	– £300

In each of the above transactions it is clear that both sides of the balance sheet remain equal in total.

3.2.2 Changes in Shareholders' Funds

The four examples just used to illustrate the double-entry principle all involved a straightforward exchange of one asset or liability for another. We now look at three examples of transactions which affect shareholders' funds. They still fall within the four categories listed in Fig. 3.3 (where the term 'liability' was used to refer to 'shareholders' funds and liabilities').

1. A company sells goods from stock. The cost of the goods was £50, and the company sells them on credit for £65. Thus there is a profit of £15. *This is attributed to shareholders' funds.* The changes on the balance sheet are as follows:

Shareholders' funds		Stocks	– £50
Profit & Loss Account	+ £15	Debtors	+ £65

2. A company issues more **shares** to increase the funds at its disposal. In return for the new issued share capital, the **shareholders** pay in £180,000 cash. From the company's point of view, this is a *receipt* of cash.

Shareholders' Funds			
Issued Share Capital	+ £180,000	Cash	+ £180,000

3. A company pays £14,000 cash on wages. This is an expense, which reduces the profit. Hence it reduces shareholders' funds on the balance sheet.

Shareholders' Funds			
Profit & Loss Account	− £14,000	Cash	− £14,000

Many transactions affect the amount of shareholders' funds in the balance sheet. The profit and loss account shows the success or failure of a company in making profits. It is a summary of all the trading transactions in a given period which affect the shareholders' funds. But as example (2) above showed, not all transactions affecting shareholders' funds are necessarily related to the profit and loss account. They would be referred to as **capital** transactions, as opposed to **revenue** transactions (see also 5.2.2).

3.2.3 Recording Business Transactions

The previous two sub-sections dealt with the balance sheet changes resulting from exchanging assets and liabilities and changes in shareholders' funds. Now we illustrate the effects of a series of business transactions on the balance sheet of a new company.

To simplify the picture, each set of transactions is supposed to occur in a different month. Apart from the initial issue of shares, the first few transactions do not affect shareholders' funds. This is a little unrealistic: in practice it would be unusual for a business to wait for three months before starting to trade.

Example: *Keith and Ray Thompson are brothers. They decide to start their own business in the baking industry. They ultimately hope to produce their own high quality bread and cakes; but plan to begin by building up three good retail shops in neighbouring towns.*

The new company is to be called Thompson Brothers Limited. It will need share capital of £60,000, and Keith and Ray agree to provide half each. Each month's transactions are set out separately below.

(a) *In January the company issues share certificates to the two brothers, each for 30,000 £1 shares, in exchange for two cheques for £30,000. A company account is opened at the bank, and the two cheques are paid in.*

Double entry:

Shareholders' Funds		Assets	
Issued Share Capital	+ £60,000	Cash	+ £60,000

(b) *In February the company buys three freehold properties for its shops. These cost a total of £78,000, half of which is paid for by raising a mortgage bond (liability) with an insurance company.*

Double entry:

Liability		Assets	
Mortgage bond	+ £39,000	Freehold property	+ £78,000
		Cash	− £39,000

Foundations of Accounting 29

At the end of February the company's balance sheet appears as shown in Fig. 3.4.

	(£)		(£)
Shareholders' Funds		*Fixed Assets*	
Issued Share Capital	60,000	Freehold property	78,000
Long-term liability		*Current asset*	
Mortgage bond	39,000	Cash at bank	21,000
	99,000		99,000

Fig. 3.4: Thompson Brothers Ltd Balance Sheet: end of February.

(c) *In March, fitting out the shops and buying the required equipment cost the company £12,000, which was paid for in the same month.*
Double entry:

	Assets	
	Equipment	+ £12,000
	Cash	− £12,000

You should be able to arrive at a new balance sheet, as at the end of March, by making suitable changes to the end-of-February balance sheet shown in Fig. 3.4.

(d) *In April, the company began trading. In the month it bought goods (bread and cake) costing £6,000 on credit, and cash sales from the three shops totalled £10,000. Each Saturday afternoon unsold stocks were given to a local orphanage, as they would be unsaleable by Monday morning. During the month, wages of £2,000 were paid.*

Double entry:

(i)	Trade creditors	+ £6,000	Stocks	+ £6,000
(ii)	*Shareholders' Funds* Profit & Loss Account	+ £4,000	Stocks Cash	− £6,000 + £10,000
(iii)	*Shareholders' Funds* Profit & Loss Account	− £2,000	Cash	− £2,000

Figure 3.5 sets out the company's balance sheet at the end of April, with the balance sheet now presented in £'000.

	(£'000)		(£'000)
Shareholders' Funds		*Fixed Assets*	
Issued Share Capital	60	Freehold property	78
Profit & Loss Account	2	Equipment	12
	62		90
Long-term Liability		*Current Asset*	
Mortgage bond	39	Cash at bank	17
Current Liabilities			
Trade creditors	6		
	107		107

Fig. 3.5: Thompson Brothers Ltd Balance Sheet: end of April

(e) During the remaining eight months of the year to 31 December, the company undertook the following transactions in total:
1. Bought goods costing £46,000, and owed suppliers £5,000 at year-end.
2. Made cash sales totalling £80,000; had no stocks left at year-end.
3. Paid wages of £16,000.
4. Paid £8,000 in respect of the mortgage bond; £4,000 in interest, and £4,000 capital repayment to reduce the size of the loan.
5. Purchased a delivery vehicle for £3,000 cash.
6. Paid £5,000 of other overhead expenses.
7. Provided for £2,000 depreciation on the equipment.

Figure 3.6 sets out the company's balance sheet as at the end of December, after all the above transactions. You should be able to check it, stage by stage.

	(£'000)		(£'000)
Shareholders' Funds		*Fixed Assets*	
Issued Share Capital	60	Freehold property	78
Profit & Loss Account	9	Equipment	10
	69	Delivery vehicle	3
Long-term Liability			91
Mortgage bond	35	*Current Asset*	
		Cash at bank	18
Current Liabilities			
Trade creditors	5		
	109		109

Fig. 3.6: Thompson Brothers Ltd Balance Sheet: end of December.

Work Section

A. Revision Questions

A1 What is the basic purpose of financial accounts?
   What do you understand by:
A2   the 'going concern' concept?
A3   the 'accruals' concept?
A4   the 'consistency' concept?
A5   the 'prudence' concept?
A6 What recent phenomenon has brought the 'money' convention into doubt?
A7 Name two implications of the 'materiality' convention.
A8 How does the law affect company accounts?
A9 What are Statements of Standard Accounting Practice (SSAPs)?
A10 Why are standard rules necessary in accounting? What are their possible drawbacks?

A11 What is the double-entry principle?
A12 What does the double-entry principle imply for the balance sheet?
A13 List the four basic ways in which transactions can affect the balance sheet.
A14 How does the double-entry principle deal with goods being sold for more than they cost?
A15 Name two kinds of transactions which affect shareholders' funds.
A16 What does the profit and loss account for a period contain?
A17 What is the essential difference between a cash and a credit transaction?
A18 Does it affect shareholders' funds differently if a transaction is for cash or on credit?
A19 Must every transaction involve a cash payment or receipt? Explain.
A20 What happens when a transaction is not for cash?
   What happens to a company's total assets when:
A21 it issues new shares to pay off a loan?
A22 it sells land to buy new machinery?
A23 it issues new shares to buy a new building?
   What happens to a company's total liabilities when:
A24 cash is used to repay a loan?
A25 a long-term loan is raised to repay a short-term loan?

B. Exercises and Case Studies

B1 Which of the following transactions will directly affect shareholders' funds?
   a. The sale of goods for more than they cost.
   b. The sale of goods for less than they cost.
   c. A loan to the company by a shareholder.
   d. The payment of last year's tax.
   e. The payment of insurance premiums.

B2 Write out the appropriate double entry for each of the following transactions, in the same way as in **3.2.3**.
   a. The purchase of a machine in cash for £26,000.
   b. The repayment of a loan of £10,000.
   c. The sale of a freehold property costing £5,000 for the same amount.
   d. The purchase of a motor lorry on hire purchase for £4,500, with a deposit of £500.
   e. The sale of goods costing £500 for £650 on credit.
   f. The payment of wages of £1,000.
   g. The sale of goods costing £800 for £650 in cash.
   h. The theft of an uninsured vehicle valued at £1,500.
   i. The purchase of raw materials on credit for £14,000.
   j. The provision for taxation of £800.
   k. The sale of some land, costing £6,000, for £17,000.
   l. The raising of extra capital by issuing 10,000 ordinary shares for £1 each.

B3 Refer to **3.2.3** (c). Draw up a balance sheet for Thompson Brothers Ltd as at the end of March.

B4 Refer to **3.2.3** (e). Draw up a profit and loss account for the year ended 31 December. (Hint: Remember the trading in April.)

B5 What balance sheet items would change (and how) in each of the following transactions?
   a. A purchase of machinery for £20,000, of which 25 per cent is to be paid at once, the balance to be paid later.
   b. The issue of 50,000 £1 $11\frac{1}{2}$ per cent Preference Shares, fully paid up.
   c. The purchase, for 65p per share, of 10,000 25p ordinary shares in a company which has a total issued share capital of 15,000 shares.
   d. The sale of goods, which cost £15,000, for £25,000, payment to be made 30 days from the date of sale.
   e. The cash sale of a piece of equipment for £3,600, which originally cost £8,000, but which has had £5,000 provided for depreciation over the five years of its life to date.

B6 Write out the double entry for each of the following transactions undertaken by Lopsided Ltd after its formation on 1 January. Give a complete balance sheet at the end, as at 30 June, incorporating the effect of all the transactions.

Foundations of Accounting

	(£'000)
a. Share capital paid in on 1 January	200
b. Land purchased on 4 January	20
c. The company built its own factory between 4 January and 16 May, incurring the following costs:	
(i) Wages paid to builders	7
(ii) Building materials	4
(iii) Subcontractors' charges:	
Electricians	2
Plumbers	3
d. On 12 June the company buys materials, ready to commence production	20
e. On 16 June machinery which it had ordered several months previously arrives, and is paid for	30
f. Up to 30 June expenditure is incurred on installing the machinery	6

Identify any assumptions you have had to make.

B7 In year 2, Thompson Brothers Ltd had the following transactions (in summary):

	(£'000)
1. Freehold property bought for two more shops	53
2. Equipment purchased for new shops	7
3. Mortgage bond increased by	30
4. Payments in respect of mortgage bond:	
Interest	7
Capital repayment	6
5. Purchases of goods	140
6. Cash sales	217
7. Paid wages	49
8. Purchased another delivery vehicle	4
9. Paid various overhead expenses	16
10. Provided for depreciation:	
Equipment	4
Delivery vehicles	2

At the end of the second year, £12,000 was owed to suppliers. You are asked to provide for taxation on the second year's profits, at an estimated rate of 50 per cent of the profit for the year.

a. Prepare a balance sheet as at the end of year 2.
b. Prepare a profit and loss account for year 2.

B8 Give *one* example of a business transaction which would immediately result in *each* of the following balance sheet changes:

Cash and profit
a. Profit   +   Cash   +

Cash not profit
b. Liabilities   +   Cash   +

Profit not cash
c. Profit   +   Assets   +
d. Profit   −   Assets   −
e. Profit   −
   Liabilities −
Neither profit nor cash
f. Liabilities −   Assets   +

NB. 'Profit' refers to the cumulative retained profits in the shareholders' funds part of the 'shareholders' funds and liabilities' part of the balance sheet.

B9 *Seven Days in May*

Clinker Ltd's balance sheet as at 1 May 1984 is set out on page 35. Each of the following events occurs on successive days in the first week of May.

2 May. 1,000 new £1 ordinary shares are issued for a total of £1,000 cash.

3 May. A tax liability of £400 is paid.

4 May. New fixed assets costing £700 are purchased, by means of:
  (i) a new long-term loan of £500
  (ii) a cash payment of £200.

5 May. £600 is received from credit customers (Debtors).

6 May. £900 is paid to creditors.

7 May. Stocks which had cost £1,000 are sold on credit to customers for £1,500.

a. Show, in the columns set out, the *change* to the balance sheet resulting from each event (*not* the new balance sheet amount). Each of the six columns should 'balance'.

b. Show in the right-hand column the balance sheet amounts as at the end of 7 May 1984. Check that your balance sheet balances.

C. Essay Questions

C1 'To give no weight to matters incapable of money valuation renders the whole basis of accounting invalid.' Support or oppose this view.

C2 Write an essay supporting Goethe's view that 'Double entry accounting is the finest invention of the human mind.'

C3 'Flexibility in financial accounting is both necessary and potentially dangerous.' Discuss.

C4 'Uniform standards for published financial accounts are both necessary and potentially misleading.' Discuss.

C5 'The concepts of consistency and prudence may conflict; if so, practical accountants prefer prudence, while academics advocate consistency.' Discuss.

Foundations of Accounting 35

Clinker Ltd

Balance Sheet as at 1 May 1984	(1) £	(2) £	(3) £	(4) £	(5) £	(6) £	(7) £	Balance sheet as at 7 May 1984
Shareholders' funds								
Issued £1 Share Capital	2,000							
Retained profits	2,600							
	4,600							
Long-term loans	2,200							
Current liabilities								
Creditors	2,400							
Tax payable	900							
Dividend proposed	300							
	3,600							
	10,400							
Fixed assets	3,700							
Current assets								
Stocks	2,600							
Debtors	3,000							
Cash	1,100							
	6,700							
	10,400							

4 The Balance Sheet

4.1 Introduction

4.2 Shareholders' Funds
4.2.1 Ordinary Share Capital
4.2.2 Reserves
4.2.3 Preference Share Capital

4.3 Liabilities
4.3.1 Long-term Liabilities
4.3.2 Current Liabilities

4.4 Assets
4.4.1 Fixed Assets
4.4.2 Current Assets

4.5 Presentation
4.5.1 Format
4.5.2 The Use of Notes to Accounts
4.5.3 Rounding Numbers
4.5.4 Comparative Figures
4.5.5 Example

Objective: *To describe the various items in balance sheets under three headings: shareholders' funds, liabilities, and assets; and to discuss how balance sheets are presented.*

Synopsis: *The balance sheet shows the financial position of a business as at a particular date. The usual modern format is 'vertical', with shareholders' funds and liabilities, and assets, shown* underneath *each other (in either order).*

Shareholders' funds consist of issued ordinary share capital, reserves, and (sometimes) preference share capital. The three main kinds of reserves arise from share premiums, revaluations, and retained profits.

Long-term liabilities are not due to be settled for more than a year from the balance

The Balance Sheet

sheet date, and thus form part of the (long-term) 'capital employed' of a business; whereas current liabilities are due for payment within one year.

Fixed assets are long-term resources owned by a business, classified between tangible, intangible, and financial (investments). Current assets are expected to be turned into cash within one year from the balance sheet date; they are usually grouped with current liabilities, and the net difference is known as 'working capital'.

4.1 Introduction

A balance sheet is a statement of the financial position of a business as at a particular date. It shows the cumulative sources and uses of funds of the business. The balance sheet is *not* intended to show the 'true worth' of a business. Even apart from serious valuation problems, many valuable assets are excluded, especially internally-generated intangible long-term assets such as business 'know-how'. In Chapter 2 we saw the **horizontal format**, with shareholders' funds and liabilities on the left-hand side, and assets on the right-hand side. Figure 4.1 shows the main balance sheet headings.

Sources of funds	*Uses of funds*
Shareholders' Funds	Fixed Assets
Long-term Liabilities	
Current Liabilities	Current Assets

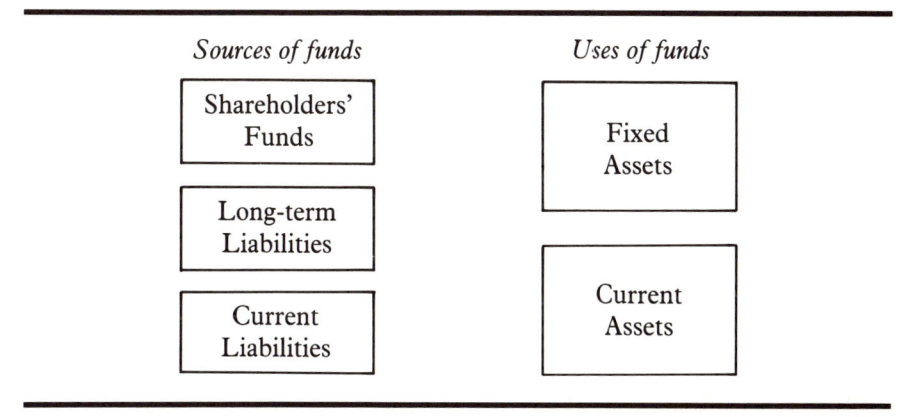

Fig. 4.1: Main headings in a horizontal balance sheet

Nowadays, however, balance sheets are usually set out in a **vertical format**, with assets shown *underneath* shareholders' funds and liabilities. (Or the other way round: treatment varies.) The totals are still equal to each other, so the balance sheet still balances!

Whether assets appear above or below shareholders' funds and liabilities in the vertical balance sheet, the items within each heading appear in order of liquidity. Thus the least liquid asset, or longest-term liability, is at the top; and the most liquid asset, or shortest-term liability, at the foot.

Figure 4.2 shows a detailed balance sheet skeleton in vertical format, setting out the items to be discussed in this chapter. This should be a useful source of reference for constructing balance sheets yourself.

Balance Sheet of (name of company) as at (date)

		(£'000)
Sources of funds		
Shareholders' Funds		
Issued Ordinary Share Capital		xxx
Reserves: Share premium	xxx	
Revaluation	xxx	
Retained profits	xxx	
	——	xxx
Ordinary Shareholders' Funds		xxx
Preference Share Capital		xxx
		—— xxx
Long-term Liabilities		xxx
Current Liabilities		
Creditors and accrued charges	xxx	
Bank overdrafts	xxx	
Taxation	xxx	
Dividends payable	xx	
	——	xxx
		xxx
Uses of funds		
Fixed Assets		
Tangible	xxx	
Intangible	xxx	
Financial	xxx	
	——	xxx
Current Assets		
Stocks	xxx	
Debtors and prepayments	xxx	
Cash and liquid resources	xxx	
	——	xxx
		xxx

Fig. 4.2: Skeleton of a vertical balance sheet

The Balance Sheet

4.2 Shareholders' Funds

Shareholders' funds are provided directly or indirectly by the owners of the business. They may be regarded as ultimate 'liabilities' of a company to its shareholders. But amounts become legally payable to shareholders only when the directors of a continuing company declare **dividends** out of profits. Thus shareholders' funds, as a rule, represent *permanent* capital.

4.2.1 Ordinary Share Capital

A new company issues **ordinary share capital** to its original shareholders, in return for cash (or other assets). To increase the total funds at their disposal, existing companies may issue more ordinary shares during their life. Each company records its shareholders and the number of shares they own, and issues numbered certificates of ownership. Shareholders may be individual persons, companies, or various financial institutions such as life assurance companies, pension funds, or unit trusts.

Shares can be of any amount, often either £1 or 25p units. Shareholders must legally authorise companies to issue share capital; and the total **authorised share capital** (shown in the Notes) may be larger (but never smaller) than the **issued share capital** in the balance sheet.

If the stock exchange 'quotes' a company's shares, any owner can sell them to someone else. The market price of each share fluctuates from day to day depending on demand and supply. The company records the change of ownership in the share register, and issues a new share certificate in place of the old one. But its total issued share capital does not change as a result of such dealings on the 'second-hand' market.

Only ordinary shareholders are normally entitled to vote at the company's general meetings, and they elect the company's directors. In large public companies, most individual shareholders (including the directors) hold only a very small proportion of the total shares issued. So if they are dissatisfied, their only choice is usually whether or not to *sell* their shares. But in smaller family companies, large shareholders may also be directors (and vice versa).

The liability of ordinary shareholders is *limited* to the fully-paid **nominal value** of their shares (hence the name limited company – or **public limited company** (plc) for larger companies). In contrast, the partners in an ordinary **partnership** firm have *unlimited* personal liability to meet the firm's debts. But if things go wrong, ordinary shareholders in a company may lose all they have invested. On a **liquidation**, they will get whatever is left over after the company has paid all amounts owing to creditors and preference shareholders. If there are not enough assets to pay creditors in full, then the ordinary shareholders get nothing.

Ordinary shareholders may be said to 'own' a company's profits; but they have no *legal* right to them unless the directors choose to declare dividends. So ordinary shareholders are really 'residual owners' of a company's assets. Sooner or later they can expect to receive anything left over after all other suppliers of finance have been paid their agreed *fixed* money amounts. Shareholders obtain a 'return' from their investment in two ways: by cash dividends from the company, and by any increase in the market value of their shares ('capital gain'). If a company does well, there is no ceiling on the possible return. (Someone who invested £1,000 in Racal in 1961 would by 1983 have owned shares worth over £500,000!)

4.2.2 Reserves

Three kinds of **reserves** are shown as part of ordinary shareholders' funds:

a. Share premiums
b. Revaluations
c. Retained profits.

(a) Share premiums
When an existing company issues more ordinary shares, it may charge more than the nominal value per share. Thus a 25p share might be issued at 60p. Such a **share premium** (in this case, of 35p per share) may equate the new shareholders with existing ones, who have allowed the company to retain 'their' profits, rather than pay them out in dividends. Any such share premium is shown separately under reserves: it is 'permanent' just like issued share capital, and can never be used for dividend payments. But only the nominal amount of each share is shown as part of issued share capital.

(b) Revaluations
Chapter 6 discusses how accounts value assets. As a rule the basis is original money cost. But in times of rapid inflation, the current value of some assets can be much higher than their original cost; and companies may wish to **revalue** them upwards in order to give a fairer picture of their financial position in the balance sheet. (Chapter 8 discusses in detail possible systems of full **inflation accounting**.) So that the balance sheet will continue to balance, the amount of any increase on a revaluation of assets will be added to ordinary shareholders' funds under **revaluation reserve** (as well as to the assets themselves).

(c) Retained profits
Cumulative **retained profits** are also included as part of the reserves. They are profits which directors decide *not* to distribute as cash dividends to ordinary shareholders. Thus they are 'retained' in the business, and attributed to ordinary shareholders in the balance sheet. Indeed, they are the most important source of funds for most UK companies. In a changing and uncertain economic environment, annual retained profits may fluctuate sharply. They can even be *negative* for a period, if dividends paid exceed the current period's profits, or if losses occur.

As stated, the three kinds of reserves described above are shown as part of ordinary shareholders' funds on the balance sheet. They represent *sources* of

The Balance Sheet

funds. But how those funds are *used* may vary. There is no reason why 'reserves' in the balance sheet should be represented on the assets side of the balance sheet by *cash* or liquid resources. More likely, they will have been invested more profitably – in other assets, such as stocks or plant and equipment. Thus Fig. 4.3 shows British Oxygen (BOC) Group's reserves of £797.6 million at 30 September 1982; but the group's liquid resources on that date amounted to only £37.8 million.

Figure 4.3 sets out the shareholders' funds part of BOC Group's balance sheet at 30 September 1982:

	(£m)	
Called up share capital		
Ordinary 25p shares	82.9	
Cumulative preference £1 shares	2.5	
		85.4
Reserves		
Share premium account	45.6	
Revaluation reserve	323.6	
Profit and loss account	398.2	
Other reserves	30.2	
		797.6
		883.0

Fig. 4.3: BOC Group plc: Consolidated capital and reserves at 30 September 1982.

4.2.3 Preference Share Capital

Both in respect of income and capital, preference shareholders rank after all other creditors, but before ordinary shareholders. For tax reasons, **preference shares** have become unpopular in recent years. Most companies have only a small number outstanding; and (unlike with ordinary shares) there is no need to have any.

Owners of preference shares become entitled to their stated amount of dividend only when the directors declare it. Preference dividends must be paid *before* any ordinary dividends can be paid. Dividends not declared for any period on **cumulative** preference shares must be fully made up later before any ordinary dividends can be paid.

On a liquidation, preference shares rank after all a company's other creditors, but before the ordinary shares. So unless preference shareholders are repaid the full nominal amount of their shares, the ordinary shareholders will get nothing.

Preference shareholders are not residual owners of the company's assets in the same way as ordinary shareholders: their rights to dividends and capital repayments are limited to fixed money amounts.

4.3 Liabilities

4.3.1 Long-term Liabilities

A company must repay amounts borrowed (liabilities) when they are due, and regularly pay the agreed amount of interest. Failure to do so will entitle the lender to take immediate legal action to recover the principal and any unpaid interest. 'Current' or 'short-term' liabilities are payable within 12 months from the date of the balance sheet. Liabilities payable later are called 'long-term'.

Five aspects of **long-term liabilities** are briefly discussed below:

(a) Public quotation

Larger companies may borrow from the public, with such loans (called **debentures**) 'quoted' on the stock exchange rather like ordinary shares. The main influence on their price will be changes in interest rates (whereas ordinary shares will also be affected by the company's profit prospects). Smaller companies will tend to borrow from a single lender, such as an insurance company or a bank.

(b) Security

Long-term borrowing may often be **secured** against particular assets. In a liquidation, the secured lender has a prior claim to the proceeds of the assets concerned. Any surplus remaining after the secured loan is fully repaid goes into the pool to pay unsecured creditors; while if there is any shortfall, to that extent the 'secured' creditor has to rank equally with other unsecured creditors.

(c) Interest rate

Recent large fluctuations in rates of inflation have made 'fixed-interest rate' loans unpopular. In effect both lenders and borrowers have had to speculate about the future rate of inflation. To avoid this need, 'variable-rate' loans have developed, with the interest rate varying in line with interest rates in general. For example, a company might borrow at '$1\frac{1}{2}$ per cent above LIBOR' (the interest rate on the London Inter-Bank market).

(d) Currency

As international business grows, more and more companies may wish to borrow foreign currencies (rather than sterling) in order to finance their overseas operations. For accounting purposes, interest and principal must be translated into sterling at the **exchange rate** at the date of the balance sheet. Obviously a sharp change in the exchange rate can have a big impact on the sterling equivalent of a foreign currency loan. (A well-known example concerns Laker

The Balance Sheet

Airways' borrowings of some $850 million. The pound's fall from $2.35 in March 1981 to $1.88 by January 1982 cost Laker about £90 million.)

(e) Conversion into equity

Sometimes loan capital is 'convertible into ordinary shares', at the option of the lender, on prearranged terms. Such **convertible loans** are shown on the balance sheet as long-term liabilities either until they are converted into ordinary shares (**equity**), or until they are repaid. After conversion, they are shown partly as issued ordinary share capital and partly as share premiums, depending on the conversion price.

4.3.2 Current Liabilities

There are four main kinds of **current liabilities** payable by a company within 12 months from the date of the balance sheet. Each is discussed briefly below.

(a) Creditors and accrued charges

Goods and services supplied by one business to another are often sold 'on credit', rather than for immediate settlement in cash. The normal period of credit ranges from one to three months after delivery of the goods. Accounting practice records the purchasing company as owning the goods supplied on credit from the moment of delivery. Goods owned but not yet paid for at the balance sheet date are shown under current liabilities as **creditors** (or 'trade creditors' or **accounts payable**). In effect the suppliers have 'lent' the purchasing company, for a short period, the funds with which to buy the goods.

Interest is not usually charged on this kind of 'loan' from suppliers; but it may implicitly carry a high annual rate of interest if there is a substantial **cash discount** for prompt payment. By *not* paying promptly, the purchasing company forgoes the cash discount that would otherwise be deducted from the amount payable. Thus, in effect, it bears interest as an **opportunity cost**.

Certain expenses accrue from day to day, but a bill (invoice) may be sent only every three months (for example, for electricity or telephones). Accountants estimate the amount of the expense relating to the accounting period and include it as an expense in the profit and loss account. It is shown in the balance sheet as an **accrued charge**, often grouped together with trade creditors.

(b) Bank overdraft

A regular source of short-term loans (for individuals as well as for companies) is the **bank overdraft**. This simply means a bank allowing its customer to spend more, by drawing cheques, than there is money in the account. Permission to borrow in this way, and the maximum amount of any such overdraft, must be agreed in advance with the bank. Overdrafts are legally repayable 'on demand', and companies show them as current liabilities in the balance sheet. It is true that in practice some bank overdrafts continue for many months, or even for years; but any customer would be foolish to assume that his overdraft would *never* be repayable!

(c) Taxation

Most unpaid taxes are included with creditors, such as local rates, national insurance, and value added tax. But taxation based on *profits* – called **corporation tax** for companies – is shown separately as a current liability. All unpaid corporation tax relating to periods up to the date of the balance sheet is normally shown as 'current', even if it is not legally payable for more than 12 months after the balance sheet date.

(d) Dividends payable

Most British companies pay an **interim dividend** out of profits during the year, with the directors recommending a **final dividend** in respect of the year. If the shareholders approve at the company's Annual General Meeting (several months later), the proposed final dividend then becomes a legal liability. In the balance sheet, the proposed final dividend is shown as a current liability on the assumption that shareholders will approve it.

Figure 4.4 shows the 'current liabilities' section of the balance sheet of Courtaulds plc at 31 March 1983:

	(£m)
Creditors	443.1
Overdrafts	17.2
Taxation	19.8
Dividends	6.2
Total current liabilities	486.3

Fig. 4.4: Courtaulds plc: Group current liabilities at 31 March 1983.

4.4 Assets

Assets are valuable resources controlled by a business, usually stated in accounts at original cost, less deductions for **accumulated depreciation**. Chapters 6 and 7 discuss the basis for valuing fixed assets and stocks.

4.4.1 Fixed Assets

Fixed assets are long-term resources of a business, used to provide goods or services over their life, rather than to be sold in the normal course of trading. Some fixed assets, like land, never 'wear out' – though they may need to be maintained in proper condition. Others have a finite limited life: either for physical reasons (like motor vehicles), or for legal reasons (like leases or patents).

The Balance Sheet

The reason for acquiring assets determines whether they are 'fixed' or 'current', not their tangible form. A company which makes filing cabinets for sale would show them as current trading stocks in the balance sheet; while one simply using filing cabinets as permanent office furniture would show them as fixed assets.

Fixed assets are now classified under three headings:
(a) tangible;   (b) intangible;   (c) financial.

(a) Tangible fixed assets

(i) Property. Most businesses need premises to operate from, which they may own outright or lease (rent). 'Freehold property' is shown either at cost or at a more recent valuation, less depreciation on buildings. Any capital sum (premium) paid for a lease appears separately as 'leasehold property', and is amortised over the period of the lease.

(ii) Plant and equipment. The heading 'plant and equipment' may cover virtually all tangible fixed assets other than land and buildings, in service industries as well as in manufacturing. It could include: all sorts of production machinery and tooling; motor vehicles; and office furniture, fittings, and equipment.

(b) Intangible fixed assets

Many fixed assets are tangible physical items, such as land and buildings, or plant and equipment. But others may be **intangible**, such as goodwill, patents, or development costs. These items may be shown in accounts at original cost less amortisation.

(i) Goodwill. **Goodwill** is shown in accounts only if a distinct *cost* can be identified: it does *not* refer to normal commercial 'goodwill' which has gradually built up over the years. Accounting 'goodwill' occurs if a company buys another business, and pays more than **book value** for the acquired assets. Some companies prefer not to show large intangible assets: they may eliminate any purchased goodwill which does arise, by deducting it from reserves in the balance sheet.

(ii) Patents, copyrights, and trade marks. Certain other intangible fixed assets may appear on the balance sheet. These include (a) patents, the sole right to make and sell a product, (b) copyrights, the sole right to publish and sell a book, and (c) the registered right to use particular trade marks. Where a company has acquired another business owning such rights, the 'goodwill' figure is likely to include their cost. Many companies treat the cost of obtaining such legal rights as a revenue expense in the year it is incurred, even if they expect future benefits.

(iii) Research and development costs. The cost of basic or applied research is normally written off at once as an ordinary business expense. But there may be a

good chance of enough future revenue to recover the costs of specific product development projects. If so, such expenditure may be carried forward as an intangible fixed asset on the balance sheet, and amortised over the periods expected to benefit. But even here, 'conservatism' often prevails over strict application of the 'matching' concept; and companies often prefer to treat all research and development expenditure as an ordinary expense.

(c) *Financial fixed assets*
A third fixed asset heading covers long-term investments in financial securities, such as holdings of ordinary shares in other companies. These are called:
  (i) investments in **subsidiaries**, if more than 50 per cent of the ordinary shares are owned;
  (ii) investments in **associated companies** if between 20 per cent and 50 per cent;
  (iii) **trade investments** if less than 20 per cent.

Sometimes there may also be long-term investments in fixed interest securities, such as government stocks. These investments may give rise to 'investment income' in a company's profit and loss account, which is shown separately from the operating (trading) profit or loss.

4.4.2 Current Assets
Current assets are short-term resources, either already in liquid form, or expected to be used up or turned into cash within 12 months from the balance sheet date. The main current asset headings are: stocks, debtors and prepayments, cash and liquid resources.

(a) *Stocks*
Stocks (inventories) represent **raw materials**; and processed goods which are either unfinished (**work in progress**) or unsold (**finished goods**) (see 7.3). Many firms also hold small stocks of supplies, such as stationery and maintenance materials, to be used up in the course of business.

The level of stocks held will vary with the nature of the business. A company which makes only to firm orders will hold low stocks of finished goods, since as soon as they are finished the goods will be delivered to customers. Similarly stocks will tend to be low if goods are highly perishable, such as bread. But if the manufacturing cycle is long, as for companies buildings ships or aircraft, then large amounts may be invested in work-in-progress.

Holding stocks can be expensive: it involves handling and storage costs, insurance, risks of deterioration or theft, as well as the financial cost of tying up funds. On the other hand, it can also be costly to run out of stocks and so be unable to satisfy customers. The art of managing stocks is to balance these conflicting costs and benefits.

(b) *Debtors and prepayments*
When firms sell on credit, the amounts owed to the company by customers at

The Balance Sheet 47

the balance sheet date are shown as **debtors** (sometimes called **accounts receivable**). The amount will depend on the volume of credit sales and on the average period of credit taken. Many businesses sell almost entirely on credit, and find the average period of credit amounts to about two months. This represents a substantial investment (use) of funds.

Certain expenses, by custom or law, have to be paid in advance – for example, insurance premiums and local rates. At the balance sheet date, part of the amount paid, say for insurance premiums, may relate to the *next* accounting period. This is called a **prepayment**, and is shown in the balance sheet as a current asset, often grouped together with debtors.

(c) Cash and liquid resources

Cash in hand (**petty cash**) consists literally of notes and coins, but **cash** in accounting also refers to balances in bank accounts. Most companies plan to keep their cash balances fairly low, since they do not normally earn any interest. On the other hand, it could be very serious to run out of cash, especially if no bank overdraft arrangements have been made. Many companies now use the general term **liquid resources** to include cash in hand and at banks, together with short-term marketable securities.

Figure 4.5 shows the working capital cycle of a manufacturing business. The business first purchases raw materials on credit, then uses labour and capital equipment (in various proportions in different industries) to convert the raw materials into finished goods. When the finished goods are sold and delivered, legal title passes to the customer. He either pays cash, or, if he buys on credit, owes the price to the selling company. The transaction is completed when the debtor finally pays cash to settle his account.

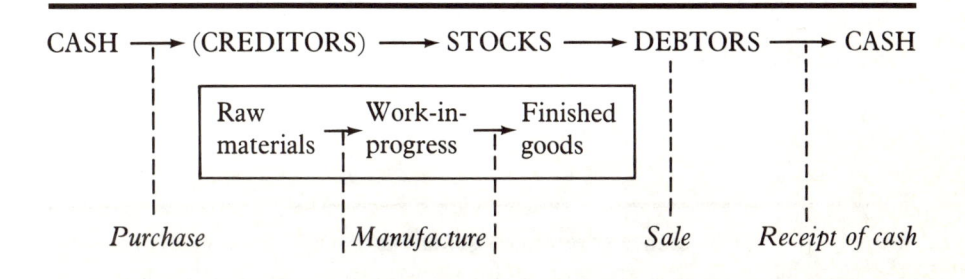

```
CASH ──▶ (CREDITORS) ──▶ STOCKS ──▶ DEBTORS ──▶ CASH
              ┌─────────────────────────────────┐
              │ Raw         Work-in-    Finished │
              │ materials ▶ progress  ▶ goods    │
              └─────────────────────────────────┘
  Purchase      Manufacture              Sale      Receipt of cash
```

Fig. 4.5: Working capital cycle of a manufacturing business

4.5 Presentation

4.5.1 Format

For larger companies, the vertical form of balance sheet has supplanted the traditional horizontal layout. Figure 4.2 (on p. 38) showed a skeleton layout for a vertical balance sheet, listing shareholders' funds and liabilities, and then assets. But the balance sheet layout shown in Fig. 4.2 is usually modified in order to show the *long-term* sources and uses of funds.

Current liabilities are now normally deducted from current assets, producing a sub-total **net current assets** (often entitled **working capital**). Each item in current assets and current liabilities is 'short-term' in nature; but the difference between total current assets and total current liabilities (the net working capital) represents a more or less *permanent* use of funds. In the same way, a hotel may be permanently full, even though no individual guest stays for long.

Figure 4.6 shows the main headings of the modified vertical format. Shareholders' funds and long-term liabilities together are described as **capital employed**; and fixed assets and working capital together as **net assets**. Of course capital employed – long-term sources of funds – must always exactly equal net assets – net long-term uses of funds.

	(£)
Long-term sources of funds	
Shareholders' funds	xxx
Long-term Liabilities	xxx
Capital Employed	xxx
Long-term uses of funds	
Current Assets	xxx
less: Current Liabilities	xxx
Working Capital	xxx
Fixed Assets	xxx
Net Assets	xxx

Fig. 4.6: Vertical balance sheet, net asset layout

4.5.2 The Use of Notes to Accounts

The main accounts themselves used to contain considerable detail, but this made it hard for non-experts to see the wood for the trees. Modern practice simplifies the accounts, by using only the main headings, and giving the required details in notes to the accounts. Most items in the balance sheet and profit and loss account contain a reference number for the relevant note. As a result of this modern practice, the notes themselves are *part* of 'the accounts', not merely a sort of 'optional extra'.

The Balance Sheet

4.5.3 Rounding Numbers

Another modern development, partly brought on by inflation, is to present accounts only to the nearest thousand pounds (or, for large companies, to the nearest million pounds). The accounts of complex businesses could not possibly be estimated with an accuracy extending 'to the nearest pound'. Even if accounts could be that accurate (which they can't), it would still be undesirable to *present* them in that much detail. That would obscure the overall view of the company's affairs which accounts are intended to show. So the general rule in accounting is to ignore tiny amounts that don't matter, group similar items together, and so on. The legal maxim *'de minimis non curat lex'* (the law is not concerned with trifles) also applies in accounting.

In this respect British accounts are probably in advance of American practice. As recently as 1975, General Motors (the largest manufacturing company in the world) still presented its accounts to the nearest dollar! (Its sales revenue in that year was reported as $35,724,911,215 and its net profit after tax as $1,253,091,965! The balance sheet contained no less than 370 digits – more than four times as many, for example, as Beecham Group's 1983 balance sheet in Fig. 4.7.)

4.5.4 Comparative Figures

Finally, company law requires accounts to show figures not only for the most recent date, but also for the preceding period. This is to give readers an easy basis for comparison. (In analysing accounts, of course, other standards for comparison may also be required, such as the performance of competitive businesses.) Separate tables of statistics often set out major accounting items over a period of five to ten years, but these are not regarded as part of the accounts themselves nor subject to audit. (And Ch. 8 explains how one needs to be careful about allowing for inflation in making comparisons over time.)

4.5.5 Example

Figure 4.7 shows an actual balance sheet (very slightly simplified) for Beecham Group plc at 31 March, 1983. Notice the comparative figures for 1982. At this stage, readers are strongly recommended to obtain a set of published accounts and examine the balance sheet and notes. (Most large companies will be glad to send a copy of their latest annual report and accounts on request.)

Beecham Group plc
Consolidated Balance Sheet 31 March 1983

	Notes	1983 (£m)	1982 (£m)
Group Capital Employed			
Ordinary Share Capital	7	163.7	163.6
Reserves	8	574.6	475.7
		738.3	639.3
Loans	9	312.9	196.9
Deferred Liabilities, etc.	10,14	18.0	16.3
		1,069.2	852.5
Employment of Group Capital			
Current Assets			
Stocks	11	312.5	252.2
Debtors and prepayments		365.7	273.2
Liquid resources	12	196.0	140.9
		874.2	666.3
Current Liabilities			
Short-term borrowings	13	88.0	27.7
Creditors and accruals		284.1	202.8
Taxation		73.6	64.4
Dividends	4	32.8	28.1
		478.5	323.0
Net Current Assets		395.7	343.3
Fixed Assets	15	430.4	325.5
Associated Companies	17	11.6	7.2
Goodwill		231.5	176.5
		1,069.2	852.5

Fig. 4.7: Beecham Group plc: Balance Sheet at 31 March 1983

Work Section

A. Revision Questions

A1 Define a 'balance sheet'.
A2 How is a vertical balance sheet set out?
A3 In what order do items appear within balance sheet headings?
A4 How does a horizontal balance sheet differ from a vertical one?
A5 What is the difference between an asset and a liability?

A6 What are the two main sources of ordinary shareholders' funds?
A7 Distinguish between authorised and issued share capital.
A8 Why are 'limited' companies so called?
A9 What do ordinary shareholders receive when a company is liquidated?
A10 How can ordinary shareholders get a 'return' from their investment?

A11 What is a share premium?
A12 How does revaluing assets upwards affect the balance sheet?
A13 Define the balance sheet item 'retained profits'.
A14 How can retained profits for a period be negative?
A15 Why are balance sheet 'reserves' unlikely to be represented by cash?
A16 Define 'preference share capital'.
A17 What are 'cumulative' preference shares?
A18 What priority do preference shares take on liquidation?
A19 Distinguish preference shares from ordinary shares.
A20 How do shareholders' funds differ from long-term liabilities?

A21 How do 'current' liabilities differ from 'long-term' liabilities?
A22 How does 'secured' lending differ from 'unsecured'?
A23 Why have variable-interest-rate loans become popular?
A24 How are foreign currency borrowings treated in sterling balance sheets?
A25 What is convertible loan stock?
A26 In what sense may trade credit involve an interest 'cost'?
A27 What are accrued charges?
A28 Define a bank overdraft.
A29 What does the current liability item 'taxation' consist of?
A30 What appears on a balance sheet as 'dividends payable'?

A31 Define an 'asset' in accounting.
A32 How are assets normally valued in balance sheets?
A33 What are the three different 'fixed asset' headings?
A34 What are 'intangible' assets? Give two examples.
A35 Define 'goodwill' in accounting.

A36 Name three kinds of long-term investment.
A37 Define a 'current asset'. What are the three main types?
A38 What are the three main kinds of stock for a manufacturing company?
A39 What is a debtor, and how does it arise?
A40 What is a prepayment? Give an example as well as a definition.

A41 Define 'working capital'.
A42 How can there be a permanent need to finance net current assets?
A43 Define 'capital employed'.
A44 Define 'net assets'.
A45 Into which four or five main categories are balance sheets classified?
A46 What is the function of notes to the accounts?
A47 Give *two* reasons why accounts are not presented to the nearest pound.
A48 What are 'comparative figures'?
A49 Why is care required in comparing figures over several years?
A50 Define 'net current assets'.

B. Exercises and Case Studies

B1 The balance sheet of Millers Emporium at 30 June was as follows:

	(£)		(£)
Share capital	10,000	Fixed assets	15,000
Retained profits	15,000	Current assets	10,000
	25,000		25,000

However, it had been forgotten that tax of £3,000 would have to be paid on the £6,000 profits for the year which had been added to retained profits, and that the shareholders were certain to approve a proposed dividend of £1,000 at the annual general meeting.
  a. Make any necessary changes to the balance sheet.
  b. Explain in your own words what you have done, and why.

B2 The following is the balance sheet of Acme Motors Ltd at 31 March:

	(£)		(£)
Share capital	15,000	Premises	10,000
Retained profits	3,500	Stocks	10,000
Creditors	1,500		
	20,000		20,000

  a. During April the company sells half of the cars in stock for £10,000 in cash. It uses this cash to extend its premises.
    (i) How does the resulting balance sheet at 30 April differ from the one above?
    (ii) What does this tell you about the nature of a reserve?

The Balance Sheet 53

    b. During May Acme Motors sells its premises for £25,000, and buys more vehicles with the cash received.
       (i) How will the balance sheet at 31 May differ from that at 30 April?
       (ii) Are the changes different in nature from those in April?
    c. Rearrange the balance sheet as set out above into the vertical format.

B3 Place a tick in the appropriate column to show in which category each of the following items belongs:

	Ordinary share capital	Reserves	Preference share capital	Long-term liabilities	Current liabilities	None of these
1. Convertible Loan Stock						
2. Preference dividend proposed						
3. Revaluation surplus on land						
4. Authorised ordinary shares						
5. Loss for the year						
6. Accounts receivable						
7. Accrued charges						
8. Interim ordinary dividend paid						

B4 Place a tick in the appropriate column to show in which category each of the following items belongs:

	Fixed Assets Tangible	Fixed Assets Intangible	Fixed Assets Financial	Stocks	Debtors	Liquid resources	None of these
1. Bank overdraft							
2. Work-in-progress							
3. Accounts receivable							
4. Freehold property							
5. Government securities							
6. Shares in subsidiary							
7. Finished goods for resale							
8. Office fixtures and equipment							

The Balance Sheet

B5 Keram Ltd starts business as a publisher of multi-coloured economic charts in January 1984. The company's transactions during its first six months of operations are summarised below. You are asked to show how the balance sheet will appear at the end of June 1984. (Hint: You may find it best to prepare a rough balance sheet summary and alter the numbers month by month, to record the separate transactions.)

- a. January. 20,000 £1 ordinary shares issued for cash at par.
- b. February. Cash used to buy equipment for £6,000, stocks of raw materials for £3,000, and leasehold premises for £8,000.
- c. March. Raw materials costing £4,000 bought on credit.
- d. April. Materials which had cost £2,000 were sold, after much processing, to customers for £5,000 cash.
- e. May. Creditors for materials were paid £4,000.
- f. June. Materials which had cost £4,000 were sold to customers for £9,000, of which £6,000 was on credit.
- g. How would the end of June balance sheet be changed if, in addition to the above, wages of £1,000 in cash were paid monthly?

B6 Place a tick in the appropriate column to show in which category each of the following items belongs:

	Shareholders' funds	Liabilities Long-term	Liabilities Current	Fixed assets	Current assets	None of these
1. Finished goods awaiting despatch						
2. Money lent out at 24 hours call						
3. Convertible loan stock						
4. Surplus on sale of land						
5. Sales director's company car						
6. Shares in subsidiary company						
7. Land held for future expansion						
8. Issued share capital						
9. Management expertise						
10. Overdraft at the bank						
11. Money owed to suppliers						
12. Petty cash in hand						
13. Unpaid customers' accounts						
14. Proposed dividend						
15. Retained profits						
16. Machinery and equipment						

The Balance Sheet

B7 Show how the following items would be set out in (part of) a horizontal balance sheet:

	(£'000)
Taxation	12
8 per cent convertible loan	50
Issued ordinary shares	80
10 per cent mortgage debenture	36
7 per cent cumulative preference shares	12
Dividends payable	5
Retained profits	161
Trade creditors	70
Share premium account	37
Bank overdraft	31

B8 Show how the following items would be set out in (part of) a horizontal balance sheet for a company manufacturing office furniture:

	(£'000)
Work-in-progress	37
Shares in associated companies	10
Leasehold property	28
Prepayments	3
Liquid resources	17
Plant and equipment	33
Accounts receivable	41
Shares in subsidiary company	8
Finished goods	24
Motor vehicles	12
Raw materials	18

B9 Show how the following items would be set out in (part of) a vertical balance sheet:

	(£m)
Dividends payable	3.6
Stocks	31.2
Cash	11.3
Taxation	9.7
Debtors	42.0
Accrued expenses	6.1
Bank overdraft	8.0
Creditors	16.3

B10 From the following information construct a balance sheet for Village Stores Ltd at 31 May 1984, using the horizontal format:
Premises £25,000; Overdraft £6,500; Goods in stock £8,900; Retained profits £10,000; Fittings £2,000; Mortgage bond £16,000; Delivery vehicle £1,000; Owed to suppliers £3,500; Owed by customers £1,700; Share capital £2,750; Cash on hand £150.

B11 See B10. Prepare a balance sheet for Village Stores Ltd at 31 May 1983 using the vertical format.

B12 The following information applies to Good Products Ltd as at 31 December 1983. Calculate the amount of shareholders' funds, and then arrange the information into a balance sheet using the vertical format:

	(£'000)
Long-term lease on factory	160
Owed to suppliers	28
Delivery vehicles	16
Loans from bank	60
Owed by customers	41
Machinery in factory	110
Taxation owed	40
Cash	2
Shares in suppliers' companies	10
Stocks of raw materials	15
Dividend proposed	15
Finished goods in stock	11
Government bonds	26
Expenditure on new patents	5
Debentures issued	80

B13 See B12. Prepare a balance sheet for Good Products Ltd as at 31 December 1983 using the horizontal format.

B14 Write out brief definitions for the following:
1. Balance sheet
2. Fixed assets
3. Current liabilities
4. Authorised share capital
5. Debtors
6. Current assets
7. Work-in-progress
8. Shareholders' funds
9. Ordinary shares
10. Prepayments

B15 From the following information as at 31 March 1984, construct a balance sheet for Domestic Appliance Manufacturers Ltd, in vertical form with appropriate headings, sub-totals and totals:

Cash and liquid assets £70,000; Ordinary shares, four million 25p shares, fully paid up; Undistributed profit £20,000; Machinery and equipment £850,000; Trade creditors £180,000; Unfinished appliances £160,000; Patents £50,000; 200,000 50p Preference shares fully paid up; 10 per cent mortgage bonds of £300,000, secured on property; Shares in subsidiary £100,000; Tax provision £50,000; Bank overdraft £12,000; Debtors £230,000; Freehold property £339,000; General reserves £250,000; Dividends payable £25,000; Raw materials and components £140,000; Accrued expenses £2,000.

B16 The following balance sheet of J. Arthur Bloggs Ltd contains ten deliberate mistakes. Please identify as many as you can, and in each case say what is wrong.

The Balance Sheet

J. Arthur Bloggs Limited
Balance Sheet for the year ended 31 March 1984

		(£'000)
Fixed Assets		
Freehold property, at valuation		420
Plant and equipment:		
Accumulated depreciation	390	
less: Cost	140	
= Net book value	——	250
Stocks of finished goods		110
		780
Current Assets		
Accounts payable	220	
Bank overdraft	70	
Stocks of raw materials	80	
	370	
Current Liabilities		
Debtors	130	
Taxation	80	
	——	210
= *Working Capital*	——	580
Net Assets		1,360
Shareholders' funds		
Issued £1 preference share capital		400
Retained profits		560
		960
Long-term Liabilities		
Loans	90	
Revaluation reserve	130	
	——	220
Other Assets		
Goodwill		180
Capital Employed		1,360

B17 From the following information (figures are in £ thousands), construct a vertical balance sheet at 30 September 1984 for Duplication Ltd:
Liquid resources 7; Creditors 59; Plant and equipment 41; Issued ordinary share capital 26; Tax 12; Goodwill --?--; Reserves 80; Land and buildings 125; Stocks 46; Long-term liabilities 62; Dividends 4; Debtors 45; Convertible loan 30.
Please insert an amount against Goodwill to balance the accounts.

B18 On 7 August 1983 a burglary took place at the head office of Francis Furniture Ltd. Among the items stolen was the only copy of the draft balance sheet as at 30 June 1983. Since the company's books of account had not appealed to the burglar(s), it would have been possible to compile the balance sheet again. But Mr Alec Smart, the assistant chief accountant, had noted on a separate piece of paper a number of balance sheet items and relationships.
See if you can reproduce the company's balance sheet at 30 June 1983, in vertical format, from Mr Smart's notes, which are shown below:
a. Stock = 2 × current liabilities
b. Long-term investments = 3 × cash
c. Issued ordinary share capital = working capital = £40,000
d. Current assets = 3 × current liabilities
e. Total liabilities + shareholders' funds = £102,000
f. Long-term liabilities = 3 × long-term investments
g. Debtors − long-term liabilities = 0
h. Net fixed assets = 1½ × retained profits
i. All items (in £ thousands) are even whole numbers.

C. Essay Questions

C1 Company chairmen sometimes say: 'Our workforce is our most important asset.' Why is this 'asset' never shown on the balance sheet? Should it be?
C2 When a company is liquidated, will the ordinary shareholders receive the balance sheet amount of 'shareholders' funds? Why or why not?
C3 Explain why balance sheets should always balance.
C4 Why are large business enterprises nearly always organised as limited companies and not as partnerships?
C5 How do 'reserves' arise in accounts, and what use are they?
C6 What are shareholders' funds, and why are they important?
C7 Discuss the reasons for the conventional classification of assets on the balance sheet.
C8 Why may the matching conflict with conservatism or intangible assets?
C9 Why are accounts not precisely 'accurate'? To what extent does it matter?
C10 'Using the historical cost of items on the balance sheet makes more sense when the latter is seen as a statement of sources and uses of funds rather than as a statement of shareholders' funds.' Discuss.

5. The Profit and Loss Account

5.1 **Introduction**

5.2 **Sales Revenue**
5.2.1 Timing
5.2.2 Accounting Entries for Sales
5.2.3 Problems in Measuring Sales

5.3 **Operating Expenses**
5.3.1 The Matching Principle
5.3.2 Expenditures: Expenses or Assets?

5.4 **Presentation**
5.4.1 Trading Account
5.4.2 Profit and Loss Account
5.4.3 Appropriation Account
5.4.4 The Overall Profit and Loss Account
5.4.5 Example
5.4.6 Other Items

Objective: *To show how sales revenue for a period is calculated; to describe the 'matching' principle and its role in determining whether expenditures are treated as assets or expenses; and to outline how profit and loss accounts are presented.*

Synopsis: *Sales revenue is recognised, as a rule, when goods are delivered to customers, rather than earlier (when production is completed) or later (when cash is finally paid). The timing of sales also determines the timing of profits.*

The matching principle deducts from sales revenue the expenses incurred in the period. Expenditures are carried forward as assets in the balance sheet only *if there are expected to be future sales revenues against which they can be matched later. Otherwise they are written off as expenses in the current period's profit and loss account.*

The three parts of the profit and loss account are often combined in practice, with much of the trading details omitted. These three parts are: the trading account, the profit and loss account, and the appropriation account. Dividends are not *an expense, but an 'appropriation' of profit.*

5.1 Introduction

Many companies buy and sell goods and services. In a year there are literally millions of transactions. If company managers succeed, they satisfy customers at a profit: if not, their companies may incur losses.

A company's profit and loss account shows how much profit or loss it has made in a given period. A profit is the excess of sales revenue over expenses for a period. A **loss** is simply a negative profit: the excess of expenses over sales revenue. Figure 5.1 illustrates.

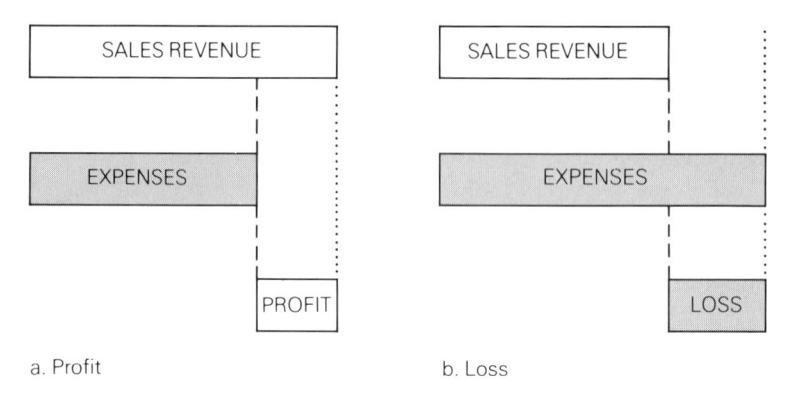

Fig. 5.1: Basic calculation of profit or loss

Companies treat any profit in two ways: they usually pay part out in cash dividends to shareholders, and keep ('retain') the rest. Retained profit increases the amount of shareholders' funds in the balance sheet (which may be regarded as an ultimate 'liability' of a company to its owners). Thus shareholders may benefit from company profits either directly, in cash dividends, or indirectly, in increased net assets owned by the company on their behalf. (Of course, a *loss* for a period *reduces* the total amount attributed to shareholders' funds in the balance sheet.)

Retained profit for a period thus represents the *link* between the balance sheets at the beginning and end of a period and the profit and loss account for that period. In Chapter 4 we saw how the balance sheet describes and classifies various items: now we look at the profit and loss account. 5.2 discusses problems in determining the amount of sales revenue in a period; 5.3 looks at operating expenses; and finally 5.4 describes the form of presentation.

5.2 Sales Revenue

5.2.1 Timing

Figure 4.5 (p. 47) set out the working capital cycle of a manufacturing business. It showed how a firm acquires materials, transforms them into finished goods,

The Profit and Loss Account 61

sells them to customers (often on credit), and finally gets paid in cash.

Figure 5.2 shows three different points in time at which company accounts might *recognise* that a sale has occurred:

1. when the production process is completed
2. when the finished goods are delivered to customers
3. when the customers pay cash

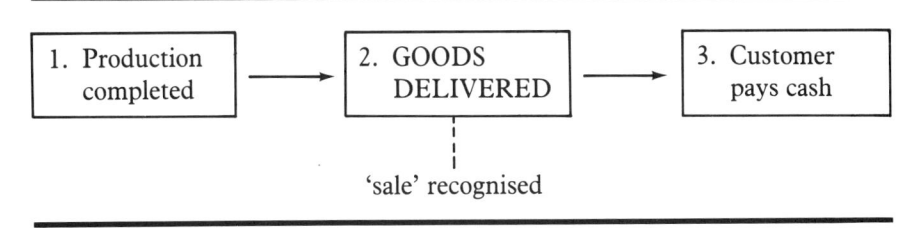

```
┌──────────────┐      ┌──────────────┐      ┌──────────────┐
│ 1. Production│ ───▶ │  2. GOODS    │ ───▶ │ 3. Customer  │
│   completed  │      │  DELIVERED   │      │  pays cash   │
└──────────────┘      └──────────────┘      └──────────────┘
                             │
                       'sale' recognised
```

Fig. 5.2: Recognition of sale in a credit transaction

Accounts generally recognise a sale as occurring at point (2) – on delivery of the goods to customers. This is important because *profit* is recognised in accounts at the same time as *sales*. This **realisation concept**, as it is known, can be justified on grounds of reasonable *certainty*.

Many businesses cannot be sure they will find customers merely because they have produced finished goods for sale. Hence accountants, who are conservative, would be reluctant to 'count their chickens before they are hatched'. They prefer *not* to recognise a sale (and hence a profit) as having been made until a definite customer has agreed to buy the goods. Until that time, the finished goods continue to be owned by the manufacturing company; it shows them in the balance sheet as current assets (stocks), and values them *at cost*. After the moment of a credit sale, the stock becomes a *debtor* – and is valued at *selling price*.

FINISHED GOODS | +   PROFIT | = DEBTOR
STOCK
at cost   *selling price*

Where a company is making goods to order, for specific customers, then stages (1) and (2) above – completion of production, and delivery – will occur at almost the same time. This is shown in Fig. 5.3.

On the other hand, waiting until credit customers had actually paid cash would be regarded as *too* conservative. If customers fail to pay, they can be legally sued for the amount of the sale price. Unless there is some good reason for non-payment (such as faulty manufacture, dispute over the price, etc.), the courts will compel them to pay up. Hence accountants recognise that a sale has been made at the moment (normally on physical delivery) when legal title to the

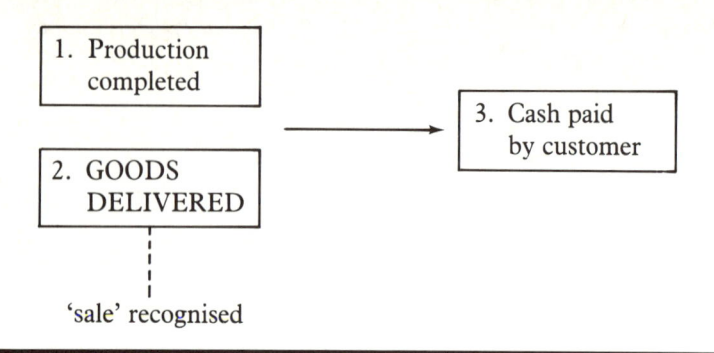

```
    ┌─────────────────┐
    │ 1. Production   │
    │    completed    │
    └─────────────────┘                ┌─────────────────┐
                        ───────────▶   │ 3. Cash paid    │
    ┌─────────────────┐                │    by customer  │
    │ 2. GOODS        │                └─────────────────┘
    │    DELIVERED    │
    └─────────────────┘
             ┆
             ┆
      'sale' recognised
```

Fig. 5.3: Recognition of sale for made-to-order goods

goods (ownership) passes from the manufacturer (seller) to the customer (buyer).

Where sales are for cash, rather than on credit, then points (2) and (3) above – delivery of the goods, and payment of cash – will occur at the same time. This is shown in Fig. 5.4.

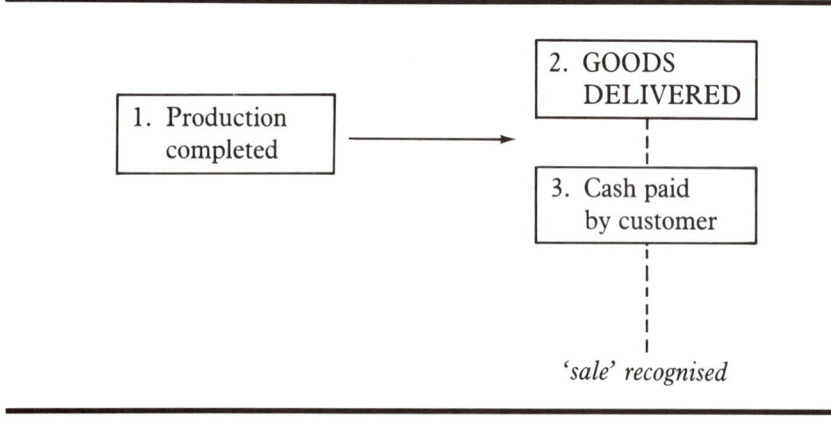

```
                                       ┌─────────────────┐
                                       │ 2. GOODS        │
                                       │    DELIVERED    │
    ┌─────────────────┐                └─────────────────┘
    │ 1. Production   │                         ┆
    │    completed    │   ───────────▶  ┌─────────────────┐
    └─────────────────┘                │ 3. Cash paid    │
                                       │    by customer  │
                                       └─────────────────┘
                                                ┆
                                                ┆
                                         'sale' recognised
```

Fig. 5.4: Recognition of sale in a cash transaction

5.2.2 Accounting Entries for Sales

When a sale is made, *two* sets of changes occur in the profit and loss accounts (P & L) and balance sheet (BS), as set out in Fig. 5.5.

Recognising a sale has two net effects: (a) to increase profit (and thus shareholders' funds, via retained profit); and (b) to increase current assets by the amount of the profit. The profit and loss account includes the sales revenue less the **cost of goods sold**, which increases profit. Cash or debtors in the balance sheet is increased by the amount of the sale, while stock is *reduced* by the *cost* of the goods sold.

The Profit and Loss Account

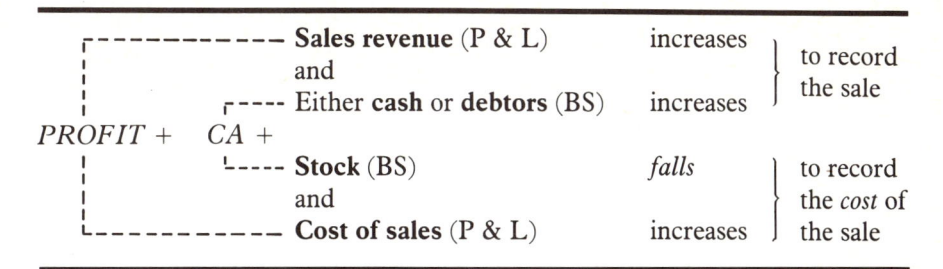

```
              ┌─────────── Sales revenue (P & L)      increases  ┐ to record
              │            and                                   │ the sale
              │   ┌─────── Either cash or debtors (BS)  increases ┘
PROFIT +   CA +
              │   └─────── Stock (BS)                  falls      ┐ to record
              │            and                                    │ the cost of
              └─────────── Cost of sales (P & L)       increases  ┘ the sale
```

Fig. 5.5: Changes in accounts when a sale is recognised

The final result of a credit sale is the same as for a cash sale: *the amount of the sale is received in cash*. But with a credit sale, this result is achieved in two stages: (1) when the sale is recognised, the customer becomes a *debtor* for the amount; and (2) when he pays, cash is received (and replaces the debtor as a current asset).

Figure 5.6 sets out the accounting entries showing that where a credit sale is made in period 1 which is paid for in period 2, the end-of-period 1 balance sheet will show a debtor for the amount. With a cash sale, of course, the cash would be received in period 1.

	Sales revenue (P & L)	+
Period 1	Debtor (BS)	+
Period 2	Debtor (BS)	−
	Cash (BS)	+

Fig. 5.6: Accounting entries for a credit sale

Thus we see the three stages of Fig. 5.2 reflected for a credit sale in the three different kinds of current asset, at each stage becoming more 'liquid':

EVENT	production completed	→	delivery of goods	→	receipt of cash
CURRENT ASSET	stock	→	debtor	→	cash

5.2.3 Problems in Measuring Sales

(a) Value added tax

Value added tax (VAT) is a tax on the supply of goods which is eventually *borne* by the final consumer. However, it is *collected* at each stage of the production and distribution chain. Trading companies simply collect the tax on behalf of the government; and the figure for 'sales revenue' in their accounts does *not* include VAT. You should therefore assume that any figures in accounts for sales revenue exclude VAT.

(*b*) *Bad debts*

Occasionally credit customers fail to pay the full amount owed for goods sold to them. Accounting practice is to treat the amount of any such **bad debt** as a separate item of expense in the profit and loss account, and to leave the original 'sales revenue' figure as it stands. When the decision is made to 'write off' the bad debt, the amount is deducted from debtors in the balance sheet, and the balance of profit for the period is reduced to the same extent.

(*c*) *Goods returned*

A deduction is made from 'sales revenue' where a customer physically returns goods (and the selling company agrees to take them back), or where an agreed allowance is made against the original price (e.g. because the goods are of inferior quality). For example, if 80 units were sold at £3 each, but there was an agreed price reduction to £2 per unit, then the original sales revenue of £240 would be reduced to £160. (Obviously the amount the debtor owes would be reduced accordingly.) Similarly if 40 units were sold at £5 each, but 10 units were returned later, the original sales revenue figure of £200 would have to be reduced to £150.

(*d*) *Errors on invoice*

The account (or bill) for goods or services sold is called an **invoice**. It is the legal document (sent with, or soon after, delivery) which tells the customers what the goods cost. The letters 'E & OE' at the foot of an invoice stand for 'Errors and Omissions Excepted'. What happens if a sale of 15 units at £12 each is wrongly charged on the invoice as £315 instead of £180 because by mistake the 15 units are multiplied by £21 instead of by £12? Answer: the original sales revenue figure of £315 must be amended to £180. This would often be done by issuing a formal **credit note** (in effect reversing part of the earlier invoice) for £135.

To summarise: (a) VAT is left out in calculating sales revenue, and (b) bad debts are treated as a separate item of expense with the original sales revenue figure left unchanged. But (c) where goods delivered are later returned or a price reduction is agreed, or (d) there is simply an error in calculation, then the original sales revenue figure needs to be amended.

The Profit and Loss Account 65

5.3 Operating Expenses

5.3.1 The Matching Principle

The **matching principle** enables accounts to determine profit or loss for a period by deducting from ('matching' against) sales revenue for the period those expenses incurred in earning it.

Example: *Mary Mullins received £15 on her birthday, which she planned to use in a part-time business venture. She bought pictures at £3 each from her big brother, who painted them as a hobby, and planned to sell them to her friends for £5 each. During the first week she bought five pictures and sold two; but was disappointed when she calculated her trading result:*

SOLD	**	2 at £5	=	£ 10
BOUGHT	*****	5 at £3	=	£ 15
		Loss for week:		£ 5

Her father, an accountant in the City, explained her mistake. Since she sold only two pictures in the first week, only the cost of those two pictures should be deducted (as cost of goods sold) from the week's sales revenue. The three remaining pictures should simply be recorded as stock in hand at the end of the week (valued at cost). Thus the week's trading actually produced a profit of £4 (£10−£6).

After four weeks, Mary had made the transactions shown in Fig. 5.7. The connecting lines show the week in which each picture bought was actually sold. The first week's profit, and the cost of the stock held at the end of that week, are shown:

	Week 1	Week 2	Week 3	Week 4
SOLD at £5 each	○ ○	○ ○ ○ ○	○ ○ ○	○ ○ ○ ○
BOUGHT at £3 each	○ ○	○ ○ ○ ○	○ ○ ○ ○	○ ○
Sales	£ 10			
Cost of goods sold	£ 6			
Profit in week	£ 4			
Cost of stock at end of week	£ 9			

Fig. 5.7: Mary Mullins, trading transactions and profit

5.3.2 Expenditures: Expenses or Assets?

The accrual principle means that accounts record items when they are legally incurred, rather than when cash is paid. This applies to **expenditures** as well as to sales revenue. Expenditures for which no cash has yet been paid appear in the balance sheet as current liabilities (creditors), just as sales for which no cash has yet been received appear in the balance sheet as current assets (debtors).

A more interesting question is whether expenditures should be treated (a) as expenses in the current period's profit and loss account, or (b) as assets on the balance sheet (usually valued at cost). Expenditure **written off** as an expense in the profit and loss account is called **revenue expenditure**; if treated as an asset in the balance sheet it is called **capital expenditure**.

A manufacturer of motor vehicles will deduct from sales revenue the costs incurred in producing the cars sold. Steel, glass, and all the other materials and components, together with the wages of factory workers, can be directly identified with specific goods, and are referred to as **product costs**. These also include production overheads, such as factory supervision, rent of factory space, factory lighting and heating costs, and depreciation of factory equipment.

But the company must incur other costs too, such as advertising, distribution, office managers' salaries. These selling and administrative expenses are general overhead expenses of running the business which *cannot* easily be identified with particular products. They may be regarded as being incurred at a definite rate *per period*, rather than varying with the number of units produced; hence they are often called **period costs**.

Many expenditures are also **expenses** in the same period, either because they are product costs relating to goods *sold* in that period, or because they are period costs relating to that period. But two kinds of expenditures are not treated as expenses in the same period. Product costs relating to products which have not yet been sold at the end of a period are 'carried forward' as stocks on the balance sheet (like Mary Mullins's pictures). Also carried forward as assets are period costs *relating to future periods*. These may simply represent 'prepayments' (such as local rates or insurance premiums paid in advance). Or they may be 'fixed assets' (such as equipment or motor vehicles) to be used by the business over several years in the future. Chapter 6 describes how expenditure on fixed assets gradually becomes depreciation expense over its whole life.

It should be stressed that not all expenditures *can* be matched against sales revenue. This may be because they are period costs rather than product costs. Or they may, in effect, simply be *losses*; for example, the cost of advertising a product that nobody buys. Expenditures are carried forward as assets on the balance sheet only if there are expected to be *future* revenues against which they can be matched. Expenditures which cannot be matched against revenues, or product costs relating to the current period's sales revenue, are written off as expenses in the current period's profit and loss account.

Figure 5.8 summarises the treatment of expenditures.

The Profit and Loss Account 67

	Product costs	Period costs
Expense (P & L)	In period when product sold	If related to *current* period
Asset (BS)	If product unsold by end of period	If related to *future* period

Fig. 5.8: Product costs and period costs

5.4 Presentation

The overall 'profit and loss account' can be split into three parts:
1. the trading account
2. the profit and loss account
3. the appropriation account.

This section discusses them in turn.

5.4.1 The Trading Account

The **trading account** consists of sales revenue less operating expenses, and the final result is the trading (or 'operating') profit for the period. The trading account is often split into two, separating cost of goods sold from selling and administrative expenses.

Figure 5.9 sets out a skeleton layout for the trading account. Published accounts would normally disclose only the first line and the last line. The detail inside the dotted-line box would be omitted.

		(£)
Sales revenue		xxx
Less: Cost of goods sold:		
Materials	xxx	
Direct labour	xxx	
Production overheads	xxx	xxx
Gross profit		xxx
Less: Selling expenses	xxx	
Administrative expenses	xxx	xxx
Trading (operating) profit		xxx

Fig. 5.9: Layout for the trading account

Management accounts, for use by managers inside the company, would of course contain much more detailed analysis. They would often contain budgets for future periods, as well as actual past results. For example, sales revenue, cost of goods sold, and selling and administrative expenses might be analysed in two kinds of ways: (a) into months; and (b) between divisions, departments, product groups, or individual factories. Expenses would also be analysed in much more detail, for example, selling expenses would be split between advertising, distribution, salesmen's expenses, selling administration. The larger the company, the more detailed information is likely to be omitted from its published accounts.

5.4.2 The Profit and Loss Account

The profit and loss account starts with trading profit, includes any non-operating income (see 5.4.6 (a)), deducts interest and taxation, and ends with profit after tax for the period. In practice the published trading account and profit and loss account are often regarded as a *single* account, of which Fig. 5.10 provides a typical layout.

	£
Sales revenue	xxx
Trading (operating) profit	xxx
Add: Non-operating income	xxx
Profit before interest and tax	xxx
Less: Interest expense	xx
Profit before tax	xxx
Less: Taxation expense	xxx
Profit after tax	xxx

Fig. 5.10: Layout for published trading and profit and loss account

Interest expense represents the 'price of time' – the rent for borrowing money for a period. Long-term liabilities and bank overdrafts bear interest charges, while other current liabilities normally don't. Interest expense is shown separately in accounts because it relates to a company's method of *financing* operations (its sources of funds) rather than to the operating results themselves (its uses of funds). Any interest receivable (for example, on short-term deposits) may either be shown as a separate item of income below operating profit, or else netted against interest payable. As we shall see in Chapter 9, in analysing company accounts we may often be concerned with profit before interest and tax.

The Profit and Loss Account

Taxation expense in company accounts refers only to corporation tax, the tax related to company *profits*. All other taxes – such as local rates or national insurance – are included under other expense headings and not shown separately. The tax rules are rather complicated, so the tax expense for a period is usually *not* simply the current rate of corporation tax applied to the company's reported profit before tax. Hence company accounts show corporation tax separately, to enable readers to look at either profit before tax or profit after tax, depending on their precise needs.

5.4.3 The Appropriation Account

The **appropriation account** (or 'profit and loss appropriation account') shows the profit after tax for a period, the amount of any dividends relating to the period (paid or proposed, on ordinary or preference shares), and the amount of profit for the period retained in the company. Figure 5.11 shows a model layout.

	(£)
Profit after tax	xxx
Less: Ordinary dividends	xx
Retained profit for the period	xxx

Fig. 5.11: Layout for appropriation account

Ordinary dividends declared out of profits *are not an expense*. They do not affect the amount of profit actually earned during the period: they merely represent one possible way of *using* those profits.

The retained profit for a period is an important item: (a) in finance, because it is a major source of new funds, and (b) in accounting, because it is the *link* between the two main financial statements – the profit and loss account and the balance sheet.

The amount of profits retained ('ploughed back') for a period is added on to the cumulative retained profits, as part of shareholders' funds in the balance sheet. Retained 'profits' for a period will be *negative* either (a) if there is a *loss* for the period, or (b) if dividends happen to exceed profits after tax (see Fig. 5.14). (The figure for cumulative retained profits in the balance sheet would in either case have to be suitably *reduced*.)

5.4.4 The Overall Profit and Loss Account

The normal published profit and loss account often combines all three separate parts: the trading account, the profit and loss account, and the appropriation account; though sometimes the appropriation account is shown separately. As noted earlier, the details of the trading account are omitted in the published figures. Figure 5.12 shows a typical skeleton layout.

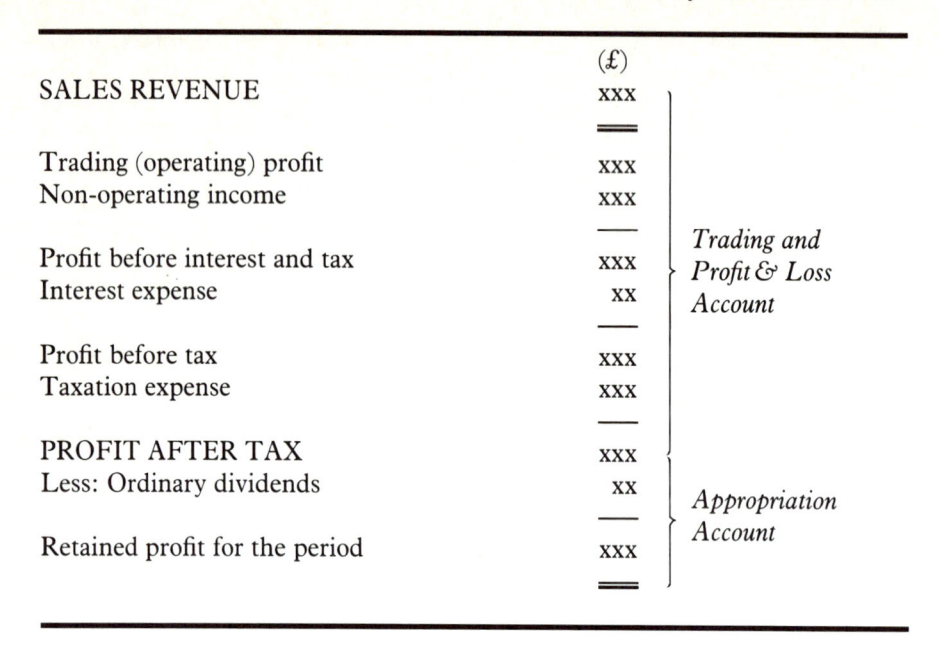

	(£)	
SALES REVENUE	xxx	
Trading (operating) profit	xxx	
Non-operating income	xxx	
		Trading and
Profit before interest and tax	xxx	*Profit & Loss*
Interest expense	xx	*Account*
Profit before tax	xxx	
Taxation expense	xxx	
PROFIT AFTER TAX	xxx	
Less: Ordinary dividends	xx	*Appropriation*
		Account
Retained profit for the period	xxx	

Fig. 5.12: Layout for the overall profit and loss account

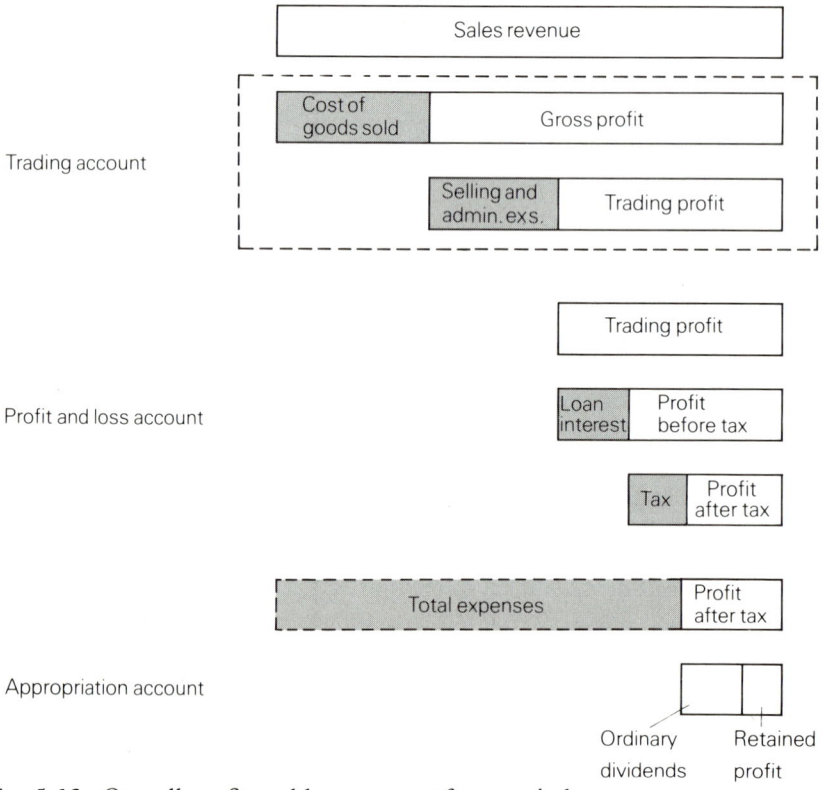

Fig. 5.13: Overall profit and loss account for a period

The Profit and Loss Account 71

The information contained in the overall profit and loss account for a period (not all of it published) can be shown graphically, as in Fig. 5.13.

5.4.5 Example

Figure 5.14 shows an example of a published profit and loss account for the Rank Organisation plc group, together with comparative figures for the previous year.

The Rank Organisation plc Group Profit and Loss Account for the year ended 31 October 1982

	Note	1982 (£'000)	1981 (£'000)
Turnover		675,182	618,402
Trading profit	2	33,167	39,144
Associated Companies:	3		
Rank Xerox Companies		57,109	85,181
Others		6,115	6,695
		96,391	131,020
Interest	4	34,867	28,264
Profit before taxation		61,524	102,756
Taxation	5	32,697	44,220
		28,827	58,536
Minority interests		2,357	5,587
Profit before extraordinary items		26,470	52,949
Extraordinary items	7	(22,466)	(1,944)
Profit attributable to The Rank Organisation plc	8	4,004	51,005
Dividends *	9	16,743	22,398
(Deficit) surplus carried forward		(12,739)	28,607

Fig. 5.14: The Rank Organisation plc: Group Profit and Loss Account for the year ended 31 October 1982.

* Preference dividends	583	583
Ordinary dividends, 8.0p per share *(10.8p)* on 202 million shares	16,160	21,815

5.4.6 Other Items

(a) Non-operating income

Many companies hold financial fixed assets (see **4.4.1** (c), p. 46), which may give rise to income from associated companies or from trade investments. As Fig. 5.14 shows, The Rank Organisation has large interests in the Rank Xerox companies, amounting to just under 49 per cent and valued in The Rank Organisation balance sheet at £235 million.

(b) Minority interests

Where a company controls subsidiary companies, it must own at least 50 per cent of the ordinary shares, but it may own less than 100 per cent. Suppose a company C owns 75 per cent of the ordinary shares in its subsidiary company S. It would be theoretically possible for C to include in its own **consolidated** (or **group**) **accounts** only 75 per cent of S's profit for the period. What happens in practice, however, is that C includes 100 per cent of S's profits in its operating profit (and deducts 100 per cent of S's taxation expense in its consolidated tax charge). A *separate* deduction from C's reported consolidated profit after tax is then made for **minority interests** – representing a deduction of the 25 per cent of S's profit after tax which does not 'belong' to the shareholders in C.

(c) Unusual items

Two kinds of items may need to be disclosed separately, either in the profit and loss account itself, or in the notes, on account of their unusual nature.
1. **Exceptional items** are unusual only on account of their *size*. Examples might be abnormally large bad debts, or stock write-offs. They are deducted in calculating operating profit; and disclosed in the notes to the accounts.
2. **Extraordinary items** arise from events or transactions *outside the ordinary activities of the business*, and are not expected to recur regularly or frequently. They should be disclosed separately in the published profit and loss account, but **below the line** – that is, *after* the line showing profit after tax for the year, and *before* ordinary dividends are deducted in the appropriation account. The major part of Rank's charge of £22.5 m for extraordinary items is attributable to closure and reorganisation costs incurred in Australia.

(d) Disclosure required

Certain items of expense must be disclosed separately, in the notes to the accounts if not elsewhere. (They are often shown in the Report of the Directors.) These items include the following:
 (i) Audit fee.
 (ii) Depreciation of fixed assets.
 (iii) Directors' remuneration.
 (iv) Charitable and political donations.
 (v) The number of persons employed, and their aggregate remuneration.

Work Section

A. Revision Questions

A1   What does the profit and loss account try to show?
A2   Define 'loss' for a period.
A3   In what two ways may profit for a period be used?
A4   How may shareholders benefit from company profits?
A5   How does retained profit link profit and loss account and balance sheet?

A6   Which three different events *might* cause recognition of a 'sale'?
A7   Which event actually causes recognition of a sale in accounting?
A8   Of the three events in A6 above, which two coincide when goods are: (a) made to order? (b) sold for cash?
A9   When does the legal title to goods normally pass to the buyer?
A10 When is 'cost of goods sold' charged as an expense?
A11 What is the difference between a cash sale and a credit sale: (a) in the profit and loss account? (b) in the balance sheet?
A12 How much do shareholders' funds change when a sale is recognised?
A13 How much do current assets change when a sale is recognised? Explain.
A14 What is a 'bad debt'? How does the profit and loss account treat it?
A15 Why might the original sales figure need amendment?

A16 What is the matching principle?
A17 What is the accrual principle?
A18 How do expenditures not made in cash affect the balance sheet?
A19 Distinguish between revenue expenditure and capital expenditure.
A20 Distinguish between product costs and period costs.
A21 Under what circumstances are product costs treated: (a) as an asset? (b) as an expense?
A22 Under what circumstances are period costs treated: (a) as an asset? (b) as an expense?
A23 Distinguish between expenditures and expenses.
A24 Name two reasons why some expenditures may not be able to be matched against sales revenue.
A25 What is the criterion for carrying forward expenditure as an asset on the balance sheet?

A26 Into what three parts can the overall profit and loss account be split?
A27 What does the trading account contain?
A28 What three main items does cost of goods sold consist of?
A29 What part of the trading account is normally not published?

A30 In what ways might management accounts analyse the trading account in more detail?
A31 What does the profit and loss account contain?
A32 Define 'interest expense'.
A33 Which liabilities do not normally bear interest? Which do?
A34 What is 'taxation expense' in accounts?
A35 How may interest receivable be treated?
A36 What does the appropriation account contain?
A37 Are ordinary dividends an expense? Why or why not?
A38 Which item links the end-of-period balance sheet and the profit and loss account for that period?
A39 Name two possible reasons for retained profits for a period being negative.
A40 How do negative retained profits for a period affect shareholders' funds?
A41 Name three expense items for which separate disclosure is required.
A42 Distinguish the definition and accounting treatment of 'exceptional' and 'extraordinary' items.
A43 What does 'below the line' mean?
A44 Define 'minority interests'. How are they treated in the profit and loss account?
A45 How is income from associated companies shown?

B. Exercises and Case Studies

B1 Is sales revenue recorded when:
    a. A debtor pays for an earlier purchase?
    b. A merchant signs a legal contract for goods?
    c. A nearby client takes delivery of an order placed last year?
    d. The factory completes all the goods for an order?

B2 Write out the double entries for each of the following:
    a. Purchase of goods for £500 in cash.
    b. Sale for £600 in cash of goods costing £400.
    c. Purchase of goods for £500 on credit, and the payment one month later to the supplier.
    d. Sale on credit for £600 of goods costing £400, and the receipt of cash two months later from the customer.

B3 Is a purchase recorded when:
    a. A company places a written order for goods?
    b. A deposit is paid on goods for later delivery?
    c. A supplier is paid by cheque for goods received last year?
    d. Goods ordered last year arrive at the company's premises?

B4 Refer to Mary Mullins and her trading activities on p. 65.
    a. Complete the table in Fig. 5.7 for weeks 2, 3, and 4.
    b. Draw up Mary's balance sheet at the end of week 4.

The Profit and Loss Account

B5 The balance sheet of Vogue Fashions Ltd at the end of 1983 is summarised below:

	(£)		(£)
Shareholders' funds	5,000	Assets	15,000
Liabilities	10,000		
	15,000		15,000

The transactions for 1984 are summarised below:

	(£)
Trading expenses	46,000
Interest paid	1,000
Sales	52,000
Ordinary dividends paid	1,000
Tax	2,000

a. Draw up a profit and loss account for 1984, and a summarised balance sheet (similar to that shown above) at the end of 1984. Liabilities at the end of 1984 total £11,000.
b. Describe and explain the changes in the end-1984 balance sheet as compared with the end-1983 balance sheet.

B6 From the following list of items for Wilfred Kelly Limited in respect of the year ending 30 September 1984, prepare a profit and loss account in a form suitable for publication.

	(£'000)
Ordinary dividend – interim paid	4
Ordinary dividend – final proposed	7
Operating profit	47
Retained profit for the year	?
Tax	18
Sales revenue	346
Interest expense	11

B7 In January, Brown makes an inquiry.
In February, Smith quotes a price.
In March, Brown places an order.
In April, Smith buys the materials.
In May, Smith completes production.
In June, Smith delivers the order.
In July, Brown queries the quality.
In August, Smith agrees to a small price reduction on the order.
In September, Smith reminds Brown of what is owed.
In October, Brown pays half the amount due.
In November, Smith demands the balance.
In December, Brown pays the balance due to Smith.

When does Smith recognise the profit on the above transaction?
(Hint: You may find it difficult to answer in a single word.)

B8 Potter Trading's balance sheet at the end of March contains only the items: cash £1,000 and issued share capital £1,000.

The company purchases goods for £1,000 and sells them for £1,300. Calculate the profit or loss and construct the new balance sheet at the end of April.

   a. If all transactions were for cash.
   b. If all transactions were on credit.
   c. If sales were for cash and purchases on credit.
   d. If purchases were for cash and sales on credit.

B9 A friend of yours buys a small country pub. After 3 months of business he asks you to help him calculate his profit on beer sales. He has had 500 gallons delivered each month. When he took over the pub (on New Year's Eve) there were 50 gallons in the cellar, and at the end of March there were still 50 gallons there. Beer costs £4.00 per gallon. His monthly output was: January 400 gallons, February 500 gallons, March 600 gallons; but 5 per cent of beer is lost in spillage, etc. The beer is sold for 80 pence per pint.

   a. Calculate the total profit on beer sales per month.
   b. Calculate the profit per pint sold.

B10 Refer to Fig. 5.7 (p. 65). At the end of week 4, Mary Mullins had no pictures left. At this point she decided it would be more profitable to pay her brother a 'wage' of £1 for each picture he painted, and for her to buy the materials for him to use, rather than buying completed pictures from him. Her brother agreed to this new arrangement. Mary estimated that her other direct production costs (such as paints, paper, etc.) would be 40p per picture, and the frames £1.20 for each picture.

In week 5, Mary purchased frames for six pictures. Her brother completed four pictures, and was paid £4 wages. The other direct production costs were in line with Mary's estimate. Mary sold three of the pictures in week 5 for £5 each.

   a. Construct a profit and loss account for week 5 (Mary's first week of 'manufacturing').
   b. Construct a balance sheet as at the end of week 5, assuming that Mary only makes deals for cash.

B11 What, if anything, should be shown on the balance sheet at 30 June 1984, and where should it be shown, in respect of each of the following items:
   a. Telephone account for quarter ended 31 May (unpaid at end of June).

Rental (3 months in advance)	£60
Calls for 3 months to 31 May	£75
	£135

The Profit and Loss Account

    b. Electricity account £96 for quarter ended 30 April (paid in June).
    c. Audit fee £850 in respect of year ended 30 June 1984 (not started until August 1984; invoice sent November 1984; paid December 1984).
    d. Motor insurance premiums £240, for year ended 30 September 1984, paid October 1983.

B12 Refer to Fig. 5.14 (p. 71), showing The Rank Organisation plc's group profit and loss account for the year ended 31 October 1982.
    a. How much has profit changed between the two years? Explain why, as briefly and clearly as you can.
    b. How have shareholders been affected, directly and indirectly, in 1982 compared with 1981?

B13 Calco, which makes electronic calculators and sells them for £15.00 each, has direct production costs as follows:

Raw materials	£33.00 per dozen units
Bought-in components	£ 5.30 per unit
Direct wages	£ 2.65 per unit
Production overheads	£ 0.70 per unit.

Calco's weekly performance in terms of sales and output, and its expenditure on materials and components, was as follows:

Week		1	2	3	4	5
Units sold		10,000	10,000	11,000	11,000	12,000
Units produced		12,000	12,000	8,000	12,000	15,000
Materials purchased	(£)	41,250	27,500	41,250	27,500	27,500
Components purchased	(£)	63,600	63,600	42,400	63,600	79,500

Calculate the gross trading profit each week.

B14 Acme Joiners Ltd produces a popular line of kitchen units. It buys several components and makes the rest of the parts itself from raw materials. Machinists perform the production operations, and assemblers put together their output plus the appropriate components bought ready-made. The units are then spray-painted and packed in cartons.

The following information is presented to the accountant by her assistant early in January 1984:

	(£'000)
Stocks on hand on 1.1.83:	
Materials	30
Components	48
Finished goods	180
Stocks on hand on 31.12.83:	
Materials	36
Components	57
Finished goods	90
Wages paid to factory personnel:	
Machinists	30
Assemblers	15

Painters	12
Packers	3
Materials received	306
Components received	489
Payments made to suppliers	759
Production overheads paid	60
Sales on credit	1050
Sales for cash	600
Received from debtors	630
Administrative overheads paid	90
Selling overheads paid	45

During 1983 the company paid a dividend of £75,000; and used most of the rest of the profits to buy new plant for a proposed expansion. Taxation is payable at 40 per cent on profits.

Construct a profit and loss account for internal use.

B15 Refer to B14.

Amend the profit and loss account to take account of the following:

a. In December 1983 an advance payment of £9,000 for a market research survey to take place in January 1984 was made. This amount was included in the selling overheads for 1983.
b. On 20 January 1984 an invoice was received for £15,000 for renovations to the buildings carried out in the previous autumn. The renovators had forgotten to invoice Acme, and nobody there had noticed the omission.
c. Debtors owing a total of £17,000 are now thought unlikely to pay in full; and a provision of £11,000 is to be made for bad debts.
d. It has been decided to recommend a final ordinary dividend of £35,000 in respect of 1983, in addition to the £75,000 interim dividend already paid.
e. It is now expected that the tax rate applying to 1983 profits will be 50 per cent, not 40 per cent.

B16 From the following list of items, prepare a profit and loss account for J. W. Hooker plc, for the year ending 31 March 1984, in a form suitable for publication:

	(£'000)
Minority interests	21
Operating profit	193
Ordinary dividend – interim paid	18
Income from associated companies	17
Sales revenue	1,242
Preference dividends paid	6
Interest expense	61

Extraordinary expenses	13
Retained profit for the year	?
Ordinary dividend – final proposed	30
Tax	71

How much is the 'profit for the year'?

C. Essay Questions

C1   Should profit be recognised in accounts when extra value is created? At what stage *is* value added by a manufacturing company?

C2   'A profit and loss account merely analyses the total expenses to be deducted from sales revenue.' Comment.

C3   Discuss the view that 'matching' is essentially a *balance sheet* concept: it requires expenditure to be carried forward as an asset at the end of a period if, but only if, it is reasonably certain to be 'matchable' against future sales revenues, otherwise to be written off as an expense in the current period's profit and loss account.

C4   'The difference between cash accounting and accrual accounting is the difference between expenditure and expense.' Discuss.

C5   Should bad debts be deducted directly from sales revenue, instead of only indirectly, as a separate item of 'expense'?

C6   Can there be any justification for treating period costs as an asset?

C7   'The profit and loss account for a period merely explains the change in one balance sheet item between dates.' Discuss.

C8   Should extraordinary items be excluded altogether from the profit and loss account? How else could they be treated?

C9   Should increases arising on revaluation of assets be regarded as profits?

C10 Why does it matter when a sale is recognised in accounts?

6 Depreciation of Fixed Assets

6.1 Depreciation
6.1.1 Purpose
6.1.2 Information Required

6.2 Methods of Depreciation
6.2.1 Straight-line
6.2.2 Declining Balance
6.2.3 Comparison
6.2.4 Other Methods

6.3 Miscellaneous
6.3.1 Profit or Loss on Disposal
6.3.2 Revaluing Fixed Assets
6.3.3 Revising Estimated Lives
6.3.4 Part-years
6.3.5 Profits and Cash Flow

Objective: *To explain the purpose of depreciation of fixed assets, to outline the information needed to determine it, and to describe the main methods.*

Synopsis: *Depreciation aims to spread a fixed asset's cost over the periods which benefit from its use. It is thus an extreme example of the 'matching' principle. A fixed asset's life may be limited by the passing of time, physical wear and tear, or technical or market obsolescence. The information needed to determine depreciation is: (1) the fixed asset's original cost; (2) its expected economic life; (3) its expected residual value (if any); and (4) the chosen method of depreciation. The many estimates required make the amount of depreciation expense somewhat subjective.*

The two main depreciation methods are: straight-line, charging an equal amount each year; and declining balance, charging a constant percentage of declining net book value. Straight-line is easily the most common method in the UK.

Depreciation of Fixed Assets

6.1 Depreciation

6.1.1 Purpose

Fixed assets are resources lasting for several years and intended to produce goods or services, not for resale. Accounts charge **depreciation** expense in order to spread a fixed asset's cost over its life in the periods which benefit from its use. Depreciation of fixed assets is thus an extreme example of the 'matching' process in accounting. The depreciation of intangible assets is usually called **amortisation**.

If a business simply charged the whole cost of a new machine as an expense in the year it was bought, profit would be understated in that year. The whole cost of a machine lasting several years would have been deducted from the first year's sales revenue. But the profit would then be overstated in later years, since there would then be no deduction from sales revenue for the use of the machine.

On the other hand, if *no* depreciation expense were charged during the machine's life, a large loss would arise in the year it was finally scrapped. Profit would have been overstated in the early years, with no charge being made for the using-up of the machine. This treatment would be suitable only for those fixed assets – like land – which do *not* lose value over time.

Accounts normally show fixed assets at their original cost less the accumulated depreciation written off (charged as an expense) to date. Any period's depreciation is charged as an expense in the profit and loss account, and added to the accumulated depreciation on the balance sheet.

Thus Fig. 6.1 shows balance sheet net book values for a fixed asset with a three-year life costing £12,000 at the beginning of 1982. Depreciation expense is £4,000 in each of the three years.

	End 1982 (£)	End 1983 (£)	End 1984 (£)
Original cost	12,000	12,000	12,000
Less: Accumulated depreciation	4,000	8,000	12,000
Net book value	8,000	4,000	—

Fig. 6.1: Balance sheet amounts for fixed asset

6.1.2 Information Required

To calculate depreciation in any period, four separate items of information are needed:

a. the fixed asset's original cost;
b. its expected economic life;

c. its residual (or scrap) value;
d. the *method* of depreciation to be used.

The first three are discussed below, and the method of depreciation in **6.2**.

(*a*) *Original cost*

The original cost of a fixed asset may simply be the amount invoiced by a supplier. But other amounts may need to be added to the 'cost', such as legal charges incurred in acquiring leasehold property, or installation costs of equipment.

There may be doubt how to treat the cost of major repairs to a fixed asset. If they merely restore an asset to its former condition, they should be treated as an expense in that period. But where repairs *improve* the asset, their cost should be **capitalised** (added to the fixed asset's 'cost'). The cost of the improvement will then itself be written off as depreciation expense over a number of future periods. (An improvement may lengthen an asset's life, increase its physical capacity, or better the quality of its output.)

(*b*) *Economic life*

The useful life of an asset may be limited by:
  i. *the passing of time* – e.g. a lease for a definite number of years, or a patent, which has a legal life of only 20 years.
  ii. *physical wear and tear* – e.g. a machine which gradually wears out as a result of physical use.
  iii. *technical obsolescence* – e.g. old-fashioned adding-machines have largely been replaced by electronic calculators, and steam-engines by diesels. Newer technology may allow a cheaper or a better-quality product, even if the outmoded assets are still physically usable.
  iv. *market obsolescence* – e.g. motor cars or clothes, whose styles go out of fashion even if no new technology is involved.

Where the life of an asset is definitely known, there is no problem. Physical wear and tear can often be estimated fairly closely by engineers with experience of similar assets; though the asset's rate of use may vary. Technical obsolescence can sometimes be estimated, though often only approximately. Finally, market obsolescence may be the hardest of all to guess, depending as it does on the subjective preferences of consumers.

Accountants tend to be conservative: if in doubt they prefer to use a shorter economic life rather than a longer one. As a rule accountants try to avoid an asset having to be sold or scrapped for much less than its net book value at the time. (They are less worried if they *under*estimate an asset's life, so that it continues in use long after its net book value has been written down to zero.)

Depreciation of Fixed Assets

(c) Residual value

A fixed asset is disposed of when it reaches the end of its economic life. Only the difference between the original cost and the expected resale value has to be charged as depreciation expense during its life. For example, a car hire firm may keep its vehicles for only three years before replacing them. If each car costs £5,400 and can be sold after three years for £1,800, then only £3,600 in total (£1,200 each year) has to be written off as depreciation. In practice a fixed asset's resale value (**residual value**) may be so small, or so uncertain, that it is ignored in estimating depreciation.

6.2 Methods of Depreciation

6.2.1 Straight-line

The **straight-line** method of depreciation is the simplest, and by far the most common. It writes off an *equal* expense each year, based on the asset's net cost (original cost less residual value) and estimated life. Note that *both* the amounts are only estimates.

Thus if a lorry costs £10,000, and is reckoned to have a useful life of five years, with a residual value at the end of £2,000, the depreciation expense each year would be £1,600:

$$\frac{£10,000 - £2,000}{5} = \frac{£8,000}{5} = £1,600.$$

Figure 6.2 shows what would appear in the accounts each year.

	Profit and loss account Depreciation expense	End-of-year balance sheet Original cost	−	Accumulated depreciation	=	Net book value
	(£)	(£)		(£)		(£)
Year 1	1,600	10,000	−	1,600	=	8,400
Year 2	1,600	10,000	−	3,200	=	6,800
Year 3	1,600	10,000	−	4,800	=	5,200
Year 4	1,600	10,000	−	6,400	=	3,600
Year 5	1,600	10,000	−	8,000	=	2,000

Fig. 6.2: Fixed asset entries in accounts: straight-line depreciation

The same information can be shown graphically, as in Fig. 6.3.

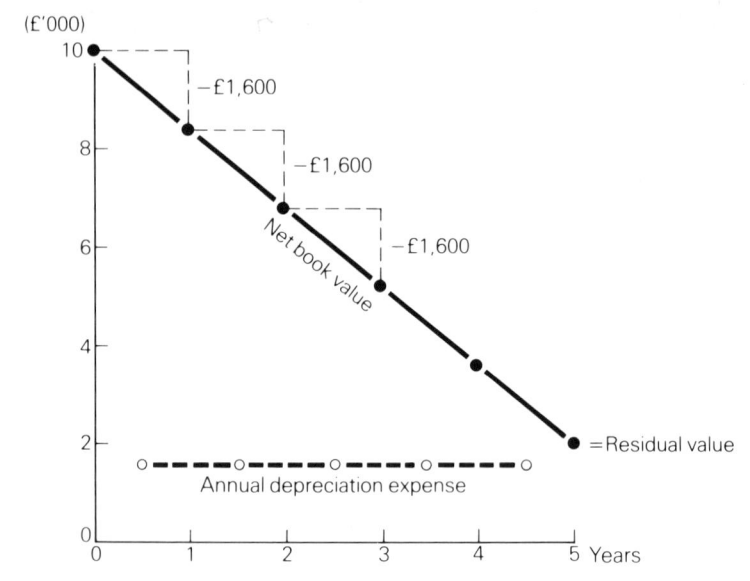

Fig. 6.3: Straight-line depreciation

6.2.2 Declining Balance

The **declining balance** method of 'accelerated' depreciation charges larger amounts to expense in the early years of an asset's life than in later years. It applies to the asset's declining net book value each year a constant percentage to reduce it (roughly) to the expected residual value at the end of its life.

For the lorry costing £10,000, lasting five years, and with an expected residual value of £2,000, the required constant declining balance percentage rate would be about 27½ per cent.* (see footnote p. 85).

Thus Figure 6.4. shows the amounts which would appear in the accounts for each of the five years.

	Profit and loss account Depreciation expense	End-of-year balance sheet		
		Original cost	Accumulated depreciation	Net book value
	(£)	(£)	(£)	(£)
Year 1	2,750	10,000	2,750	7,250
Year 2	1,994	10,000	4,744	5,256
Year 3	1,446	10,000	6,190	3,810
Year 4	1,048	10,000	7,238	2,762
Year 5	760	10,000	7,998	2,002

Fig. 6.4: Fixed asset entries in accounts: declining balance depreciation

Depreciation of Fixed Assets   85

Figure 6.5 shows the declining balance information graphically.

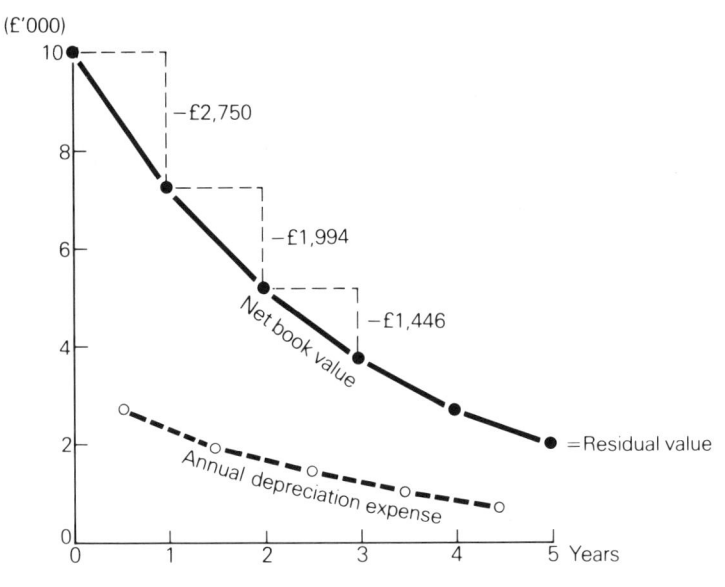

Fig. 6.5: Declining balance depreciation

6.2.3 Comparison

Both straight-line and declining balance depreciation methods aim to charge as an expense over the expected economic life of a fixed asset its net cost to the business. But the *pattern* varies year by year, both the depreciation expense and the net book value.

Most British companies use the straight-line method; most United States companies the declining balance. The choice between them is partly a matter of custom. Two arguments are sometimes suggested in favour of the declining balance method. For many assets, maintenance and repair costs tend to grow as the asset becomes older. Hence using declining balance depreciation tends to result in a more equal *total* expense each year for fixed-asset-related expenses (maintenance plus depreciation).

A second argument is that many assets tend to lose second-hand market value faster in the early years. Thus declining balance **net book values** more closely reflect the pattern of decline in the market value of the assets. (But the purpose of depreciation is not to reduce an asset's net book value to its net realisable value at *each* balance sheet date; merely to do so by the *end* of its economic life. On the assumption that a fixed asset will be held until the end of its economic life, depreciation is a process of allocating its net cost over its life.)

---

* The exact percentage can be calculated by solving the equation:

$$\text{Rate of depreciation} = (1 - \sqrt[n]{\frac{\text{Residual value}}{\text{Cost}}}) \times 100 \text{ per cent}$$

where n = the number of years of useful life.

A higher percentage rate is needed to write an asset off using the declining balance method rather than the straight-line method. This is because the declining balance percentage (27½ per cent for the lorry) is applied to the *declining net book value* each year, whereas the straight-line percentage is applied to the original cost. (For the same reason, the declining balance method will never reduce an asset's net book value quite to zero. But when the net book value becomes very small in relation to original cost, it can be written off entirely in a single year.)

Clearly two similar companies with identical fixed assets can produce different accounting results by using different depreciation methods.

Example: *Two companies, Laurel Ltd and Hardy Ltd, are in the same business, and both regularly make profits (before depreciation) of about £30,000 a year. (To simplify the example, we ignore tax.) Both companies acquire identical equipment at a cost of £40,000.*

Laurel's technical director believes that the equipment could soon be outdated. He proposes that the company should write it off over three years, allow for a residual value of £5,000, and use declining balance depreciation in case the equipment becomes obsolete even sooner than expected. The required percentage depreciation rate to apply to the declining net book value is 50 per cent each year.

Hardy's production manager, on the other hand, expects his equipment to last for five years, after which time he thinks it should be saleable for about £10,000. The company uses straight-line depreciation.

This example shows the impact of opinion (expectations) on reported accounting results. The widely different figures shown in Fig. 6.6 for the two companies represent the *same physical facts*. But the two managers take different views about the uncertain future.

		Profit and loss account		End-of-year balance sheet	
		Depreciation expense	Net profit	Accumulated depreciation	Net book value
		(£'000)	(£'000)	(£'000)	(£'000)
	Year 1	20	10	20	20
	Year 2	10	20	30	10
LAUREL	Year 3	5	25	35	5
	Year 4	2½	27½	37½	2½
	Year 5	1¼	28¾	38¾	1¼
	Year 1	6	24	6	34
	Year 2	6	24	12	28
HARDY	Year 3	6	24	18	22
	Year 4	6	24	24	16
	Year 5	6	24	30	10

Fig. 6.6: Comparison of two depreciation methods

Depreciation of Fixed Assets

6.2.4 Other Methods

(a) Sum-of-the-years' digits

In the United States the **sum-of-the-years' digits** method also charges more in the early than in the later years of a fixed asset's life. If an asset has a five-year life, the sum-of-the-years' digits is 15 (= 5 + 4 + 3 + 2 + 1). In the first year the depreciation charge would be 5/15 of the original cost, in the second year 4/15 of the original cost, in the third year 3/15, and so on. The overall effect is similar to the declining balance method.

(b) Machine hour (usage) method

Physical wear and tear may be the main cause limiting an asset's life. It may then be appropriate to relate depreciation expense to the amount of *use* an asset receives in any accounting period. Suppose that a machine is expected to produce 50,000 units over its life before being worn out. The machine costs £22,000, and will have a residual value of about £2,000. Then, under the **usage method**, the depreciation expense may be reckoned as 40p per unit produced (= £20,000/50,000 units). If in the first year 14,000 units are produced, the depreciation expense will be £5,600; if in the second year only 8,000 units are produced, then depreciation in that year will be only £3,200; and so on. The same approach may be used for other assets, such as motor vehicles (on a mileage basis).

6.3 Miscellaneous

6.3.1 Profit or Loss on Disposal

When fixed assets are finally disposed of, the sales proceeds may differ from the balance sheet net book value. Indeed this is likely unless both the economic life and the residual value have been guessed precisely right in advance. Any excess is a profit on disposal (or any deficit a loss on disposal). In effect these are *adjustments* of prior years' depreciation charges, and are usually subtracted from (or added to) the total depreciation charge for the current year. But very large profits or losses on disposal may be disclosed separately, as 'exceptional items' (see **5.4.6 (c)**).

6.3.2 Revaluing Fixed Assets

Chapter 8 on inflation accounting discusses whether and how to revalue fixed assets to allow for inflation. But some fixed assets may be revalued above original cost even in 'historical cost' accounts. Many companies formally revalue all their freehold and leasehold property every five years or so. If the new valuation exceeds the fixed assets' net book value, the excess is added to shareholders' funds as a revaluation reserve (see **4.2.2(b)**). *It is not regarded as a* *profit*. Similar revaluations are rarer for other fixed assets, such as plant and equipment. This may be because any future depreciation charges would have to be based not on the fixed assets' original cost, but on the new higher valuation. The effect would be to reduce reported profit. Clearly it is difficult to compare the results of different companies if some have revalued their fixed assets while others continue to use original cost.

6.3.3 Revising Estimated Lives

Some companies revise their estimates of asset lives from time to time. Imperial Chemical Industries, for example, includes this statement in its Annual Report:

'Estimates of asset lives cannot be made with precision and in practice a range of possible lives exists. Reviews are made periodically of the estimated remaining lives of individual productive assets, taking account of commercial and technical obsolescence as well as normal wear and tear.'

Where a fixed asset's life is revised, the net book value should be written down to estimated residual value over the revised remaining life. Where the original estimated life was too long there would otherwise be a loss on disposal. Where, however, the estimated life was too *short*, a company may carry on its books fixed assets which are fully written off. (That means the accumulated depreciation equals the original cost, and the net book value is zero.) As long as an asset remains in use, its original cost continues to be included in the total cost of fixed assets (and the accumulated depreciation total may include that same amount). Cost and accumulated depreciation for a specific fixed asset are eliminated from the books only when it is disposed of or retired from active use.

6.3.4 Part-years

Companies buy and sell fixed assets all through the year, not only right at the start. Some companies charge a full year's depreciation in the year of acquisition, and none in the year of disposal; while others do the opposite. Or depreciation may be charged pro rata, so that if an asset is bought after four months of the accounting year, 4/12ths of a full year's depreciation is charged in the first year. Whichever practice is used, it should be followed *consistently*.

6.3.5 Profits and Cash Flow

Profit is not the same as cash. Many a business has collapsed through failing to distinguish the two. Profit is an accounting measurement of the surplus on trading for a period, calculated by deducting all business expenses from sales revenue. If a business sells goods for more than their total cost, it has made a profit. But until the customers *pay* for the goods, the business may have no cash. Even if the customers have paid, the whole profit for a period may be distributed in cash dividends to shareholders. Cash, on the other hand, is a liquid asset owned by a business. A company may have been losing money, but by closing down an unprofitable factory may generate plenty of cash.

Depreciation of Fixed Assets

Depreciation of fixed assets is a striking example of the difference between profits and cash. Depreciation expense is deducted from sales revenue in the profit and loss account, along with all other expenses. The larger the depreciation expense in a period, the smaller the profit. But depreciation does *not* involve any payment of cash in the period: it is merely an allocation to expense of part of the original cost of a fixed asset.

Indeed, the *acquisition* of fixed assets also illustrates the difference between profits and cash. For the whole cost of a fixed asset will involve a cash payment at the time of acquisition. Yet profits are only reduced gradually over the whole life of the asset. Thus the *timing* is very different; and we must not expect to be able to equate profit and cash for any single accounting period.

The financial press often refers to the term **cash flow** as a shorthand description meaning 'retained profits plus depreciation' for a period. Confusion is sometimes caused by this practice of apparently treating depreciation expense as if it were somehow a positive inflow of cash to a business. Depreciation is neither a source nor a use of cash. Depreciation is a book-keeping allocation, not a cash payment *or* receipt.

It is worth noting that increasing the company's depreciation charge *does not affect the charge for taxation*. (If it did, it would indirectly increase the cash position, by reducing the amount to be paid out for tax.) The Inland Revenue has its own rules for calculating **capital allowances** (depreciation for tax purposes); and they *completely ignore* the company's own method of estimating depreciation.

Work Section

A. Revision Questions

A1 Define a fixed asset.
A2 What is the purpose of depreciation?
A3 What is the difference between depreciation and amortisation?
A4 How are fixed assets normally valued in balance sheets?
A5 Distinguish between depreciation expense and accumulated depreciation.
A6 What four items of information are needed to estimate depreciation?
A7 Give two reasons why depreciation is usually only an estimate.
A8 When might 'repairs' be partly or wholly added to the cost of fixed assets in the balance sheet?
A9 Name three possible reasons why an asset's useful life may be limited.
A10 Why is residual value relevant in estimating depreciation?

A11 What are the two main methods of depreciation?
A12 Distinguish between the two main methods of depreciation.
A13 Name two arguments for using declining balance depreciation.
A14 What is the 'usage method' of depreciation?
A15 When may the usage method be especially suitable?

A16 How can a profit or loss arise on disposal of a fixed asset?
A17 How does the profit and loss account normally treat a profit or loss on disposal of a fixed asset?
A18 Explain in two different ways how much is charged in total as an expense in respect of a fixed asset over its whole life.
A19 How can revaluing fixed assets affect future depreciation charges?
A20 Name two possible ways to calculate first-year depreciation expense when a company buys a fixed asset in the middle of the year.
A21 Why do sales not necessarily result in a receipt of cash in the same period?
A22 What cash flows are directly associated with a fixed asset? When do they occur?
A23 What is meant by 'cash flow'?
A24 Explain why increasing depreciation expense does not affect cash flow.
A25 Explain why increasing depreciation expense does not affect tax.

B. Exercises and Case Studies

B1 A firm of solicitors acquires a four-year lease for £24,000.
  a. What depreciation expense should be charged each year?
  b. How will the lease appear on the balance sheet at the end of each year?

Depreciation of Fixed Assets

B2 Marcel et Cie uses straight-line depreciation. It buys a new machine for weighing chemicals. The machine costs 120,000 francs at the beginning of 1983, and is expected to last for six years.
   Show how the machine will appear in Marcel's balance sheet at the end of 1984:
   a. if no residual value is assumed.
   b. if residual value of 30,000 francs is allowed for.

B3 Kenneth Barker buys a new typewriter for £600. He plans to use it for four years, after which time he anticipates it will have a trade-in value of about £150. He proposes to depreciate the machine using the declining balance method, with a percentage rate of 30 per cent.
   a. What will the depreciation expense be each year?
   b. What will the net book value be at the end of each year?

B4 James Carter pays £12,000 for a truck with an estimated life of four years. Residual value of £2,000 is expected, and straight-line depreciation is used. After three years the truck is sold for £4,000.
   a. Calculate the profit or loss on disposal.
   b. Prepare a table showing how the truck's total net cost over its whole life is charged as an expense year by year.
   c. What would the profit or loss on disposal have been if residual value had been ignored in charging depreciation?

B5 Peterborough Printers Ltd buys photogravure equipment for £11,000 at the beginning of 1984. It makes £8,000 a year profit before charging depreciation. The company's manager expects the equipment will last for five years, and will then have a scrap value of £1,000.
   a. Draw up a table showing the net profit year by year:
      (i) using straight-line depreciation;
      (ii) using declining balance depreciation at 35 per cent a year.
   b. Comment on the magnitude of the percentage rate used for the declining balance method, compared with straight-line depreciation.
   c. How might you have dealt with depreciation if the equipment had been bought halfway through 1984?

B6 Jones Car Hire Ltd purchases new cars which are kept for three years before being sold second-hand, for about one-third of the original price. In 1983, 1984, and 1985 the company buys four, two and five new vehicles respectively, for £6,000 each.
   a. Construct a table showing total depreciation expense each year for these cars, using straight-line depreciation.
   b. Construct a similar table using declining balance depreciation.

B7 Reliable Transport Ltd acquires a lorry for £14,000 which it expects to last for four years, at the end of which time it will be sold for about £2,000. The lorry's mileage each year is as follows:

	(*'000 miles*)
Year 1 (part)	14
Year 2	20

Year 3	24
Year 4	10*
Year 5 (part)	12

*Off the road for the second half of year 4, due to engine problems.

   a. Draw up a table comparing the depreciation expense each year under:
      (i) the usage method;
      (ii) the straight-line method.
   b. What information would be needed at the start of the lorry's life in order to calculate depreciation under each method?
   c. Show the accounting results, under each method, if the lorry had actually been sold for £1,000 when it first broke down in the middle of year 4.

B8 Robertson Engines plc invests £150,000 in tooling which it expects to last for five years and to have a residual value of £25,000. The company uses straight-line depreciation.
   a. Prepare a table showing year by year over the asset's expected life:
      (i) depreciation expense;
      (ii) accumulated depreciation;
      (iii) net book value.
   b. Prepare a similar table for a competitor company, Paynter and Sutcliffe Ltd, which buys identical tooling for £150,000, but estimates only a four-year life and a residual value of £20,000, and which uses declining balance depreciation.

B9 Adam Blair & Sons use the sum-of-the-years' digits method to depreciate a machine costing £75,000 with an estimated four-year life.
   a. Prepare a schedule of the year-by-year depreciation charge and net book value of the asset.
   b. What is the accounting result if the machine is sold at the end of year 6 for £4,000?

B10 Simon Fisher Inc. buys machinery for $200,000, which is expected to last for three years and to have a residual value of $60,000.
   a. Using the formula at the foot of p. 85, calculate a suitable annual percentage rate of declining balance depreciation.
   b. Confirm your arithmetic by setting out the net book value of the machine for each year of its three-year life, using the rate of depreciation calculated in (a) above.

B11 George Viner Ltd depreciates its office building, which originally cost £300,000, over 20 years, using straight-line depreciation and ignoring any possible residual value. After 15 years it realises that too short a life has been used; and the building's remaining life is re-estimated at 15 years.
   a. What is the annual depreciation expense for the early years of the building's life?
   b. What will it be for the later years?
   c. What would it have been throughout, if the life had been 'correctly' estimated to begin with?

Depreciation of Fixed Assets

B12 Oregon Yards acquired equipment for £30,000 which was expected to last for 10 years, and would be written off on the straight-line basis, with no residual value allowed for. After six years the company reckoned its equipment still had eight years of useful life remaining, and decided to adjust its future depreciation charges accordingly.
  a. What would the annual depreciation charge be:
   (i) in years 1 to 6?
   (ii) in years 7 to 14?
  b. What difference would it make if in each case a residual value of £6,000 was allowed for?

B13 The lorry discussed in **6.2.1** and **6.2.2** was actually sold for £3,000 at the end of year 4.
  a. Show the profit or loss on disposal:
   (i) using straight-line depreciation;
   (ii) using declining balance depreciation.
  b. Calculate the total 'depreciation' charged over the lorry's whole life, by combining the depreciation expense for each year with the profit or loss on disposal:
   (i) using straight-line depreciation;
   (ii) using declining balance depreciation.

(Hint: The total 'depreciation' ought to come to the original cost, less the net proceeds; i.e. the same total amount in each case.)

B14 Hudson Ltd's summarised profit and loss account for 1984, and an estimate of 'internally-generated cash flow', is shown below. In the original accounts £20,000 depreciation expense was charged; but as the company is short of cash, and as the finance director thinks that 'depreciation is a source of funds', he decides to increase the depreciation charge by 50 per cent in order to increase the cash flow by £10,000! Demonstrate that altering the depreciation expense will make no difference at all to cash flow.

	(£'000)
Profit before depreciation	60
Depreciation expense	20
Profit before tax	40
Corporation tax	14
Profit after tax	26
Ordinary dividends	12
Retained profit for the year	14
Retained profit for the year, as above	14
'Add back' depreciation expense	20
= 'Internally-generated cash flow'	34

B15 With £6,000 he received as a redundancy payment, James Palmer decided to start a travelling greengrocer's business. He bought a second-hand van for £4,800; and used the remaining £1,200 to buy his initial trading stock.

Each morning he went to the wholesale market to buy vegetables and fruit for his day's sales. All his purchases and sales were for cash. Each weekend Mr Palmer threw out any remaining stock. He kept aside the £1,200 he would need to buy new stocks on Monday morning, and regarded any excess over that amount as profit which he spent on living expenses (and on tax).

After five years the van was on its last legs, and a garage offered £800 for it as a trade-in against a replacement costing £4,800. But Mr Palmer was quite unable to raise the extra £4,000 cash required, so his business collapsed.
   a. Was the cash taken for personal use really his business profit?
   b. What steps could Mr Palmer have taken to avoid the collapse of his business?

B16 In 1974 Plant Hire Ltd paid £10,000 for a crane with an estimated life of 10 years. Using the straight-line method, the company charged £1,000 a year depreciation to overheads. Plant Hire's policy was to finance all fixed asset purchases out of profits, and to distribute 50 per cent of its profits in dividends to shareholders. Operating profits were usually about 10 per cent of sales revenue.

When the crane had to be replaced in 1984, the company found the price was £30,000.
   a. Calculate the extra volume of sales the company must make to finance the increased price of the crane if it wishes to follow its normal financing and dividend policy. (Assume that corporation tax is 40 per cent of profits before tax.)
   b. How, if at all, could the company have avoided this problem caused by a trebling of plant prices over 10 years?

B17 TXW Plastics Ltd buys a computer for £800,000. It is expected to last four years, and to have a residual value of £100,000.
   a. Prepare a table showing depreciation expense and net book value year by year if declining balance depreciation is used.
   b. After three years, at a cost of £160,000, an improvement extends the computer's life to six years in all. The new residual value is expected to be £60,000. Prepare a revised schedule of declining balance depreciation for years 4 to 6 inclusive.
   c. The computer breaks down at the end of year 5, and is sold for only £20,000. What is the profit or loss on sale? Prepare a table showing how the year-by-year expenses charged over its whole life amount in total to the net cost of the computer.

Depreciation of Fixed Assets

C. Essay Questions

C1 Why is it necessary to charge depreciation?

C2 Would it matter if a business simply charged the whole cost of fixed assets as an expense in the year of acquisition? Why or why not?

C3 How would you try to estimate (a) the useful life, (b) the residual value, of a new machine?

C4 Why does the disposal of fixed assets usually give rise to profits or losses on disposal?

C5 How are profits or losses on disposal of fixed assets treated in accounts? How should they be treated?

C6 What are the main arguments for and against the usage method of depreciation?

C7 Are fixed assets merely prepaid depreciation expenses?

C8 Should intangible assets be shown on balance sheets? How should they be amortised?

C9 'The subjective estimates and arbitrary choices of method in calculating depreciation make reported profits or losses unreliable as measures of economic performance.' Discuss.

C10 As accountant of a plant hire firm, write a memo to the managing director of your company, putting the case for changing from straight-line to declining balance depreciation.

7 Valuing Stock

7.1 Stock Valuation and Accounts
7.1.1 Lower of Cost or Net Realisable Value
7.1.2 Effect of Stock Valuation on Accounts

7.2 Methods of Identifying Stock
7.2.1 FIFO and LIFO
7.2.2 Average Cost

7.3 Manufacturing Stocks
7.3.1 Three Kinds of Manufacturing Stock
7.3.2 Full Costing and Marginal Costing
7.3.3 Long-term Contracts

Objective: *To describe the basis for valuing stocks in accounts; to outline its impact on the determination of profit; and to explain the First In First Out method of identifying stock, and the full costing approach to manufactured stocks.*

Synopsis: *Stocks are normally valued at cost in accounts, unless net realisable value is lower (due either to physical damage or loss, or to a change in market conditions). Stock valuation directly affects the amount of cost of goods sold, and therefore the amount of profit.*

The First In First Out (FIFO) method of stock valuation assumes that the earliest purchases are consumed first, so that the stock remaining at the end of a period is that most recently purchased. (Last In First Out (LIFO), which is not used in the UK, makes the opposite assumption.)

The 'cost' of partly-completed and finished manufactured goods may not be easy to determine. UK companies are required to use the 'full costing' approach, which allocates production overheads to products, as well as direct materials and labour costs. (In contrast, the 'marginal costing' approach, which is not *used in financial accounts, treats production overheads as 'period costs'.)*

Valuing Stock 97

7.1 Stock Valuation and Accounts

There are several reasons why goods may not seem to be physically on hand in stock even though they have not been sold:

a. the opening stock figure may have been incorrect;
b. the physical count may have been wrong;
c. they may have physically disappeared (e.g. evaporated);
d. they may have been scrapped, as obsolete or damaged;
e. they may have been lost;
f. they may have been stolen.

Companies need to take suitable precautions against all the above. Many companies physically check their stock from time to time against their accounting records. If satisfied that the records are reasonably accurate, they may then derive their end-of-period physical stock at least partly from the records. That avoids the need to make a physical check of all their stock at a single date, which can be inconvenient.

From now on we assume a correct physical stock count. The problem in valuing stock for accounting purposes is to attach a money value to each item of stock physically on hand. It is simplest to begin with a trading business which buys and sells finished goods. Later we look at the more complex problems that arise where raw materials are processed into finished goods before being sold.

7.1.1 Lower of Cost or Net Realisable Value

Accounts normally value stocks at cost, unless **net realisable value** is lower. This is the estimated net selling price, less (a) all further costs to completion and (b) all marketing, selling and distributing costs. The basis for the rule is prudence: accountants are reluctant to recognise profits in accounts until they are reasonably certain that they have been earned.

A profit-seeking business presumably aims to sell each item at a higher price than was paid for it. (At this stage we are looking only at trading companies.) But there are two reasons why net realisable value of trading stocks might be *lower* than cost:

a. physical damage may have reduced the saleable value;
b. market conditions may have changed for the worse since purchase.

Examples
(a) Physical damage

Ovoids Limited trades in eggs. In April it buys one million eggs for 4p each. It has sold half of them for 6p each when the air-conditioning plant breaks down. The remaining half million eggs left in stock all go bad. Clearly their value at the end of the month is not as much as 4p. Nobody is going to buy rotten eggs at any price at all! So Ovoids must write off the unsaleable eggs as an expense in April, and reduce the value of the closing stocks to zero.

(b) Market conditions change

Peregrine owns a ladies fashion boutique. He buys 100 high fashion dresses for £40 each, which he hopes to sell for £80. At the end of the year he has only sold 90 of the dresses, and the new season's dresses are due in soon. How should he value the remaining 10 out-of-fashion dresses? Clearly he cannot now expect to sell them for as much as £80 each. On the other hand, there are always people who will buy unfashionable clothes to get a bargain. The key question is whether the net realisable value of the 10 dresses will be as high as their £40 cost. If so, then the dresses should be valued at cost in the accounts. But if the net realisable value will probably be less than £40 each, then that lower figure should be used to value the closing stock. Clearly Peregrine will need to use his judgement here, based on intuition and past experience.

The 'lower of cost or net realisable value' rule applies to each item of stock *separately*: it is not a question of comparing the aggregate cost of the stock with the aggregate net realisable value. Thus all losses are provided for as soon as a serious possibility is first noticed. One of the problems in accounting is that judgement is needed to estimate when there *is* a 'serious possibility' of a loss.

7.1.2 Effect of Stock Valuation on Accounts

Stock valuation matters in accounting because the cost of goods sold depends on the closing stock value. We know that the profit for a period depends on the cost of goods sold charged against that period's sales revenue. *So profit for a period depends on the closing stock value.* Stock valuation also, of course, affects the amount of current assets shown in the balance sheet.

We can identify the cost of goods sold in a trading business as follows:

	(Cost of)	opening stock	£ xxx
+	(Cost of)	purchases in period	£ xxx
=	(Cost of)	goods available	£ xxx
−	(Cost of)	closing stock	£ xxx
=	(Cost of)	goods sold in period	£ xxx

We may assume that a firm has correctly counted and valued its opening stock, and that it knows the cost of its purchases in the period. That establishes the cost of the goods becoming 'available for sale' in the period; from which we deduct the cost of the goods still left in stock at the end. We then know the amount to be charged as an expense against sales revenue as 'cost of goods sold' in the period.

Example: *Trendy Footwear's normal 'mark-up' on cost was 50 per cent; thus a pair of shoes purchased for £10 would normally be sold at £15 – giving a 'gross profit' of £5. The shop then had to deduct its various running expenses in order to calculate its net operating profit.*

At the end of 1983, Trendy had several thousand pairs of shoes in stock, valued

Valuing Stock

(at cost) at £20,000. During 1984 further purchases of shoes cost £80,000, and the shop's sales revenues totalled £90,000.

Obviously we can't say the shop made a gross loss of £10,000 in 1984, because (like Mary Mullins – see 5.2.1) we have not yet allowed for the closing stock. Suppose the purchase cost of the shoes left in stock at the end of the year totalled £40,000. Then the cost of goods sold in 1984 was £60,000, and the gross profit was £30,000.

Make sure you understand how (a) cost of goods sold and (b) gross profit are calculated:

a. Cost of goods sold (£60,000) is made up from:
   Opening stock + Purchases – Closing stock
   £20,000   + £80,000   – £40,000
b. Gross profit (£30,000) consists of:
   Sales revenue – Cost of goods sold
   £90,000   – £60,000.

This is set out in Fig. 7.1

Sales £90,000	Gross profit £30,000	Less: Closing stock £40,000	Purchases £80,000
	Cost of goods sold £60,000		Opening stock £20,000

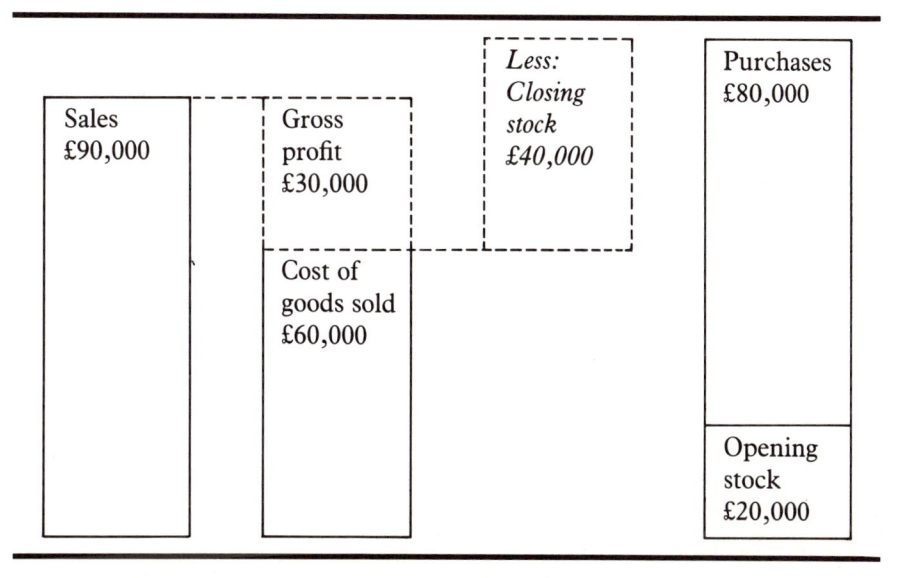

Fig. 7.1: How closing stock affects gross profit

Now suppose that when Trendy's manager looked closely at the closing stock of shoes, he found that many pairs were slightly damaged, and that others would have to be sold at somewhat less than original cost due to a change in fashion. He considered the closing stock of shoes item by item, in each case taking the lower of cost or estimated net realisable value. As a result the manager reckoned the closing stock of shoes should be valued in total at only £30,000.

The reduction in value of the closing stock from £40,000 to £30,000 also reduced the gross profit for the year by £10,000, from £30,000 to £20,000. This is set out in

Fig. 7.2, with the 'difference' of £10,000 shown as the shaded area. You can see that the reduction of £10,000 in the closing stock valuation has, in effect, been added on to the cost of goods sold; *it has thus* reduced *1984's gross profit to the same extent.*

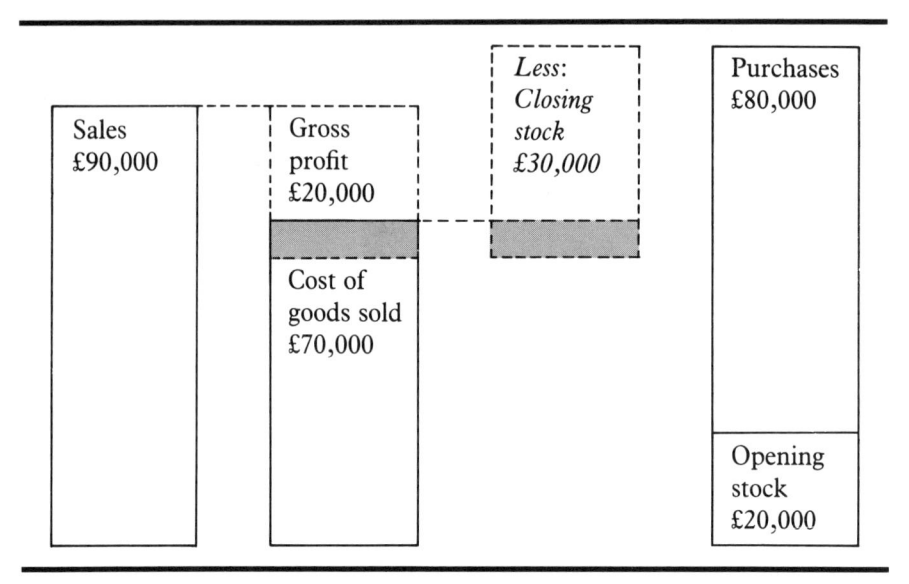

Fig. 7.2: How reducing closing stock reduces gross profit

Changing the stock value at one moment of time does not affect the total profit reported over the whole life of a business. (That will be sales revenues less total expenses.) What it does is *shift* the reporting of some profit from one accounting period to another. After all, one period's closing stock must be the next period's opening stock. Reducing the closing stock valuation reduces the earlier period's reported profit. But it also reduces the later period's *opening* stock, which *increases* the later period's reported profit. (Trendy's reduced profit would probably have been discovered next year, when some shoes could not be sold at their normal prices.)

7.2 Methods of Identifying Stock

7.2.1 FIFO and LIFO

So far we have assumed that we can identify the 'cost' of goods in stock; but in practice this can present problems, especially where prices are changing. In this section we shall assume that prices are *rising* over time; but it should be obvious that similar problems arise if prices are falling.

The normal way to identify stocks in the United Kingdom is to use the **First**

Valuing Stock

In First Out (FIFO) method. This method assumes that the first items of stock purchased ('in') are the first items to be sold ('out'). Thus the earliest purchases are used up first (starting with any opening stock), leaving in stock at the end of a period the latest purchases during the period.

The implications of using the FIFO method of identifying stock may become clearer if we contrast it with another possible method, known as **Last In First Out** (LIFO). Again, the name explains what happens. The LIFO method assumes that the first items to be sold are the *last* to have been purchased. So they will have been purchased at the *most recent* prices. It should be emphasised that LIFO *is not normally used in the UK* (partly because the Inland Revenue do not permit LIFO to be used to compute **taxable profits**).

Very often FIFO may be closer to the *physical* flow of goods; but the method used for *accounting* purposes need not be the same. Obviously FIFO should be the physical method actually used to move goods when they are perishable; but for durable goods other physical patterns of flow may be appropriate. For example, coal may be dumped before all existing stocks have been used up; and withdrawals from the surface may then leave a 'core' of older coal.

Example: *Quickflo Pumps Ltd operates a petrol filling station. At the end of May the storage tanks contained 30,000 gallons of petrol, which had cost 50p per gallon (excluding tax). During June the company received two deliveries each of 20,000 gallons, costing 60p per gallon. At the end of June 30,000 gallons were left in the tanks, the same amount as at the start of the month. Competitive market conditions prevented Quickflo from increasing the selling price of petrol: it remained at 70p per gallon (excluding tax) all through June. The question is: how much profit did Quickflo Pumps make in June?*

Clearly we need to make an assumption about which petrol was left at the end of June. Was it (a) the 30,000 gallons in the tanks at the beginning of the month? Or (b) part of the two deliveries of 20,000 gallons each made in the month of June? These amount to using (a) LIFO and (b) FIFO. Figure 7.3 shows how the profit for June is £3,000 higher using FIFO.

	'000 galls	price	FIFO (£'000)	LIFO (£'000)
Opening stock	30	50p	15	15
Purchases	40	60p	24	24
Petrol available	70		39	39
Less: Closing stock	30	60p	18	50p 15
Cost of petrol sold	40		21	24
Sales revenue	40	70p	28	28
Gross profit			7	4

Fig. 7.3: Quickflo Pumps Ltd. Gross profit for June.

It should be clear why, if prices are *rising*, using LIFO produces a *lower* figure for gross profit. LIFO charges against sales revenue the more recent (that is, the higher-priced) purchases. But LIFO results in a balance sheet figure for stock which may be very out-of-date. This can cause problems if closing stock is lower in volume than opening stock; part of the cost of goods sold will then consist of *very* out-of-date costs, thus distorting the profit and loss account.

FIFO, on the other hand, uses recent costs in the balance sheet valuation of stock; but somewhat out-of-date costs in the profit and loss account. Thus FIFO may be regarded as 'overstating' profit. That is why the Inland Revenue, which does not permit LIFO, used to allow UK companies to deduct **stock relief** in computing taxable profits.

Figure 7.4 shows that both FIFO and LIFO have disadvantages. In a period of rising prices, FIFO overstates the current period's profit, while LIFO understates current assets on the balance sheet.

	Profit and loss account	*End-of-period balance sheet*
FIFO	Out-of-date costs	Cost of most recent purchases
LIFO	Cost of most recent purchases	Very out-of-date costs

Fig. 7.4: FIFO versus LIFO.

7.2.2 Average Cost

Apart from FIFO, which is the most common method used in the UK, and LIFO, which is hardly used at all, there is a third method of identifying stock for valuation purposes. This is **average cost**; and again the name describes it well. This method simply assumes that the *average* cost – recalculated on every purchase – forms the basis for valuing closing stock. The average cost method is quite widely used in the UK. Figure 7.5 shows how Quickflo Pumps would calculate its petrol stock value on this basis.

Thus closing stock is valued at £17,667 using the average cost method, compared with £18,000 using FIFO and £15,000 under LIFO. Of course, whichever method a company uses it must do so *consistently*.

Valuing Stock

	'000 galls	price	(£)
Opening stock	30	50 p	15,000
Issued	20	50 p	10,000
	10	50 p	5,000
First delivery	20	60 p	12,000
	30	*56.7p	17,000
Issued	20	56.7p	11,333
	10	56.7p	5,667
Second delivery	20	60 p	12,000
Closing stock	30	*58.9p	17,667

*calculated

Fig. 7.5: Quickflo Pumps in June, using the average cost method.

7.3 Manufacturing Stocks

7.3.1 Three Kinds of Manufacturing Stock

Until now we have been looking at the stock of a trading company which buys and sells finished goods only. Now we move on to consider some of the special problems of a manufacturing company's stocks. The most obvious difference is that there are three different kinds of stock held in a manufacturing company:

a. Raw materials stocks
b. Work-in-progress
c. Finished goods stocks.

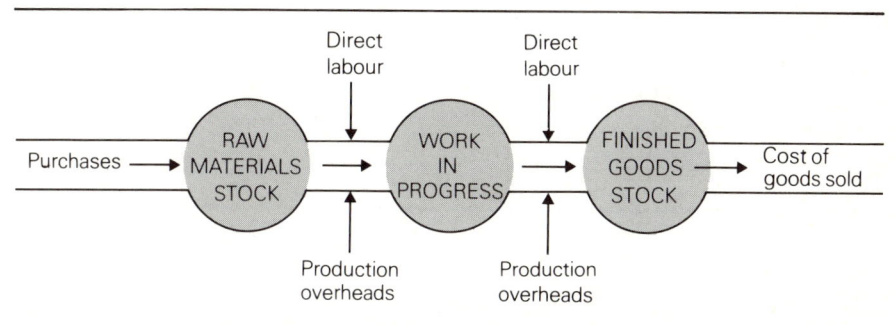

Fig. 7.6: Flow of material through a production process.

The relationship of these three kinds of stock is illustrated in Fig. 7.6, which shows the flow of materials through a manufacturing process.

The shaded areas in Figure 7.6 show the three kinds of manufacturing stock. Raw materials stock is valued at cost. (For simplicity we ignore the use of net realisable value if lower than cost, which applies to all kinds of stocks.) But work-in-progress and finished goods stocks are harder to value because their cost includes not only raw materials, but also the costs of direct labour and of production overheads (see 7.3.2).

Figure 7.7 shows how the three kinds of manufacturing stock relate to different stages of production: (A) raw materials used up; (B) costs of goods manufactured; and finally (C), cost of goods sold. Cost of goods sold equals raw materials purchases, direct labour, and production overheads in a period, plus opening stocks minus closing stocks. Thus a net *increase* in combined stocks (of raw materials, work-in-progress, and finished goods) reduces cost of goods sold, while a net decline in stocks increases cost of goods sold:

	Raw materials	Work-in-progress	Finished goods
Opening finished goods stock			**
Opening work-in-progress		**	
Opening raw materials stock	**		
+ Purchases of raw materials	xx		
= Raw materials available	xx		
Less: closing raw materials stock	**		
(A) = Raw materials used in production		xx	
Direct labour		xx	
Production overheads		xx	
		xx	
Less: closing work in progress		**	
(B) = Cost of finished goods made			xx
= Finished goods available			xx
Less: closing finished goods stock			**
(C) = Cost of goods sold			xx

Fig. 7.7: Detailed composition of cost of goods sold.

Valuing Stock

Opening stocks	**
Raw materials purchased	xx
Direct labour	xx
Production overheads	xx
Less: Closing stocks	(**)
= Cost of goods sold	xx

7.3.2 Full Costing and Marginal Costing

There are two approaches to valuing manufacturing stocks, known as full costing and marginal costing. The last section discussed LIFO, which is not used in the UK, in order to bring out more fully the implications of the FIFO method. So, *even though marginal costing is not acceptable in the UK*, we discuss it here in order to bring out the implications of full costing.

Full costing values manufacturing stocks by including *all* costs incurred in bringing stocks into their present condition. This includes the cost of materials, plus direct labour, plus production overheads (based on the normal level of activity). In contrast, **marginal costing** values manufacturing stocks by including only materials costs and direct labour. The difference between the two methods is that full costing includes production **overheads** as part of the cost of stocks, whereas marginal costing does not. In the UK full costing is now required in published financial accounts; though some companies use marginal costing in their internal management accounts.

Example: Jones Packaging Ltd makes wooden crates from second-hand timber. The company produces 400 crates per month at a direct cost of £40 (£25 timber, plus £15 direct labour); and plans to sell them for £80 each to removal firms. The company also incurs production overheads amounting to £8,000 per month. These include the production director's salary, depreciation of production equipment, factory lighting, and other production expenses.

In its first three months of operations the company sold 300, 450, and 350 crates. How much profit did it make for the quarter? What is the value of stock on hand at the end of the third month? (The answer to the first question, of course, depends on the answer to the second.) Figure 7.8 shows the alternative results using: full costing; marginal costing.

Marginal costing values each crate at direct cost only (£25 timber, plus £15 direct labour), whereas full costing also includes £20 per crate in respect of production overheads. This is simply the £8,000 per month divided by the 400 crates produced each month. Thus closing stock is valued at £6,000 using full costing (100 crates at £60 each), but only at £4,000 using marginal costing (100 crates at £40 each). The difference of £2,000 in the closing stock valuation, and hence in the profit for the quarter, represents the 100 crates in stock multiplied by the production overheads of £20 per crate.

Marginal costing treats production overheads, in effect, as 'period costs' (see 5.3.2), and writes them off as expenses in the period in which they are *incurred*.

	Full costing (£'000)	Marginal costing (£'000)
Opening stock	–	–
Raw materials (timber)	30	30
Direct labour	18	18
Production overheads	24	24
Total production costs	72	72
Less: closing stock	6	4
Cost of goods sold	66	68
Sales revenue	88	88
Gross profit	22	20

Fig. 7.8: Jones Packaging Ltd results for first quarter.

Full costing, however, treats production overheads as 'product costs', and writes them off as expenses only when the goods are *sold*. This is now regarded as according better with the matching principle.

7.3.3 Long-term Contracts

We have seen that accounts normally value stocks at 'the lower of cost or net realisable value'. There may be alternative ways of computing 'cost', and judgement may be needed in estimating the amount of net realisable value; but the intention is clear. No profit should be recognised in accounts until the goods are actually sold. This applies in manufacturing companies to all three kinds of stock: raw materials, work-in-progress, and finished goods.

But there is an important exception, in respect of long-term contracts. Construction of buildings, or civil engineering projects such as dams, motorways, or power stations, may last for two or more years. It would be unrealistic to regard none of the profit on such long-term contracts as being earned until the date of completion; yet this would be the result if contracts in progress were valued at cost.

Instead, work-in-progress on long-term contracts is valued at cost plus attributable profit, less any foreseeable losses. 'Attributable profit' is the profit fairly attributable to work performed at the balance sheet date, assuming the final outcome of the contract can be foreseen with reasonable certainty. Thus if a project was two thirds completed at the balance sheet date, and no particular problems were expected in future, then about two thirds of the estimated total

Valuing Stock

profit on the project should be included in the valuation of work-in-progress.

'Foreseeable losses' are defined as losses estimated to arise over the whole duration of the contract. Thus profits are recognised only to the extent 'earned'; but losses are recognised in full as soon as they are anticipated. Where there is a conflict, 'prudence' usually outweighs the 'matching principle' in accounting.

The use of the above approach is now mandatory in the UK. It does, however, have certain disadvantages:

a. A contract normally requires completion before ownership passes to the purchaser. Half a ship is not much use.
b. It may be hard to apportion profit between different parts of a project.
c. Many contracts contain uncertainties right up to the time of completion, in respect of labour problems, exchange rate fluctuations, etc.
d. It may give management more opportunities to present misleading profit figures, either in apportioning profit or in estimating future losses.

Work Section

A. Revision Questions

A1 What are the two separate aspects of arriving at a value for stocks?
A2 Name three reasons why unsold goods may not be physically on hand.
A3 What is the general rule for valuing stock in accounts?
A4 Define 'net realisable value'.
A5 Why may net realisable value be lower than cost?
A6 Why does stock valuation matter in accounts?
A7 Define 'cost of goods sold'.
A8 Explain carefully how the value of closing stock affects profit.
A9 If stock value falls, is the difference (a) added to or (b) deducted from the period's purchases in computing cost of goods sold? Explain why.
A10 Why may subjective value be needed in valuing stock?

A11 Define FIFO.
A12 What is the FIFO method trying to do?
A13 Define LIFO.
A14 How does FIFO differ from LIFO as regards: (a) the profit and loss account? (b) the balance sheet?
A15 If prices were falling, which method would produce a higher stock valuation: FIFO or LIFO? Explain why.
A16 What is the 'average cost' method of valuing stock?
A17 Why isn't LIFO used in the UK?
A18 What assumption does LIFO make about the date of acquisition of closing stock?
A19 What happens under LIFO if closing stock is less than opening stock?
A20 What is the main disadvantage of (a) FIFO? (b) LIFO?

A21 What are the three different kinds of manufacturing stock?
A22 In a manufacturing company why are raw materials stocks easier to value than the other two kinds of stock?
A23 Distinguish full costing from marginal costing.
A24 Which of full costing or marginal costing will result in higher profits if the volume of stocks held is: (a) rising? (b) stable? (c) falling?
A25 Why is full costing normally used in the UK, and marginal costing not?
A26 Which costs does full costing include in stock valuation?
A27 Which costs does marginal costing include in stock valuation?
A28 Full costing produces a higher stock value than marginal costing; what other balance sheet difference is there between the two methods?
A29 How are long-term contracts in progress valued in accounting?

Valuing Stock

A30 How is the required method of valuing long-term contracts in progress inconsistent as between profits and losses?

B. Exercises and Case Studies

B1 Non-Ferrous Metals Ltd started 1983 with £200,000 worth of stock; during the year the company purchased altogether 2,500 tonnes of copper costing £2.4 m. Sales for 1983 were £1.6 m; and at the end of the year the company had 800 tonnes of copper in stock. This was all purchased at £1,200 per tonne during a price boom late in the year. Shortly afterwards, before Non-Ferrous Metals Ltd had sold any of its stock, the market price fell to £1,000 per tonne as a result of over-supply on the market.
 a. How should the company value its copper stocks at the end of 1983?
 b. What was the company's gross profit for 1983?

B2 George Bull speculates in commodities. In June 1983 his purchases of platinum were as follows:

		(£'000)
Week 1. 2,000 ounces at £290	=	580
Week 2. 1,500 ounces at £280	=	420
Week 3. 1,000 ounces at £270	=	270
Week 4. 2,000 ounces at £260	=	520
6,500		1,790

His opening stock at the beginning of June was 1,500 ounces, valued at £450,000. During the month he sold 4,500 ounces of platinum, for a total of £1,250,000.

What was George Bull's profit or loss on platinum deals for the month of June 1983 (a) using LIFO? (b) using FIFO?

B3 Simpson Eagle Equipment Ltd makes television sets. Materials amount to £80 per unit, and direct labour to £40 per unit. The production overheads total £400,000 per month. The company had no opening stock at the start of 1985 because the Christmas rush in 1984 had exhausted supplies. In January 1985 production was at the normal rate of 5,000 sets per month. During the month 3,500 sets were sold, for a total of £850,000.
 a. What was the company's gross profit for January 1985:
  (i) using full costing? (ii) using marginal costing?
 b. Explain the difference between the two profit figures.

B4 During the first three years of its existence, the Libman Company's manufacturing costs, closing stocks, and sales were as follows:

Year	Manufacturing costs (£'000)	Closing stocks (£'000)	Sales revenue (£'000)
1.	80	80	none
2.	90	130	60
3.	30	none	250.

Ignoring all other costs and revenues, determine the company's gross profit for each of the three years.

B5 From the information below, calculate what is the profit or loss for Ecco Trading for each of the first three years:

	Year 1 (£'000)	Year 2 (£'000)	Year 3 (£'000)	Year 4 (£'000)
Sales	30	70	90	—
Purchases	40	80	60	—
Opening stock	—	20	50	30.

B6 Imperial Imports Ltd bought 5,200 tonnes of sugar in the year to 31 March, 500 tonnes at £200 and the rest at £180 per tonne. By the end of the financial year, 31 March, the market price for sugar had jumped to £400 per tonne. In the year to 31 March sales were 4,500 tonnes at an average of £230 per tonne. Stocks at the beginning of the year had been 800 tonnes valued at £170 per tonne.
  a. What was the value of closing stocks of sugar at 31 March?
  b. What was the profit for the year?
  c. Comment on the implications of the rise in price to £400.

B7 Bernard Deel, a second-hand car trader, constructs his balance sheet and profit and loss account as follows:

End-of-year balance sheet   *Profit and loss account for year*

End-of-year balance sheet	(£'000)	Profit and loss account for year	(£'000)	
Shareholders' funds	20	Sales revenue		134
Loans	30			
	—	Opening stocks	28	
	50	Purchases	106	
	=		134	
Stocks	30	Less: Closing stock	30	
Debtors	22		—	104
Cash	1			—
	—			30
	53	Overhead expenses		20
Less: Creditors	3			—
	—	Profit		10
	50			=
	=			

The auditor, however, notes that a number of cars, included in closing stock at cost at a total of £18,000, have been in stock for more than six months. When he asks why, Mr Deel tells him the cars are probably priced too high. The standard mark-up of one third on cost has been applied in setting their selling prices.
  a. Draw up a new set of accounts, assuming that the selling prices of the old stock have to be reduced by 33⅓ per cent.
  b. What difference would it make if the selling prices had to be reduced (i) by 25 per cent; (ii) by 20 per cent?

Valuing Stock

B8 Old Mistresses Ltd was started by two spinster sisters, Belinda and Caroline, to trade in pictures and antiques. The company's financial year ended on St Cecilia's Day. Details were recorded of each item dealt in, showing the date of purchase, name of supplier, and cost. When it was sold, the date and amount and (usually) the name of the customer were recorded. Thus the sisters were able to prepare a list of every item which had not yet been sold at any time, together with its original cost.

At the end of the 1984 accounting year, stock lists were prepared showing items apparently unsold with a total cost of £23,700. This figure was included as closing stock in the draft 1984 accounts. In the course of the audit (by a female chartered accountant), the following queries arose. Please identify for each one what adjustment, if any, is needed to the closing stock figure; and calculate what the total closing stock valuation should be in the final accounts.

a. A notebook containing a short story which had been thought to be by Daisy Ashford on an off-day turned out to be by Jane Austen. Its selling price was accordingly raised from £25 to £200 (which compared with a cost of £5).

b. No trace could be found of a number of small items of jewellery which, according to the records, ought to have been in stock. They had cost £215 in total, and none of them had been sold since the end of the financial year. Belinda reckoned the sales proceeds would have totalled about £430, but Caroline believed the jewellery would probably have realised closer to £500.

c. A rather dented silver coffee pot (Queen Anne), which had cost £300, had been in stock for over a year. Because of its poor condition it had been written down to £160 in the 1983 accounts. Its selling price was currently set at £360, but Caroline didn't think Old Mistresses Ltd would be able to sell it for more than £180.

d. The business had in stock a pair of Constable water colours, which together had cost £200. Unfortunately, they were now attributed to Maria not to John Constable; and as a result their selling price had had to be reduced from £1,200 to £80.

B9 In preparing the accounts of Harper Hardware for the year ending 30 September 1984, the chief accountant had to decide at what figure the closing stock should be stated. From the company's books he knew that opening stock at 1 October 1983 had amounted, after some adjustments, to £34,800; and that purchases for the year had cost a total of £105,400. The total of the stock sheets summarising the physical stock check taken on 30 September 1984 was £43,200, but two items needed special consideration.

A quantity of kettles remained in stock which had been bought more than two years earlier. They had been slightly damaged in a fire soon after purchase (for £1,600); and their value had been written down to £400 in the 1983 accounts. It had been decided that they were now valueless and should be completely written off.

More significant, a large consignment of dustbins had been acquired to sell to a local council; but when the collection of rubbish was privatised, it proved difficult to sell them. The dustbins had cost £3,200, but it was thought the most they could now be sold for was £1,800 instead of their original selling price of £5,000.

Calculate Harper Hardware's cost of sales for the year 1984.

B10 At 1 April 1984 Snip Snaps Ltd had 30 units of a particular type of camera in stock. They were shown as costing £16 each. In the year ended 31 March 1985, three batches of cameras were purchased. In June 1984, 40 cameras at £17 each; in October 1984, 20 cameras at £19 each; and in December 1984, 30 cameras at £20 each.
1. Calculate the closing stock valuation at 31 March 1985, when there were 60 cameras in stock.
2. Compute the cost of goods sold for the year ended 31 March 1985.
3. Verify your computation by identifying the volume of cameras and related costs per camera assumed to be sold.

Answer the above three questions:
a. using the FIFO method of stock valuation;
b. using the LIFO method.

B11 Dorchester Decorations was a wholesaler of wallpaper. It replenished its stock of a certain type of paper (known as Rainbow) at the end of each quarter. For the calendar year 1984, opening stock was 1,200 metres, and the quantities purchased were 1,800 metres in March, 2,400 metres in June, 1,200 metres in September, and 1,800 metres in December. The cost attributable to the opening stock was £4.20 per metre. Purchase prices per metre through the year 1984 were £3.60 (March), £3.00 (June), £5.00 (September), and £4.00 (December).

The quantities sold each quarter were as follows: March quarter 900 metres; June quarter 1,700 metres; September quarter 1,400 metres; and December quarter 1,900 metres. The closing stock at 31 December 1984 amounted to 2,500 metres of Rainbow wallpaper.

The company used the average cost method of valuing stock, and its practice was each quarter to deduct the issues from stock (in respect of sales during the quarter) *before* adding on the purchases for that quarter, which were made right at the end of each quarter.

Calculate:
a. the value of closing stock of Rainbow wallpaper at 31 December 1984;
b. the cost of Rainbow wallpaper sold during the year 1984.

B12 Skyline Construction Ltd signed a contract on 1 January 1983 to build an office block for White Elephant Enterprises Ltd for a total of £6.0 m. Skyline estimated that the job would take three years to complete, and that construction would cost £4.8 m. At the end of the first year, on

Valuing Stock

31 December 1983, the job is on schedule, and costs incurred, at £1.2 m, are also on target.

What profit, if any, should Skyline Construction report in its 1983 accounts in respect of the White Elephant contract:
a. on the basis of the information above?
b. if progress payments totalling £1.3 m have been received by 31 December 1983?
c. if, on review, the directors of Skyline conclude that unexpected delays and cost increases mean that overall the contract will show a loss of £0.5 m instead of a profit of £1.2 m?

B13 Presto Sums Ltd was formed to produce small electronic calculators. Sales were estimated at some 5,000 units per quarter, at an average price of £30 per unit; so production was set at this level. Stocks were planned to build up at the start, since the first quarter's sales were not expected to exceed 3,500 units. By the end of the first quarter it seemed that even that sales estimate was too optimistic, and production was accordingly cut back to 2,000 units for the second quarter.

Direct costs of production averaged £20 per unit, and fixed production overheads amounted to £20,000 per quarter. The company sold 2,000 units in the first quarter and 4,000 (at a price reduced by 5 per cent) in the second. When the managing director saw the company's profit and loss accounts (set out below) for the first two quarters, he was astonished.

	1st quarter (£'000)		2nd quarter (£'000)	
Sales revenue		60		114
Opening stocks	–		72	
Cost of production	120		60	
	120		132	
Less: closing stocks	72		30	
Cost of goods sold		48		102
Gross profit		12		12

a. Write a brief but clear memo to the managing director explaining why profits were the same in each quarter despite sales volume having doubled.
b. How could a different accounting treatment of stocks produce different results?
c. Compare the half-year's profits under the two methods, and explain the difference.
d. Which of the two accounting methods do you think does a better job of giving a 'true and fair view'? Why?

e. Comment on the business performance of Presto Sums in its first six months.

B14 Fred Makepiece, a car dealer, sold a new car for £4,000 plus the value of an old car traded in by the customer. The new car had cost Fred £3,100. After repair work on the traded-in car costing £600, it was sold for £2,200.
   a. How much profit did Fred make? (Ignore tax: Fred does!)
   b. What information would you need if the traded-in car had been sold in a later accounting period, so that it was held in stock at the end of Fred's financial year?

B15 Kostov Sails Ltd's turnover was £120,000 in Year 1; in Year 2 there was a 25 per cent increase; and in Year 3 sales were £20,000 higher than in Year 2. Purchases in Year 2 were £96,000 – 20 per cent higher than in Year 1, but 20 per cent lower than in Year 3. Stocks fell by £12,000 in Year 1 (comparing the closing stock with the opening stock), rose by £16,000 in Year 2, and rose by £12,000 in Year 3.

What was the profit in each of the three years?

B16 Refer to 7.3.2 and Fig. 7.8 (p. 105).
Calculate for Jones Packaging for each of the three months *separately:*
   (i) closing stock value;
   (ii) cost of goods sold;
   (iii) gross profit;
using:
   a. the full costing approach;
   b. the marginal costing approach.
Confirm that the total of the profits for the three months equals the total profit for the quarter shown in the text for each method.

B17 From the following information prepare a statement of cost of goods sold for Interweave Ltd for 1984, in a format similar to that used in Fig. 7.7 (p. 104).

	(£'000)
Production overheads	320
Closing WIP	65
Opening raw materials stock	50
Raw materials used in production	280
Purchases of raw materials	260
Direct labour	200

Opening finished goods stock was twice the value of the opening raw materials stock; opening work-in-progress amounted to half as much as closing raw materials stock; and closing finished goods stock was double the value of the closing raw materials stock.
   a. What is the overall percentage change in stocks during 1984?
   b. If closing raw materials stock value was reduced by 40 per cent, how, in detail, would that affect your answer?
   c. What is the raw material content in closing finished goods stock?

Valuing Stock

C. Essay Questions

C1 One period's closing stock is the next period's opening stock. What does this imply in relation to the valuation of stock?

C2 Should UK manufacturing companies be allowed to use marginal costing in valuing stock? Why or why not?

C3 Should production overheads be treated as 'product costs' or as 'period costs'? How would you try to convince someone who took the opposite view?

C4 Discuss the problems facing a producer of fashion shoes when valuing its year-end stocks.

C5 What accounting principles, if any, are contravened by the rule requiring stock to be valued at 'the lower of cost or net realisable value'? Might it be better always to value stocks either (a) at cost, or (b) at net realisable value? Why or why not?

C6 In a period of rising prices, management performance often appears better using FIFO stock valuation rather than LIFO. Yet it makes more sense to base selling prices on the unit costs of the latest purchases. Try to explain this apparent paradox.

C7 Bearing in mind that physical stock levels have recently been falling in many UK businesses, should LIFO be permitted as a method of valuing stock?

C8 Write a memo to the managing director of a construction company arguing against a proposal to account for profit on long-term projects year by year.

C9 How can professional accountants be expected to audit estimates by company directors, who have to exercise their own special expertise and judgement in valuing stocks?

C10 Should companies ever be allowed to *change* their methods of valuing stocks, in order to substitute better methods for poorer methods? If so, under what conditions? If not, how can accounting practice improve?

8 Accounting for Inflation

8.1 Inflation
8.1.1 What Is Inflation?
8.1.2 Measuring Inflation
8.1.3 How Does Inflation Affect Accounts?

8.2 Constant Purchasing Power Accounting (CPP)
8.2.1 The Basic CPP Rules
8.2.2 CPP Accounts
8.2.3 Fixed Assets and Depreciation
8.2.4 Monetary Gains and Losses
8.2.5 Comparisons Between Years

8.3 Current Cost Accounting (CCA)
8.3.1 CCA Adjustments to HC Profits
8.3.2 CCA Cost Of Sales Adjustment
8.3.3 CCA Comparisons Between Years

8.4 Conclusion
8.4.1 CPP versus CCA
8.4.2 The Future

Objective: *To explain how inflation affects accounts, and to describe two proposed methods of dealing with the problem.*

Synopsis: *The pound has lost more than 80 per cent of its value since 1967. As a result two different methods of 'inflation accounting' have been proposed.*

Constant Purchasing Power (CPP) accounting challenges the convention of using money as the unit of account. It treats money of different dates as 'foreign currencies', and proposes to use the Retail Price Index as a measure of general inflation to translate all money amounts into units of constant purchasing power.

Current Cost Accounting (CCA) challenges the convention of using historical costs as the basis for valuing assets and expenses, and proposes instead to use estimated current replacement costs. It continues to use money as the unit of account, and is thus not a method of adjusting accounts for general inflation.

Both methods require both A-adjustments, affecting the Accounts of a single year, and B-adjustments, to allow comparisons Between years.

Accounting for Inflation

8.1 Inflation

8.1.1 What Is Inflation?

There are two main explanations of the causes of **inflation**, which are not entirely unrelated: demand-pull and cost-push.

a. **Demand-pull** inflation stems from increasing the quantity of money. With 'too much money chasing too few goods', purchasers bid up prices so that in the end most retail prices rise, though not all at the same time or to the same extent. This view is complicated by time-lags and by problems in defining the 'money supply'.
b. **Cost-push** inflation means that firms increase their selling prices when their costs rise. The cost-push may stem from various sources, such as trade union pressure for wage increases, a rise in the cost of imports, or tax changes. It seems clear that some prices are 'sticky' downwards. If some prices are free to rise, but others don't fall, then the *average* ('general') level of prices must increase. On the other hand, one might expect competition to help keep prices down.

From an accounting point of view we may regard inflation as meaning a general increase in the money prices of most goods and services. Another name for the same thing is **currency debasement**; this refers not to the increase in money prices, but to the fall in the value (**purchasing power**) of money.

8.1.2 Measuring Inflation

The usual measure of inflation in the UK is the **Retail Price Index** (RPI). This monthly index represents a weighted average of the prices of a typical 'basket' of goods and services. The current retail price index, based on January 1974 = 100.0, reached 342.6 by January 1984. The average rate of inflation since 1974 amounts to 13 per cent a year, which is extremely high by any historical standard.

Figure 8.1 shows the annual rate of increase in the retail price index for each year from 1974 to 1982. In seven of the nine years the annual rate exceeded 10 per cent; indeed, in more than half the years the rate of inflation was over 15 per cent a year.

There has been inflation in the UK every year since 1934, so nobody under the age of 50 can remember a year without it. Historically this is a modern phenomenon: apart from the period around the Napoleonic Wars, the UK experienced virtually no inflation between 1660 and 1914. Prices rose from time to time, but they *fell* too. So there was no persistent *cumulative* increase in the general level of prices.

The rate of inflation accelerated fast after the sterling devaluation of 1967. The pound's purchasing power had halved (prices in general had doubled)

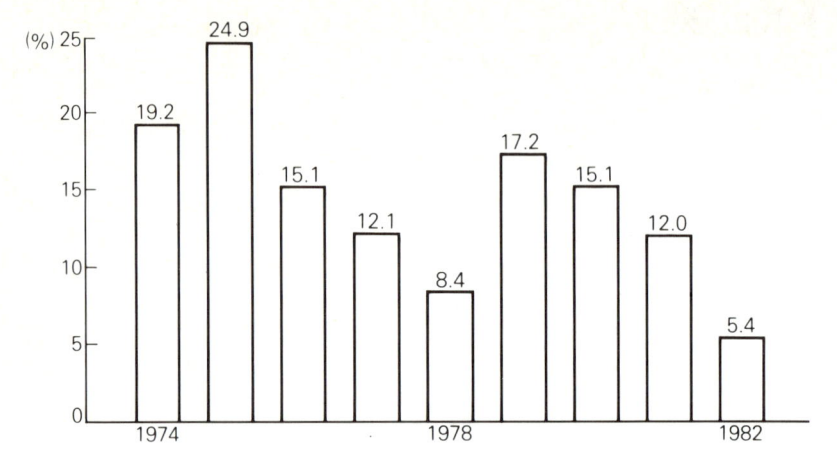

Fig. 8.1: Annual rates of inflation, 1974 to 1982.

between 1945 and 1965; it halved again between 1965 and 1975; and it halved *again* between 1975 and 1980. Thus the historical 'half-life' of the pound was 20 years in 1965, 10 years in 1975, and a mere five years in 1980.

At the rate of inflation between 1975 and 1980, one pound would be worth less than one hundredth of a penny at the end of a normal lifetime. This is not merely an academic point. Professor Hayek, the famous economist, showed his students in 1963 what a stable currency meant by producing in class an 1863 penny which he had recently received in change. It was still in circulation after a

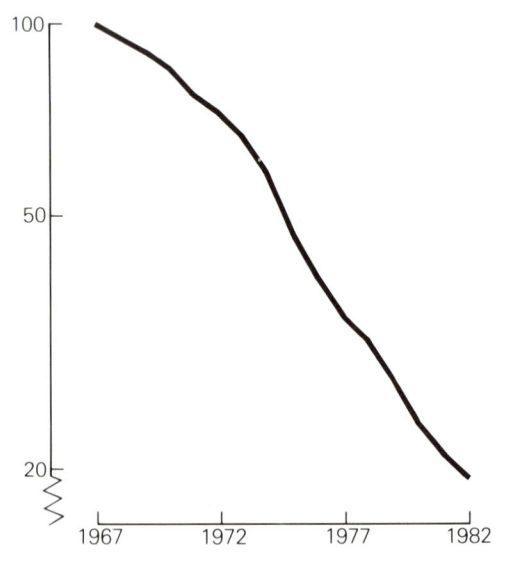

Fig. 8.2: Purchasing power of the pound, 1967 to 1982.

Accounting for Inflation

century. (His students, being German, must have found this impressive: in the hyperinflation of 1922/23 prices rose by five hundred thousand million times (by 500,000,000,000 times) in two years!)

By 1982 the pound had lost more than 80 per cent of its purchasing power in 1967, only 15 years earlier. This is shown in Fig. 8.2.

8.1.3 How Does Inflation Affect Accounts?

Inflation has caused serious problems for accounting. The solution to these problems has proved unexpectedly difficult, because there has been sharp disagreement over which of the traditional accounting conventions needs to be changed to allow for inflation. Two distinct systems of 'inflation accounting' have been developed as a result.

Constant purchasing power (CPP) accounting challenges the convention of accounting in money terms. When the value of money is falling rapidly, it is argued, the monetary unit no longer serves as an adequate unit of accounting measurement. Hence CPP uses an index of general purchasing power (the retail price index) to 'translate' all money amounts in accounts into 'units of constant purchasing power', depending on the date when they occurred. Once the basic indexing has been done, all the other concepts and conventions which we have been using until now continue to apply. (They were summarised in **3.1.1** and **3.1.2**)

Current cost accounting (CCA) challenges the convention of accounting, as a rule, in historical cost terms. Even when there is no general inflation, it is argued, the **current values** of a company's assets are likely to be different from their original cost. This is because in ever-changing markets, the specific prices of particular goods and services vary as conditions of supply and demand fluctuate over time. CCA therefore continues to use money as the unit of measurement, but substitutes current values (current costs) for historical costs.

In the rest of this chapter we first discuss constant purchasing power (CPP) accounting, in **8.2**; then current cost accounting (CCA) in **8.3**. Finally, in **8.4**, the two different methods of accounting for inflation are compared, and possible future developments are reviewed. Students who are grappling with the subject for the first time may think it a pity there has been no agreement on this topic. Many teachers, who have had to cope with two detailed sets of arguments for more than 10 years, would agree with them!

8.2 Constant Purchasing Power (CPP) Accounting

8.2.1 The Basic CPP Rules

As explained in **8.1.3**, constant purchasing power (CPP) accounting regards the problem of accounting for inflation as being to do with the unit of measurement used in accounts. If there were no general inflation, if the purchasing power of money were stable, advocates of CPP say there would be no need for inflation accounting. (But of course the problems of historical cost (HC) accounting, which we have discussed in earlier chapters, would remain.)

It makes no sense to add together dollars and pounds, and not a single multinational company does so. These different currencies must first be translated, by means of the foreign currency exchange rate between them, into terms of the *same* currency unit. In effect, in times of inflation CPP regards money of different dates as being 'foreign currencies'; and uses the retail price index as the exchange rate over time.

It makes no sense to add together Belgian francs, French francs, and Swiss francs – *even though they are all called 'francs'*. Similarly, a 1983 pound is *called* 'a pound', just as a 1984 pound is; but they do not have the same purchasing power. So in CPP accounts these different currencies must be translated into terms of the *same* unit – of 'constant' purchasing power.

There are three basic CPP rules:
1. Always 'date' monetary units.
2. Use a general index of purchasing power (the retail price index) to translate monetary units of different dates into units of constant purchasing power.
3. Only add and subtract and compare units of the *same* purchasing power.

We shall now see how to apply these rules.

8.2.2 CPP Accounts

CPP accounts are normally expressed in terms of purchasing power as at the end-of-year balance sheet date. This requires certain adjustments to the HC profit and loss account and balance sheet.

(a) Profit and loss account

The HC profit and loss account for a year is expressed in 'average-for-the-year' pounds. That is, all items in an HC profit and loss account for the year ending on 31 December 1983 are, in effect, expressed in end-June 1983 pounds. For 1983's CPP accounts all these amounts must be translated into December 1983 pounds, by multiplying each of them by the December 1983 RPI divided by the June 1983 RPI. This will roughly allow for half a year's inflation.

In addition to this comprehensive adjustment to every item in the HC profit and loss account, two other special adjustments will be needed: to depreciation of fixed assets (see **8**.2.3) and for monetary gains and losses (see **8**.2.4).

(b) Balance sheet

Balance sheet items fall into three main groups: (i) shareholders' funds, (ii) monetary assets and liabilities, and (iii) **real** assets (stocks and tangible fixed assets).

(i) *Shareholders' funds*. Shareholders' funds in the 1982 CPP balance sheet (expressed, of course, in December 1982 pounds) must be restated into terms of December 1983 pounds, to form the *opening* balance for 1983. The retained

Accounting for Inflation

profit for 1983 will result from the various CPP adjustments (outlined above) to the 1983 HC profit and loss account. And any capital transactions in 1983, such as issuing new shares, will be 'dated' and translated into December 1983 pounds by using the appropriate retail price index numbers.

(ii) Monetary assets and liabilities. The CPP profit or loss on monetary assets and liabilities is discussed in 8.2.4. No adjustment is required to the HC balance sheet, since all monetary assets and liabilities (such as cash, debtors, and all liabilities) are *already* stated in the December 1983 HC balance sheet in terms of December 1983 pounds.

(iii) 'Real' assets. Where the 'holding period' for stocks is only two or three months, it may not be worth adjusting HC stock values for inflation. For example, if on average three months' stock is held, with inflation of 8 per cent a year, the required increase in the HC stock value would be only 1 per cent. (Of course, the adjustment might be much larger if LIFO were used: see 7.2.1 and Fig. 7.4).

But a major adjustment will normally be needed to the HC net book value for fixed assets, where the 'holding period' can cover many years. We now go on to describe the necessary CPP fixed asset adjustments in detail in 8.2.3.

8.2.3 Fixed Assets and Depreciation

The historical cost of a fixed asset acquired some years ago must be translated, for CPP accounts, into purchasing power units of the latest year's accounts; and the appropriate rate of depreciation is then applied to that new amount. The 'restatement' of the fixed asset's HC net book value is exactly 'balanced' by a similar restatement of shareholders' funds.

Example: *Alan Hampton Ltd writes off all equipment over 15 years, using straight-line depreciation and assuming no residual value. The company buys a machine in 1971 for £90,000, on which it charges £6,000 HC depreciation expense. In the 1971 HC balance sheet the machine's net book value appears at £84,000.*

The retail price index doubles between 1971 and 1976; and doubles again between 1976 and 1982. How will the machine be shown in Hampton's CPP accounts? The cost, *which was actually £90,000 in 1971, must be thought of in CPP terms as being $_{71}$£90,000. In CPP accounts all money amounts must be dated.*

Since the RPI has doubled, in Hampton's 1976 CPP accounts the machine's cost will appear as $_{76}$£180,000; and the depreciation expense will be based on that amount. The same principle will be used in the 1982 CPP accounts. Figure 8.3 shows how Alan Hampton Ltd will treat the machine in each of the three years' CPP accounts. It should be clear how all the numbers in Fig. 8.3 are calculated. The column headed 'n' represents the number of years' depreciation expense (in pounds of that *year's purchasing power) included in accumulated depreciation.*

E

Year	Cost	Depreciation expense	n	Accumulated depreciation	Net book value
	(£'000)	(£'000)		(£'000)	(£'000)
1971	₇₁£ 90	×1/15 = ₇₁£ 6	× 1 =	₇₁£ 6	₇₁£ 84
....	.....	.....		.....	.....
1976	₇₆£180	×1/15 = ₇₆£12	× 6 =	₇₆£ 72	₇₆£108
....	.....	.....		.....	.....
1982	₈₂£360	×1/15 = ₈₂£24	×12 =	₈₂£288	₈₂£ 72

Fig. 8.3: The machine in Hampton's CPP accounts.

In times of rising prices, the 'restated' cost in constant purchasing power units of the latest balance sheet date will always be higher than the historical cost money amounts. This applies to the gross cost, accumulated depreciation, and net book value. When inflation is rapid, or the assets have a long life, the difference can be large. In the next chapter we shall be looking at ratios, such as return on investment, to help interpret business performance. Clearly it makes a difference whether the amount of 'investment' on which a business needs to earn a return in 1982 is £18,000 (HC) or ₈₂£72,000 (CPP).

The precise scale of such understatement of depreciation varies with the life of the asset, the rate of inflation, and the method of depreciation. The scale of the overstatement of profit depends on these three, together with the relationship between depreciation expense and profit after tax in the HC accounts. It should be noted that all inflation adjustments, whether to depreciation or to other items, are *disallowed* for tax purposes. Thus in effect they are all 'after-tax' adjustments.

Given recent UK rates of inflation, HC depreciation of plant and equipment would probably need to be increased by at least 50 per cent in CPP accounts. In some companies this alone would eliminate the entire HC profit after tax! There may also need to be other CPP adjustments further reducing the HC profit (see 8.2.4). So it is clear that CPP adjustments can often cause big reductions to reported HC profits.

The principles of CPP as applied to fixed assets and depreciation are not too hard to understand, but the arithmetic can seem complicated. So it is worth examining precisely how one year's CPP net book value turns into the next year's net book value in CPP accounts.

Example: *Let us assume 10 per cent inflation between 1982 and 1983. In preparing Hampton's 1983 balance sheet there are two steps: (1) restate the end-of-1982 CPP balance sheet into terms of 1983 purchasing power units; and (2) enter the 1983 transactions, in terms of 1983 purchasing power units. These two steps (which cannot be taken before the end of 1983) are set out in Fig. 8.4. They*

Accounting for Inflation   123

	Cost	Depreciation expense	Accumulated depreciation	Net book value
	(£'000)	(£'000)	(£'000)	(£'000)
End-of-1982 balance sheet	$_{82}$£360		$_{82}$£288	$_{82}$£ 72
(1) Restate in 1983 £s	$\times \dfrac{110}{100}$		$\times \dfrac{110}{100}$	$\times \dfrac{110}{100}$
Start-of-1983 balance sheet	$_{83}$£396		$_{83}$£316.8	$_{83}$£ 79.2
(2) Enter 1983 transactions		$\times\ 1/15 =\ _{83}$£26.4	$_{83}$£ 26.4	($_{83}$£ 26.4)
= End-of-1983 balance sheet	$_{83}$£396		$_{83}$£343.2	$_{83}$£ 52.8

Fig. 8.4: Calculating 1983 CPP net book value.

show how the 1983 net book value for Hampton's machine is calculated at $_{83}$£52,800 (i.e. cost $_{83}$£396,000 less accumulated depreciation $_{83}$£343,200). The accumulated depreciation of $_{83}$£343,200 is 13 years' worth of the annual depreciation expense of $_{83}$£26,400.

8.2.4 Monetary Gains and Losses

We now come to an unfamiliar item: gains and losses on monetary liabilities and assets. It is unfamiliar because we are used to historical cost accounts where money is the unit of account. But in CPP accounts we are reckoning in terms of units of constant purchasing power. If the purchasing power of money is falling (as it will be in times of inflation), a company which holds money will be losing purchasing power. CPP accounts record this loss as an expense in the profit and loss account.

Example: *Graham Nash holds £20,000 in cash at the end of 1982, and continues to hold the same amount of money all through 1983. During the year the retail price index rises by 10 per cent. Figure 8.5 shows how in Nash's 1983 CPP accounts there will be a* **monetary loss** *of $_{83}$£2,000.*

Although Nash holds the same amount of *money* at the end of 1983 as at the beginning of the year, *he holds less purchasing power*. In times of rapid inflation this is obvious. If Rip Van Winkle had put £1,000 in £1 notes in a sock under his bed in 1967, when he woke up in 1982 he would have found his £1,000 still

	HC accounts		CPP accounts
Start of year	£20,000	(= ₈₂£20,000)	= ₈₃£22,000
End of year	£20,000	(= ₈₃£20,000)	= ₈₃£20,000
Monetary loss	—		₈₃£ 2,000

Fig. 8.5: Calculation of G. Nash's monetary loss in 1983.

there. But with the retail price index five times as high in 1982 as it had been in 1967, his money would have lost 80 per cent of its purchasing power.

Where the amount of money – or **monetary assets** such as debtors – varies during the year (as it normally will), the actual calculation is somewhat more complicated. Then we have to use averages. But the principle is the same. And if a company happens to have net **monetary liabilities**, by *owing* more money than it is owed or possesses, then in CPP accounts its profit will be *increased* by a **monetary gain**. (Everyone who borrows a mortgage on his house benefits from this.)

Given the overall 'half-year' CPP adjustment to all HC profit and loss account items (see **8.2.2(a)**), it will normally be appropriate to treat opening and closing stocks as if they were 'monetary' assets for the purposes of CPP accounts.

8.2.5 Comparisons Between Years

Two different kinds of CPP adjustments are needed to financial statements to allow for inflation. So far we have been discussing the first kind, CPP adjustments to the current year's HC accounts: (a) the comprehensive 'average' to 'end-of-year' purchasing power adjustment to all HC profit and loss account items, and the two special CPP adjustments (b) to depreciation of fixed assets, and (c) to allow for losses (or gains) on net monetary assets (or liabilities). We may call these the **A-adjustments**: they are made to HC Accounts to translate them into CPP Accounts.

The second kind of CPP adjustments, which we consider now, are needed to allow a proper comparison of financial amounts *between different years*. We may call these the **B-adjustments**: they are made, to all sorts of financial statistics, to allow comparisons *B*etween years.

Example: *Gordon Mitchell's salary was £8,000 in 1980, £9,000 in 1981, and £10,000 in 1982. Obviously it has been increasing in money terms; but he wants to know whether he is better off in 'real' terms, after allowing for inflation. (For simplicity, we ignore tax and other complications.)*

To answer Gordon Mitchell's question we can use the CPP approach, adjusting his money salary each year by reference to the retail price index for that year. The retail price index (based on January 1974 = 100) averaged 264 in 1980, 295 in

Accounting for Inflation

1981, and 320 in 1982. We want to translate the money amount of Gordon's salary for each year into terms of 'constant purchasing power units' which can be compared directly with each other. So we adjust each of the earlier years' figures into terms of purchasing power of the most recent year, as in Fig. 8.6.

Year	Money salary	Adjustment	'Real' salary in terms of 1982 purchasing power
	(£)		(£)
1980	8,000	× 320/264	= 9,697
1981	9,000	× 320/295	= 9,763
1982	10,000	× 320/320	= 10,000.

Fig. 8.6: Restating Gordon Mitchell's salary.

After these B-adjustments, we see that Gordon's salary in 'real' terms increased by less than 1 per cent in 1981, and by about $2\frac{1}{2}$ per cent in 1982. Of course we don't change the 1982 salary figure, since it is already expressed in terms of 1982 purchasing power.

In times of rapid inflation, this kind of B-adjustment is needed to allow comparisons over time (*B*etween years) in 'real' terms. It is used in many published economic statistics, such as the Gross National Product, the Financial Times Share Indices, and so on.

In accounting we make such adjustments to different years' CPP accounts in order to translate all the different years' CPP figures into terms of the *same* CPP units. Then proper trends can be calculated and comparisons over time made. Pictures, graphs, and other comparisons over time which do *not* allow for inflation are very likely to mislead the reader.

8.3 Current Cost Accounting (CCA)

Current Cost Accounting (CCA) continues to use money as the unit of account, but translates historical costs into *current* costs, both in the profit and loss account and in the balance sheet. To do so, CCA uses a variety of specific indices for stocks and fixed assets.

Assets are stated at current cost in the CCA balance sheet, rather than at historical cost, any increase (or decrease) to stocks or fixed assets being added to (or subtracted from) shareholders' funds as a separate revaluation reserve. Expenses in the CCA profit and loss account are based on current costs not on historical costs, which requires (a) a depreciation adjustment, and (b) a cost of sales adjustment.

8.3.1 CCA Adjustments to HC Profits

CCA profit and loss accounts start with HC operating profit, and then deduct (or add) the current cost adjustments. Any non-operating income will then be added, and interest payable and taxation deducted, to arrive at CCA profit after tax.

There are four basic CCA adjustments to HC profits:

a. depreciation adjustment;
b. cost of sales adjustment;
c. monetary working capital adjustment;
d. gearing adjustment.

The CCA depreciation adjustment is similar to CPP's (see **8.2.2**). But instead of using the retail price index for all items, CCA uses a variety of specific indices for different fixed assets, depending on how their own costs have changed since the date of acquisition. In general, CCA aims to use the current **replacement cost** for each fixed asset in place of its actual historical cost; and this then forms the basis for CCA depreciation. The CCA 'depreciation adjustment' is simply CCA depreciation less the HC depreciation already charged in calculating HC operating profit.

Clearly not all prices change at exactly the same rate. If the general rate of inflation is 10 per cent in a period, some prices of assets will rise by 10 per cent, others by 15 per cent, others by 5 per cent; and some asset prices may double, while others actually fall. (Even when prices-in-general are *stable* – when there is *no* general 'inflation' – the specific prices of particular goods and services will still fluctuate.) Thus the numbers used for CCA will differ from those used for CPP; but the nature of the accounting adjustment for fixed assets and depreciation is similar.

There have already been several versions of 'Current Cost Accounting' in less than 10 years since 1975. Originally only two current cost adjustments were required to HC profits – those for depreciation and for cost of sales. Since it is likely that CCA will be further modified, it seems unnecessary to go into detail about (c), the monetary working capital adjustment and (d), the gearing adjustment. Between them these somewhat complicated CCA adjustments try roughly to encompass the same kind of adjustment as CPP makes for monetary gains and losses (see **8.2.4**), even though CCA continues to use money as the unit of account.

8.3.2 CCA Cost of Sales Adjustment

The usual method of calculating the **cost of sales adjustment** (COSA) is to assume that any purchases of stock consumed in the same period are already shown at 'current cost' (in effect, 'average-for-the-year' costs). So a CCA adjustment is needed to HC cost of sales only in respect of the *change* in the stock level during a period.

Example: *Charles Fox Ltd deals in brushes. In a year in which the retail price index rises by 5 per cent, the specific index relevant for brushes rises from 100 at the*

Accounting for Inflation

beginning of the year to 120 at the end, with an average for the year of 110. In the HC accounts, opening stocks were valued at £8,000 and closing stocks at £10,000.

We already know (see 7.1.2) that in HC accounts any increase in stock levels is in effect (a) deducted *from cost of goods sold*, and therefore (b) added *to reported HC profit for the period*. CCA aims to charge against sales revenue the current cost of sales, not the historical cost. So CCA splits *the increase in money value of stocks during the year into two parts: volume changes and price changes*. Only the increase in the volume of stocks, valued at current costs, is counted as a deduction from CCA cost of sales. CCA eliminates any increase in money stock values due to price increases (sometimes called **stock appreciation**).

How is the CCA cost of sales adjustment actually calculated? Both the opening and the closing stocks are translated into 'average prices for the year'; the difference is then regarded as the volume ('real') change in stocks during the year (valued at average current costs for the year). Any residual amount left is attributed to price changes during the year, and deducted from sales revenue (actually from HC operating profit) as an additional CCA expense – the cost of sales adjustment (COSA). *In this way it is not treated as a 'real' increase in stocks during the period. (If specific prices of stocks fell, then the COSA would be a negative CCA adjustment, and would have to be* added *to HC operating profit. It should be evident that this could happen, even during a time of general inflation.) Figure 8.7 shows how to calculate Charles Fox's cost of sales adjustment.*

Closing stock	£10,000	× 110/120 =	£9,167
Opening stock	£ 8,000	× 110/100 =	£8,800
Price *and* volume change:	£ 2,000	Volume change:	£ 367★
Less: volume change:	£ 367★		
Cost of sales adjustment (= price change)	£ 1,633		

Fig. 8.7: Cost of sales adjustment for Charles Fox Ltd.

8.3.3 CCA Comparisons Between Years

In adjusting accounts to allow for inflation by the CCA method, we need to make both the A-adjustments *and* the B-adjustments (see **8.2.5**). That is, we need first to adjust HC accounts into CCA accounts; and second to adjust those CCA accounts into terms of the *same* purchasing power units in order to compare CCA accounts over a number of years. Figures 8.8 and 8.9 illustrate the effect over five years. (Not all CCA advocates are completely happy with the

B-adjustments to CCA accounts; they are not sure about the precise *meaning* of 'constant purchasing power units'. But most people accept the need for the B-adjustments to allow comparison between years.)

Example: *Imperial Chemical Industries plc reported HC profit before tax of £259m in 1981, and of £335m in 1982. The company also published CCA figures, after making the necessary A-adjustments. ICI's CCA profit before tax was reported as £84m in 1981 and £99m in 1982.*

But we cannot directly compare ICI's reported CCA profits of £84m in 1981 and £99m in 1982. Although each year's figures on their own have been A-adjusted for inflation, using CCA, the £84m is expressed in terms of 1981 pounds, while the £99m is in 1982 pounds. It is like comparing Gordon Mitchell's 1981 salary of £9,000 with his 1982 salary of £10,000.

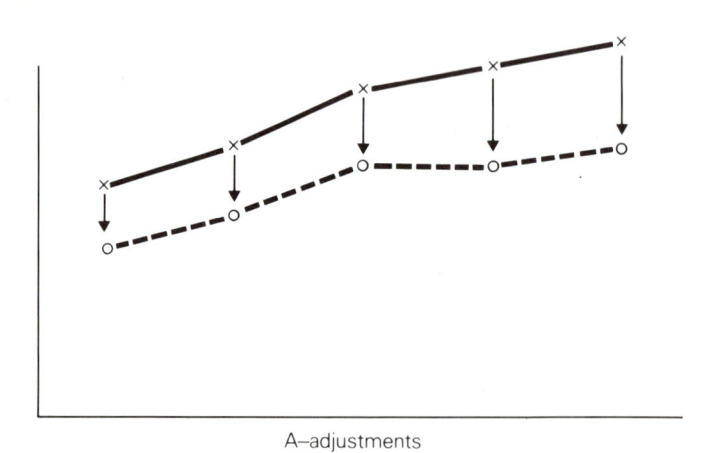

Fig. 8.8 A-adjustments

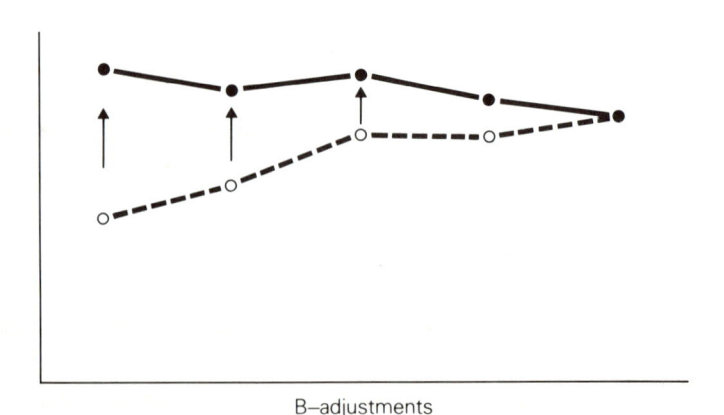

Fig. 8.9 B-adjustments

Accounting for Inflation

So ICI B-adjusts its 1981 CCA profit of £84m into terms of 1982 pounds, in exactly the same way that we did with Gordon's salary:

1981 CCA Profit	B-adjustment	1981 CCA profit in terms of 1982 pounds
£84m	320/295	£91m

Now at last we *are able to make a proper comparison between the two years' AB-adjusted accounts: ICI's 1982 CCA before-tax profit of £99m compares with its 1981 CCA profit of £91m (expressed in 1982 pounds). And this is what ICI says in its Annual Report.*

8.4 Conclusion

8.4.1 CPP versus CCA

We noted in **8.1.3** that inflation has caused serious problems for accounting, and that two different systems of 'inflation accounting' have been proposed. Constant purchasing power (CPP) accounting challenges the accounting convention of using money as the unit of account, and proposes instead to translate all items in HC accounts into terms of 'constant purchasing power units'. To do so, CPP regards money of different dates as 'foreign' currencies, and uses the retail price index (a general index of purchasing power) to translate all money amounts of different dates into CPP units of the *same* date. Current cost accounting (CCA) challenges the accounting convention of valuing assets and expenses at historical cost, and proposes instead to translate all items in HC accounts into terms of current costs. To do so, CCA uses a variety of different specific indices showing the historical changes in the replacement costs of many kinds of stocks and fixed assets.

Figure 8.8 summarises the position. Traditional HC accounting is shown in the top left-hand quadrant, using money as the unit of account and historical costs. CPP is shown in the bottom left-hand quadrant, using a CPP unit of account and historical costs. CCA is shown in the top right-hand quadrant,

| Unit of account | Basis of valuing assets and expenses ||
	Historical cost	Current cost
Money	Historical cost (HC)	Current cost accounting (CCA)
Unit of constant purchasing power	Constant purchasing power (CPP)	CCA/CPP combination

Fig. 8.10: Different kinds of inflation accounting.

using money as the unit of account and current costs. Finally, in the bottom right-hand quadrant is shown a possible *combination* of CPP and CCA accounting. This would change *two* of the accounting conventions, preparing accounts in terms of constant purchasing power units (like CPP) but also using current costs (like CCA) rather than historical costs.

Throughout the book we have been measuring a company's profit for a period by deducting expenses from sales revenue. An alternative approach (which would reach the same result) would be to ask: ignoring dividends and all capital transactions, how much would shareholders' funds have changed during the period? In other words, after maintaining the amount of 'capital' attributable to shareholders at the start of a period, how much increase (or decrease) has resulted from profit-and-loss-account transactions during the period?

In HC accounting the definition of the 'capital' to be maintained is the money amount of shareholders' funds. In CPP accounting it is the purchasing power amount of shareholders' funds: until shareholders' funds have been maintained in terms of constant purchasing power, the company has not made any CPP profit. The CCA definition of 'capital' is a *physical* one: until a company has maintained the physical productive capacity of its business, it has not made a CCA profit. Which of these definitions of 'capital' is thought more useful ultimately depends on what one believes the purpose of a business enterprise to be.

Both the proposed methods of inflation accounting have advantages and disadvantages. CPP has the advantage of using the same readily available 'general' index of inflation (the retail price index) to apply to all items in accounts; and it also allows proper comparisons of financial statements and amounts over time. On the other hand, its 'CPP unit of account' is artificial, and may be difficult for some readers of accounts to understand.

CCA has the advantage of continuing to use the familiar monetary unit as the unit of accounting measurement; but as a result it is not strictly a method of accounting for general inflation. It may be argued that current costs are more relevant for assessing business performance than historical costs; but because it is not always easy to tell which is the best specific index of cost changes to use, CCA is more subjective than CPP. CCA is also more complicated to apply than CPP: it brings a number of difficult technical problems which could be hard for smaller businesses to deal with. And some of the CCA procedures are still the subject of vigorous debate. (ICI for instance, whose CCA profit figures were used in **8.3.3**, actually produces its own preferred version of its CCA profits, in addition to the 'standard' CCA figures which we used.)

8.4.2 The Future

In 1973, after about five years of rapid inflation, the UK accountancy bodies proposed CPP accounting. At that time the government was opposed to **indexation**; so it set up a committee to consider 'whether, and if so how, company accounts should allow for changes (including relative changes) in costs and prices'.

Accounting for Inflation

In 1975 the government committee (chaired by Francis Sandilands) issued its report, rejecting CPP and proposing CCA instead. The name 'current cost accounting' was new; but for many years a similar system (called 'replacement cost accounting') had been used by a number of Dutch companies. The accountancy bodies officially 'welcomed' the Sandilands report; but said there was still a role for 'general index' adjustments, which the report had completely ruled out.

The government then instructed the accountancy bodies to implement a form of CCA, but the resulting CCA Exposure Draft was very complicated (with a guidance manual of more than 400 pages!); and in 1977 the members of the English Institute of Chartered Accountants passed a motion that 'the members of this Institute do not wish any system of CCA to be made compulsory'.

The offending Exposure Draft was withdrawn, and after much discussion a new one appeared proposing a revised form of CCA, by now quite far removed from the original Sandilands recommendations. In 1980, further modified, it became a Statement of Standard Accounting Practice to run for an experimental period of three years. SSAP 16 required companies with sales exceeding £5m a year to publish supplementary CCA accounts in addition to their ordinary HC accounts.

Paragraph 33 of SSAP 16 itself stated that CCA 'is not a system of accounting for general inflation'; and a report in 1983 indicated that many companies, including some which had been keen on CCA, were now doubtful about its value. So the accountancy bodies set up a new working party to look again at the whole question of accounting for inflation. There was obvious reluctance to abandon CCA; but there was much opposition to it, both in the accountancy profession and in industry generally. By now the government's former strong resistance to CPP-type general indexing seemed to have abated.

At the time of writing there seem to be at least four possible outcomes to the long debate over inflation accounting:

1. Carry on with CCA, somewhat modified from SSAP 16. But smaller companies would probably not be required to use CCA; and in several industries it would be difficult to apply.
2. Carry on with CCA; but combined with CPP at least for comparisons over time, and possibly in other ways.
3. Abandon CCA, after protracted efforts to make it workable and useful; and reintroduce a proposal for CPP. In the 1970s this was rejected not by accountants, but by the government and its committee.
4 Abandon both forms of inflation accounting, and continue to use only HC accounting. This might be acceptable if the rate of inflation, which has fallen sharply since 1980, stays permanently below 5 per cent a year. Without (much) inflation there would be less need for inflation accounting.

After all the debates of the previous decade, only a brave person would venture to predict the final result. The arguments may continue for some time yet.

Work Section

A. Revision Questions

A1   What do you understand 'inflation' to mean?
A2   Define 'currency debasement'.
A3   What are two main explanations of the causes of inflation?
A4   What is 'demand-pull' inflation?
A5   What is 'cost-push' inflation?
A6   How is inflation measured in the UK?
A7   How is the retail price index calculated?
A8   What annual rate has UK inflation averaged since 1974?
A9   What does the 'half-life' of the pound mean?
A10 What is the rate of currency debasement if prices triple?
A11 Which accounting convention is challenged by CPP?
A12 What problem is addressed by constant purchasing power accounting?
A13 Which accounting convention is challenged by CCA?
A14 What problem is addressed by current cost accounting?
A15 What briefly are the essential differences between CPP and CCA?
A16 In what sense is CPP like international accounting?
A17 What are the three basic CPP rules?
A18 Why are CPP comparisons over time normally made in terms of units of constant purchasing power of the most recent period?
A19 What three groups of balance sheet items were distinguished for the purposes of CPP accounting?
A20 Why is only a small inflation adjustment likely to be needed for stocks in the balance sheet?
A21 Why is no adjustment needed to translate monetary items in the end-of-year HC balance sheet into CPP terms?
A22 Name two variables which affect the size of the depreciation adjustment in the inflation-adjusted profit and loss account.
A23 Why are inflation adjustments to the profit and loss account 'after-tax'?
A24 What is meant in CPP accounting by a 'monetary loss'?
A25 Explain in words how an employee could compare his salary in 'real' terms over the past five years.
A26 How can a 'monetary gain' arise in CPP accounts?
A27 What are the two different kinds of inflation adjustments to HC accounts?
A28 What was meant by A-adjustments and B-adjustments? What do the letters A and B stand for?
A29 Why would making only B-adjustments to HC accounts be inadequate?

Accounting for Inflation 133

A30 Why may a graph showing financial information over time be misleading?
A31 How does CCA value assets on the balance sheet?
A32 When a CCA adjustment increases the net book value of fixed assets, how does the CCA balance sheet still balance?
A33 Name two current cost adjustments to the HC profit and loss account.
A34 What is the essential difference between the depreciation adjustment for CCA and that for CPP?
A35 Why do all prices not change at exactly the same rate?
A36 What is the purpose of the CCA cost of sales adjustment?
A37 Into which two component parts does CCA split a change in the money value of stocks?
A38 Define 'stock appreciation'.
A39 Explain in words how ICI compared its performance in 1981 and 1982, starting from HC profit figures.
A40 Which two kinds of adjustments are needed to HC accounts to produce CCA accounts which can be compared between years?
A41 Which two accounting conventions would *both* be challenged by a system of inflation accounting which combined CPP and CCA?
A42 What definition of the 'capital' to be maintained before reckoning profit or loss is used:
  (a) by HC? (b) by CPP? (c) by CCA?
A43 Name two advantages of CPP.
A44 Name two advantages of CCA.
A45 What four possibilities for the future of inflation accounting were suggested?

B. Exercises and Case Studies

B1 You are left £25,000 by an aunt. Assuming that inflation will average 6 per cent a year in future, which of the following investment strategies would you choose (ignoring the problem of tax)? Explain why.
  a. Keep the cash in a safe place.
  b. Use the cash to purchase a fixed-interest government security returning 3 per cent a year.
  c. Buy a piece of land which will appreciate on average at 10 per cent a year, but will give no cash return meanwhile.
  d. Buy a country cottage which will appreciate in line with inflation and which will also yield an annual rental of £500.
B2 Refer to Fig. 8.6 (p. 125). Restate Gordon Mitchell's money salary for 1980, 1981, and 1982 into terms of constant 1980 pounds.
B3 Reed Water Ltd acquires a machine in September 1978 for £40,000 when the retail price index (January 1974 = 100) stands at 200. The machine is expected to last 10 years and to have no residual value. The company uses

straight-line depreciation, and charges a full year's depreciation in the year of acquisition.
   a. What will the CPP depreciation expense be for the year ending 31 December 1983 if the retail price index stands at 350 in December 1983?
   b. What will the machine's CPP net book value be at 31 December 1983? What will the machine's HC net book value be on that date?

B4 In March 1984 the Financial Times-Actuaries 500 Share Index hit a new 'all-time peak' of 578. In that same month the retail price index (January 1974 = 100) reached 345. A previous peak in the FT-Actuaries Index had been reached in August 1972; the FT-Actuaries Index then reached 228, with the RPI then at 86.
   a. Approximately what proportion of the August 1972 level did the FT-Actuaries Index reach in March 1984 in terms of constant purchasing power?
   b. How much of its 'real' value had the FT-Actuaries Index lost at the time of its March 1984 'all-time peak', compared with its starting point (at 100) in April 1962 (when the RPI was 53)?

B5 African Traders Ltd prepare current cost accounts which contain a summary of the current year's results together with comparative figures for the previous two years. These comparative figures are not adjusted for changes in the value of money. Summarised figures from the balance sheets and profit and loss accounts are shown below as they appeared in the current cost accounts at the end of year 3. The value of money, as measured by the retail price index, had fallen over the period. The retail price index stood at 100 at the end of Year 1, at 110 at the end of Year 2, and at 120 at the end of Year 3.

	Year 1 (£)	Year 2 (£)	Year 3 (£)
Balance sheet			
Fixed assets	10,000	15,000	17,000
Current assets	9,000	8,000	8,000
Current liabilities	(500)	(1,000)	(1,500)
Shareholders' funds*	18,500	22,000	23,500
Profit and loss account			
Net profit before tax	4,000	6,000	4,500
Tax	2,000	3,000	2,250
Ordinary dividends	1,000	1,000	1,250

* Share capital is unchanged throughout.

Accounting for Inflation 135

    a. Adjust the comparative figures to allow for inflation.

    b. What conclusions can you draw from comparing your results with those published?

B6 A company begins life with a share capital of £100 which it immediately uses to purchase a £100 machine. Using historical cost accounting, it then makes a profit of £20 in the first year, £24 in the second, £28.80 in the third, etc. (i.e. the profits rise in line with inflation which is considered to be 20 per cent a year). There is no taxation, and all profits are immediately paid out at the end of each year in cash dividends; depreciation is calculated on the straight-line basis at £10 a year.

    a. Illustrate what happens to the shareholders' funds year by year, and to the assets.

    b. Are shareholders receiving a constant, falling, or rising real return through their dividends?

    c. Comment on the shareholders' situation as reflected in shareholders' funds in the balance sheet.

    d. What problems is the company creating for itself by its method of accounting?

    e. Describe the sort of changes you would wish to make to overcome the problems you have described in (d).

B7 Refer to Fig. 8.8 and 8.9 (p. 128).

Eastman Kodak reports its HC profits (in $ millions) as: 1,001 in 1979, 1,154 in 1980, 1,239 in 1981, and 1,162 in 1982.

The company reports its CPP profits (in $ millions of each year) as: 777 in 1979, 962 in 1980, 1,064 in 1981, and 983 in 1982.

The consumer price index used for CPP adjustments in the United States averaged 217.4 in 1979, 246.8 in 1980, 272.4 in 1981, and 289.1 in 1982.

Prepare charts similar to Figs 8.8 and 8.9 to reflect the position.

B8 The General Electric Company Ltd holds large liquid resources. At the end of March 1981 these amounted to £689m, at March 1982 to £1,075m, and at March 1983 to £1,350m. The rate of inflation was 10.4 per cent in the year ending March 1982, and 4.6 per cent in the year ending March 1983. The company's CCA adjustments (in accordance with SSAP 16) made no adjustment for any 'monetary loss' in respect of the liquid resources.

    a. Calculate GEC's 'monetary loss'

      (i) for the year ending March 1982

      (ii) for the year ending March 1983

    b. Restate GEC's CCA results, including the 'monetary loss', on a comparable basis for 1982 and 1983.

    c. Calculate the percentage change between 1982 and 1983 in (i) profit before tax, and (ii) profit after tax, according to your restated figures. How do these percentage changes compare with those stemming from GEC's published CCA profit figures (i) before tax? and (ii) after tax?

A summary of GEC's CCA profit and loss accounts for the years 1982 and 1983 is shown below:

	1983 (£m)	1982 (£m)
HC operating profit	531	497
Less: CCA adjustments	108	116
Current cost operating profit	423	381
Add: Interest receivable (net)	139	87
CCA profit before tax	562	468
Less: Taxation	270	219
CCA profit after tax	292	249

B9 Refer to the Alan Hampton example in 8.2.3 (p. 121).
Assume the rate of inflation is 10 per cent between 1983 and 1984.
  a. Starting from the machine's net book value of $_{83}$£52,800 at the end of 1983, prepare a statement similar to Fig. 8.4 (p. 123) showing step by step how you would calculate the machine's net book value in the end-1984 CPP balance sheet.
  b. Referring back to Fig. 8.3 (p. 122), prepare a statement comparing the machine's CPP net book value as at the end of 1971, 1976, 1982, 1983, and 1984.

B10 Refer to the Charles Fox example in 8.3.2 (p. 126). Assume that in the following year:
  1. The specific index for brushes rises from 120 at the start of the year to 150 at the end of the year, with an average for the year of 138.
  2. The retail price index averaged 163 in the first year and 188 in the second.
  3. The HC closing stock at the end of the second year was £15,000.
  a. Prepare a statement, similar to that in Fig. 8.7, showing the calculation of the cost of sales adjustment for the second year.
  b. Compare the COSA for years 1 and 2.

C. Essay Questions

C1 How would a change from historical cost to inflation accounting affect the main users of accounting information?

C2 Write a memo to the manager of a medium-sized business arguing for a change from historical cost to current cost accounting.

C3 Write a memo to the manager of a medium-sized business arguing for a change from historical cost to constant purchasing power accounting.

Accounting for Inflation

C4 Would the best solution to the problem of accounting for inflation be a combination of CPP and CCA?

C5 Write an essay defending the continuing use of historical cost accounting, as opposed to either CPP or CCA.

C6 If there is no inflation will there be no need for inflation accounting?

C7 'It is just common sense that when the value of money is falling fast enough the monetary unit becomes useless and irrelevant as a unit of account. CPP accepts and builds on this obvious point: CCA denies it.' Discuss.

C8 Comment on the following statement in the Sandilands Report: 'In determining a change in the "purchasing power" of money it is necessary to know on what it is spent...a general index of the "purchasing power" of money is unlikely to be helpful.'

C9 'The index method (CPP) is not strictly a proposal for a change from accounting based on historical cost.' Institute of Chartered Accountants in England and Wales, 1952. Discuss.

C10 Who should decide how best to account for inflation: the government, the accountancy profession, or some other group?

9 Analysing Accounts

9.1 Using Ratios
9.1.1 The Use of Ratios
9.1.2 Standards for Comparison
9.1.3 Main Kinds of Ratios

9.2 Case Example
9.2.1 Background
9.2.2 Accounts

9.3 Ratio Analysis
9.3.1 Performance (Efficiency) Measures
9.3.2 Gearing and Liquidity Measures
9.3.3 Shareholder Measures
9.3.4 Summary of Ratios
9.3.5 Problems in Using Ratios

9.4 Funds Flow Analysis
9.4.1 The Funds Flow Statement
9.4.2 Interpreting Funds Flows

9.5 Views of Different Users
9.5.1 Shareholders
9.5.2 Creditors
9.5.3 Lenders
9.5.4 Employees

Objective: *To explain the purpose of ratio analysis and funds flow analysis in interpreting financial accounts, and to describe the commonest accounting ratios.*

Synopsis: *Accounting ratios are a useful way to summarise financial relationships. They allow comparisons over time, with other firms, and with internal budgets.*

Ratios can be split into three groups: performance (efficiency) measures, gearing and liquidity measures, and shareholder measures. There are problems in using ratios: they raise questions rather than providing definite answers.

Analysing Accounts 139

Funds flow analysis may be useful to lenders in identifying a company's sources and uses of funds for a period. It may also help in forecasting future financial needs.

A case example illustrates the kinds of questions which may be of interest to different users of accounts: shareholders, creditors, lenders, and employees.

9.1 Using Ratios

9.1.1 The Use of Ratios

Much of Chapters 3 to 8 has dealt with *preparing* accounts: the basic accounting concepts and conventions (Ch. 3); the detailed presentation of balance sheets (Ch. 4) and profit and loss accounts (Ch. 5); and key problem areas in fixed assets and depreciation (Ch. 6), in valuing stocks (Ch. 7), and in allowing for inflation (Ch. 8). Now we move on to consider how to interpret and analyse accounting information contained in the published financial accounts.

One piece of information may not mean very much all by itself. For example, GKN reported profits in 1982 of £800,000. Is a profit of just under £1m 'good' of 'bad'? It may be easier to form a view when we learn that GKN's total assets exceeded £1,000m. Thus the 1982 profit was less than 1/10th of 1 per cent of total assets, which looks rather poor. It means that on average every £100 of GKN's assets earned only 8p profit! In contrast, Vosper reported 1982 profits of £1.8m, more than twice as much as GKN. But this represented 10 per cent of Vosper's total assets of £18m. Obviously this is a much better result, with every £100 of Vosper's assets earning on average a profit of £10.

A 'ratio' is simply a method of *comparing* one number to another. An accounting ratio has meaning only if there is some reason to expect a definite relationship between the two. There *is* some reason to expect profit to be related to total assets, or to sales revenue. But, for example, if we were to divide accumulated depreciation by interest payable, the result would be meaningless. There is no reason to expect the two numbers to be related.

Accounting data can often be related to another piece of information. Using a common format, by expressing the comparison as a ratio or as a percentage, makes comparisons with a particular standard much easier (see **9.1.2**). The 'ratio' may simply be one number as a *percentage* of another. Or we might *divide* one number directly by another. Vosper paid dividends of £0.3m in 1982, so the 'dividend cover' ratio was six (that is, profits 'covered' the dividends six times over).

It will be evident that the value of accounting ratios must partly depend on the accuracy of the underlying data. Thus HC return on investment ratios are probably misleading in times of inflation, because both parts of the ratio are distorted by inflation. As we saw in Chapter 8, the HC 'return' (profit) will probably need to be reduced by inflation adjustments, and the HC 'investment' (net assets, capital employed) will probably need to be *increased* by inflation adjustments. Thus the 'real' (inflation-adjusted) percentage return on investment will often be *much* lower than the HC percentage.

Ratios need not consist only of financial information. We can calculate 'fixed assets' per employee for a manufacturing company, or 'sales per square metre of space' for a retail store. In schools a commonly used ratio is 'number of pupils per teacher'. Even a single ratio on its own may not tell us very much. In order to interpret the meaning of most ratios we need *standards* for comparison.

9.1.2 Standards for Comparison

(*a*) *Over time*

One obvious way to compare ratios is over time, between years. Figures for past periods are likely to be available on a consistent basis. Comparisons over time enable us to detect *trends*, to see whether things are getting 'better' or 'worse', or staying much the same. This can help us to interpret financial (and other) information, though we should not assume that the future need be like the past. In other words, trends go on until they stop!

We have already seen, in Chapter 8, how two different kinds of inflation adjustment may be needed to accounting information: what we called A-adjustments to translate a company's HC Accounts for a period into CPP or CCA terms; and B-adjustments to permit comparison *B*etween years. Accounting *ratios* (as opposed to money amounts) may be comparable over time without the B-adjustments, since both parts of the ratio (both the 'numerator' on top, and the 'denominator' on the bottom) may be expressed in the same way (i.e. either both in CPP units of the same date, or both in current costs). Thus CCA percentage profit margins on sales could properly be compared over time, even though the CCA profit figures themselves could *not* be compared between years without the necessary B-adjustments. But the A-adjustments for inflation may still be needed in order to calculate meaningful ratios in the first place: the HC profit margin on sales is likely to overstate the 'real' percentage margin, since at least depreciation adjustments and cost of sales adjustments are needed to HC profit figures.

(*b*) *Interfirm comparisons*

Another useful standard is the performance of other firms in the same industry. A company's rate of profit to assets employed, for example, may be slowly increasing over time. But it may still be much lower than the rate of return which other companies in the same industry are earning. That is useful to know, because it provides an *external* standard by which to judge performance. If other companies in the same industry can do much better, we would like to know the *reasons*. They may give us some clues as to possible improvements in our own performance. This topic is discussed at more length in **11**.3.4.

Each firm is unique: the mix of products, the technical nature of the equipment, and so on, will tend to vary from one firm to the next. Moreover, as we have seen, accounting methods may not always be the same for different companies. This should warn us not to place *too much* weight on ratio analysis: it can probably do no more than give us approximate clues (see **9**.3.5).

Analysing Accounts   141

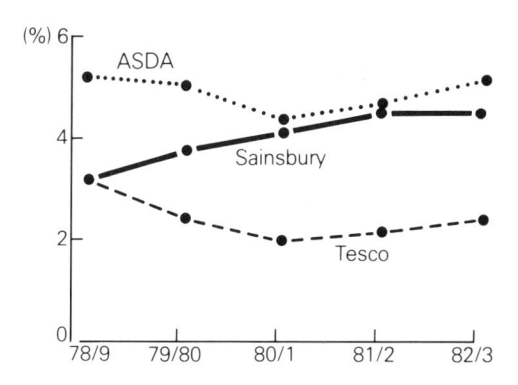

Fig. 9.1: Profit margins of three food retailers, 1978/79 to 1982/83.

(c) Interfirm comparisons over time

An obvious extension is to *combine* these two standards: interfirm comparisons over a period of years. Thus Fig. 9.1 compares the profit margin on sales of three food retailing companies over a five-year period.

What does Fig. 9.1 show? ASDA's profit margin has been about 2 percentage points above Tesco's throughout, so that the trend lines run nearly parallel. In a low-margin rapid-turnover business like food retailing, a difference of as much as 2 percentage points seems fairly high. (Incidentally, because turnover is rapid, and because depreciation of fixed assets is relatively low in this business, the HC profit margins which we are using here are probably not misleading. In a manufacturing business it would be much better to use inflation-adjusted profit margin percentages.) Sainsbury's profit margin actually increased in 1979/80 and 1980/81, whereas the other two companies' margins fell slightly in each year. As a result, while Sainsbury's started the five-year period with a profit margin close to Tesco's, after two years it had nearly reached the same level of margin as ASDA. One piece of information we would like to know is whether Sainsbury's sales revenues increased as rapidly as ASDA's and Tesco's. (The answer is: after the first year, faster.)

(d) Internal budgets

For management accounting purposes, another useful standard for comparison is the company's own internal budgets. Unlike published financial accounts, they should be available in considerable detail; thus enabling the analyst to interpret performance much more thoroughly than is possible with aggregate accounting information. (Fig. 1.3, p. 5, listed the essential differences between financial accounting and management accounting.)

The more care is spent on preparing budgets, the more they can later be relied on as standards; though one still needs to allow for changes in conditions since the budgets were prepared. We shall be discussing budgets in detail in Chapter 10; in particular the technique of **variance analysis**, which compares actual with budgeted performance, and tries to explain *reasons* for any differences.

9.1.3 Main Kinds of Ratios

When we come to calculate the main accounting ratios, in **9.3**, you may feel concerned at *how many* of them there seem to be. This merely emphasises how much information accounts contain, and how many different aspects of a business may be important. In trying to remember the main ratios and their precise definitions, you may find it helpful to split them into three groups:

1. Performance (efficiency) measures.
2. Gearing and liquidity measures.
3. Shareholder measures.

1. Performance measures

These attempt to reveal how well the business is being run. (They are sometimes referred to as 'efficiency' measures.) These key ratios are of interest to nearly all readers of accounts. The two main measures are both to do with *profit*: they relate profit (i) to the amount of investment in a company, and (ii) to the sales revenue in a year. In general, the higher both these ratios are the better. In business, a large profit is 'better' than a small profit (and better still than a loss!).

2. Gearing and liquidity measures

These look at a company's financial position, both in the short term and the longer term. The liquidity measures relate a company's short-term assets to its short-term liabilities, basically to test how well able the company is to pay its bills as they become due. We already know that profit and cash are both important to a business – but they are different. The measures of short-term liquidity are of special concern to short-term lenders, such as trade creditors (suppliers) and bankers. The **gearing** measures look at the long-term capital structure of a business, seeing how much capital comes from shareholders and how much from outside lenders. The larger the proportion of total capital coming from outside lenders, the 'riskier' the financial structure of the business. (But this risk may be compensated by higher rates of return on shareholders' funds as a result.)

3. Shareholder measures

These are of particular concern to equity investors and the stock market generally. They are concerned not only with the total profitability and financial position of the company, but with how well the *shareholders* are doing on their investment in the company. Hence these measures take account not only of the numbers in the accounts, such as profits and dividends, but also of the market price of the equity shares in the company.

Analysing Accounts 143

9.2 Case Example

9.2.1 Background

Hamilton Pumps Ltd had been in business for 25 years. In 1981 Lewis Jack, the founder of the company, retired in favour of his son David, who took over as Chairman and Managing Director. More ambitious and less conservative than his father, David Jack decided to expand production capacity and move into new overseas markets. He arranged for the company's shares to be quoted on the Unlisted Securities Market as from March 1982; and at the same time the Jack family sold to the public 1½ million of the 4 million shares then in issue, all of which had been owned by members of the family.

By the beginning of 1984 there were rumblings of discontent. Shareholders had complained of being kept in the dark about the company's plans; there had been some critical comments in the financial press about the quality of management; and the share price had fallen steadily throughout 1984, from 150p at the beginning of the year to 50p by December 1985. At the same time one or two major creditors had shown reluctance to allow any further build-up of outstanding credit accounts; the company's bank had refused to extend the overdraft as much as requested, and had insisted on some of the funds being raised by medium-term loans; and there were signs of dissatisfaction about wage levels from employees' representatives.

The company's 1984 accounts were published in mid-April 1985, with the AGM due to be held at the end of May. Around the same time, David Jack had arranged three other important meetings: (a) to see the company's major supplier of goods; (b) to visit the company's bank manager to discuss further increasing the bank overdraft; and (c) to meet representatives of the employees to discuss future prospects and wage levels.

9.2.2 Accounts

Hamilton Pumps Ltd's 1984 accounts are shown in 9.2.2. Then in 9.3 we work through the calculation of some basic accounting ratios arising from then. In 9.4 we look at an analysis of the company's funds flows in 1984. Finally, in 9.5 we return to see how David Jack's various meetings turned out.

Hamilton Pumps Ltd
Balance Sheet at 31 December 1984

1983 (£'000)			1984 (£'000)
	FIXED ASSETS		
600	Freehold property		750
1,350	Plant and equipment		2,250
1,950			3,000
	CURRENT ASSETS		
1,050	Stocks	1,350	
1,300	Debtors	1,850	
250	Liquid resources	100	
2,600		3,300	
	LESS: CURRENT LIABILITIES		
1,400	Creditors	1,600	
–	Bank overdraft	900	
350	Taxation	250	
100	Dividends payable	50	
1,850		2,800	
750	NET WORKING CAPITAL		500
2,700	NET ASSETS		3,500
	SHAREHOLDERS' FUNDS		
1,000	Issued ordinary 25p shares		1,000
1,200	Retained profits		1,400
2,200			2,400
	LONG-TERM LIABILITIES		
500	Mortgage debenture	500	
–	Other loans	600	
			1,100
2,700	CAPITAL EMPLOYED		3,500

Fig. 9.2: Hamilton Pumps Ltd: Balance Sheet at 31 December 1984.

Analysing Accounts

Hamilton Pumps Limited
Profit and Loss Account for the year 1984

	1983 (£'000)			1984 (£'000)
	6,500	Sales		6,750
	950	Operating profit *		725
	75	Interest payable		175
	875	Profits before tax		550
	350	Taxation		250
	525	Profit after tax		300
		Ordinary dividends:		
50		Interim, 1.25p *(1.25p)*	50	
100		Final, 1.25p *(2.50p)*	50	
—	150		—	100
	375	Retained profit for the year		200

* After charging depreciation £375,000 *(£250,000)*

Fig. 9.3: Hamilton Pumps Ltd: Profit and Loss Account for the year 1984.

9.3 Ratio Analysis

We now proceed to calculate a number of accounting ratios for Hamilton Pumps Ltd (for 1983 as well as 1984), under the three main groups listed in **9.1.3**: (1) performance (efficiency) measures; (2) gearing and liquidity measures; and (3) shareholder measures. Under each ratio there are a few brief comments. Please check the company's accounts (pp. 150/151) to make sure you understand how each ratio has been calculated, and where each of the numbers used has come from.

In **9.3.4** is a list of all the ratios we have calculated in this section, together with their definitions. Then in **9.3.5** some of the limitations of **ratio analysis** are discussed. An important part of interpreting company accounts is the analysis of funds flows, which is covered in **9.4**. Finally, in **9.5** we see how different interested parties outside the company react to Hamilton Pumps Ltd's performance in 1984.

9.3.1 Performance (Efficiency) Measures

$$\phantom{\text{Return on net assets}}\quad\quad\quad\quad\quad\quad\quad 1984 \quad\quad\quad\quad 1983$$

1. **Return on net assets** $= \dfrac{\text{Operating profit}}{\text{Net assets}} \quad \dfrac{725}{3{,}500} = 20.7\% \quad \dfrac{950}{2{,}700} = 35.2\%$

This basic measure of operating return on investment ignores taxes, because they are affected by non-operating factors. It also ignores interest paid on loan capital, being concerned with the total amount invested, whether in equity capital or loans. 1984's rate of return is significantly down on 1983.

2. **Profit margin** $= \dfrac{\text{Operating profit}}{\text{Sales}} \quad \dfrac{725}{6{,}750} = 10.7\% \quad \dfrac{950}{6{,}500} = 14.6\%$

This is another basic performance measure, relating operating profit (as before) to sales revenue. Again there is a definite reduction in 1984 compared with 1983.

3. **Asset turnover** $= \dfrac{\text{Sales}}{\text{Net assets}} \quad \dfrac{6{,}750}{3{,}500} = 1.93 \text{ times} \quad \dfrac{6{,}500}{2{,}700} = 2.41 \text{ times}$

The number of times that net assets are 'turned over' in a year in sales revenue is one measure of the 'productivity' of assets.

Notice the relationship of the above three ratios:

	profit margin	× asset turnover	= return on net assets
1984:	10.7%	× 1.93 times	= 20.7%
1983:	14.6%	× 2.41 times	= 35.2%

Different industries have very different characteristics. Thus a retailing chain might have an asset turnover as high as 3.0 (annual sales three times as large as net assets employed), but only a small profit margin on sales. On the other hand, a heavy engineering group might expect to have a much lower asset turnover of perhaps 1.0 to 1.5, while hoping for much larger profit margins on sales.

4. **Stock turnover** $= \dfrac{\text{Sales}}{\text{Stocks}} \quad \dfrac{6{,}750}{1{,}350} = 5.0 \text{ times} \quad \dfrac{6{,}500}{1{,}050} = 6.2 \text{ times}$

A high rate of stock turnover is normally better than a low one, though if it is too high there may be a risk of running out of stock. Because stocks are valued at cost (or lower), while sales revenue, of course, is 'valued' at selling prices, this ratio does *not* represent the physical rate of turnover. Still, it can be useful indicator of trends.

5. **Days' sales in debtors** $= \dfrac{\text{Debtors}}{\text{Sales}/365} \quad \dfrac{1{,}850}{6{,}750/365} = 100 \text{ days} \quad \dfrac{1{,}300}{6{,}500/365} = 73 \text{ days}$

This measure, like stock turnover, helps to show how well a company is managing its current assets. If debtors take too long to pay it can cause financial problems; so the big increase in 1984 is worrying.

Analysing Accounts

9.3.2 Gearing and Liquidity Measures

$$\text{6. Gearing ratio} = \frac{\text{Long-term liabilities}}{\text{Capital employed}} \quad \begin{array}{c}1984\\ \frac{1,100}{3,500} = 31.4\%\end{array} \quad \begin{array}{c}1983\\ \frac{500}{2,700} = 18.5\%\end{array}$$

The gearing ratio reflects how much financial risk a company runs in the way it finances the business, as between equity and debt. If short-term bank overdrafts were also included, the 1984 gearing ratio (2,000/4,400 = 45.5%) would show twice as big an increase over 1983.

$$\text{7. Interest cover} = \frac{\text{Operating profit}}{\text{Interest payable}} \quad \frac{725}{175} = 4.1 \text{ times} \quad \frac{950}{75} = 12.7 \text{ times}$$

The gearing ratio is a balance sheet measure of financial risk, while the interest cover is a profit and loss account measure. It shows how many times operating profit 'covers' the fixed interest payments legally due on long-term borrowings. The amount of financial risk that is acceptable varies with different kinds of business.

$$\text{8. Current ratio} = \frac{\text{Current assets}}{\text{Current liabilities}} \quad \frac{3,300}{2,800} = 1.18 \quad \frac{2,600}{1,850} = 1.41$$

The current ratio reflects **liquidity**, how well a company's short-term assets cover its short-term obligations. As a rule of thumb, the current ratio should probably be between 1½ and 2. If it is too low there is a danger of running out of cash; while if it is too high, then money may be tied up unprofitably in excess current assets.

$$\text{9. Acid test ratio} = \frac{\text{Liquid assets}}{\text{Current liabilities}} \quad \frac{1,950}{2,800} = 0.70 \quad \frac{1,550}{1,850} = 0.84$$

The acid test ratio is an even more severe test of liquidity than the current ratio. It compares liquid assets (cash plus debtors) to current liabilities. Both debtors and cash should be turned into cash fairly soon after the balance sheet date (hence they are sometimes called **quick assets**), while stocks may be much *less* liquid. As a rule of thumb, the acid test ratio should not be much below 1.0.

9.3.3 Shareholder Measures

	1984	1983

10. **Return on equity** = $\dfrac{\text{Profit after tax}}{\text{Shareholders' funds}}$ $\dfrac{300}{2,400} = 12.5\%$ $\dfrac{525}{2,200} = 23.9\%$

This 'return on investment' measure relates to the ordinary shareholders. It divides profit after interest and after tax by the amount of shareholders' funds (owners' equity) in the balance sheet. The 1984 ratio is only half the 1983 level.

11. **Dividend cover** = $\dfrac{\text{Profit after tax}}{\text{Dividends}}$ $\dfrac{300}{100} = 3.0$ times $\dfrac{525}{150} = 3.5$ times

This measure shows how many times more dividend could have been paid out of current earnings. (As with all these HC figures, one wonders what the inflation-adjusted measure would look like.) A shareholder's 'return' from his investment consists of dividends *plus* any capital gains in the share price. So if a company can reinvest its earnings profitably, a shareholder may be content not to get a higher dividend in the current year.

12. **Earnings per share** = $\dfrac{\text{Profit after tax}}{\text{Number of shares}}$ $\dfrac{300}{4,000} = 7.50\text{p}$ $\dfrac{525}{4,000} = 13.1$

This measure doesn't mean much on its own, but we shall use it later to compare with the stock exchange market price. Notice that the *number of shares* issued is 4 million not 1. The balance sheet shows £1m issued share capital; but each share has a nominal value of only 25p.

13. **Dividends per share** = $\dfrac{\text{Dividends}}{\text{Number of shares}}$ $\dfrac{100}{4,000} = 2.50\text{p}$ $\dfrac{150}{4,000} = 3.75\text{p}$

This measure, like earnings per share, is published in a company's annual report. Dividend cover can also be calculated on a 'per share' basis:
 Earnings per share/dividends per share = 7.50/2.50 = 3.00 times.

14. **Price/earnings ratio** = $\dfrac{\text{Market price}}{\text{Earnings per share}}$ $\dfrac{50}{7.50} = 6.7$ $\dfrac{150}{13.1} = 11.4$

The market price per share (in pence), which fluctuates from day to day, is not published in the annual report; it can be found in the financial section of a newspaper. The price/earnings ratio may be taken as an indicator of confidence in the future prosperity of a company: the higher the ratio the better. We also need to know how the stock exchange as a whole has been doing recently.

15. **Dividend yield** = $\dfrac{\text{Dividends per share}}{\text{Market price per share}}$ $\dfrac{2.50}{50} = 5.0\%$ $\dfrac{3.75}{150} = 2.5\%$

This measure is complicated by tax (which we ignore here). The dividend yield has doubled because the share price has fallen by two thirds while the dividends per share have fallen by 'only' one third.

Analysing Accounts

9.3.4 Summary of Ratios
For convenient reference, we list all 15 ratios, with definitions, in Fig. 9.4.

---

a. Performance (efficiency) measures

1. Return on net assets $= \dfrac{\text{Operating profit}}{\text{Net assets}}$

2. Profit margin $= \dfrac{\text{Operating profit}}{\text{Sales}}$

3. Asset turnover $= \dfrac{\text{Sales}}{\text{Net assets}}$

4. Stock turnover $= \dfrac{\text{Sales}}{\text{Stocks}}$

5. Days' sales in debtors $= \dfrac{\text{Debtors}}{\text{Sales}/365}$

b. Gearing and liquidity measures

6. Gearing ratio $= \dfrac{\text{Long-term liabilities}}{\text{Capital employed}}$

7. Interest cover $= \dfrac{\text{Operating profit}}{\text{Interest payable}}$

8. Current ratio $= \dfrac{\text{Current assets}}{\text{Current liabilities}}$

9. Acid test $= \dfrac{\text{Liquid assets}}{\text{Current liabilities}}$

c. Shareholder measures

10. Return on equity $= \dfrac{\text{Profit after tax}}{\text{Shareholders' funds}}$

11. Dividend cover $= \dfrac{\text{Profit after tax}}{\text{Dividends}}$

12. Earnings per share $= \dfrac{\text{Profit after tax}}{\text{Number of shares}}$

13. Dividends per share $= \dfrac{\text{Dividends}}{\text{Number of shares}}$

14. Price/earnings ratio $= \dfrac{\text{Market price per share}}{\text{Earnings per share}}$

15. Dividend yield $= \dfrac{\text{Dividends per share}}{\text{Market price per share}}$

Fig. 9.4: List of 15 ratios.

9.3.5 Problems in Using Ratios

Ratios are not a panacea. They can be useful in suggesting *questions* to look into; but they are unlikely on their own to provide complete answers. Below are listed some of the main problems in using ratios to interpret published accounts.

(*a*) *Comparisons over time*

1. Inflation has to be allowed for (see Ch. 8).
2. Changes in accounting methods can hinder comparisons over time. (If a company were to change from straight-line to declining balance depreciation, the apparent trend of reported profits might be misleading.)
3. If product groupings change, figures on the new basis may not be available for earlier periods.
4. We cannot assume the future will be like the past. Business conditions change in unpredictable ways.
5. One needs to interpret apparent trends over time in the light of changes in other factors, such as the overall economic environment.

(*b*) *Interfirm comparisons*

1. Individual firms, even in a single industry, will not be exactly the same as each other. There may be differences in product mix, or in business objectives and strategies.
2. Accounting methods and definitions may vary. For example, unlike other engineering companies, for many years GKN used to charge current cost depreciation as an expense in their HC accounts.
3. Financial years may end on different dates.
4. Judgement may not always be exercised in the same way. Some large international banks are optimistic about possible losses from lending to Mexico, Brazil, etc.; while others are much more conservative in providing for bad debts in their accounts. This makes it hard to compare the reported profit results of different banks.
5. Finally, there may be other unknown factors causing firms to be different which published information does not reveal.

(*c*) *General*

1. Most accounting figures are not precisely 'correct': they often include an element of personal judgement.
2. Not all relevant information is published. Sales revenue consists of volume times price; but published accounts (unlike internal budgets) hardly ever split the sales figure between the two.
3. Accounts record only matters which can be expressed in financial terms. This may exclude vital business information. Hence it is always important to use other sources of information in interpreting accounts, such as the directors' report, chairman's statement, etc. (see **2.4**).

Analysing Accounts 151

9.4 Funds Flow Analysis

9.4.1 The Funds Flow Statement

After looking at the accounting ratios (in **9.**3), an important further step in analysing Hamilton Pumps Ltd's 1984 accounts is to look at the flow of funds during the year. What does this mean? Simply from what *sources* the company obtained funds during the year to finance its business, and how the company *used* those funds (invested them).

The funds flow statement set out in Figure 9.5 shows profit before tax as the starting point. It will be appreciated that strictly speaking the *source* of the funds is sales to customers; but all the costs of sales and other operating expenses have to be deducted as uses of funds. So only the *net* figure for source of funds from operations is shown.

Hamilton Pumps Ltd
Funds Flow Statement for the year 1984.

			1984
			(£'000)
	SOURCES OF FUNDS		
Internal	Profit before tax	550	
	Add: Depreciation (see **6.**3.5)	375	
		——	925
External	Bank overdraft	900	
	Long-term loans	600	
		——	1,500
			2,425
	USES OF FUNDS		
	Taxation paid	350	
	Dividends paid	150	
		——	500
	New fixed assets acquired		1,425
	Net increase in working capital:		
	Stocks	300	
	Debtors	550	
	Creditors	(200)	
	Reduction in liquid resources	(150)	
		——	500
			2,425

Fig. 9.5: Hamilton Pumps Ltd: funds flow statement for the year 1984.

9.4.2 Interpreting Funds Flows

The major sources and uses of funds become more apparent when a separate funds flow statement lists and classifies balance sheet changes. Figure 9.5 makes it clear that Hamilton Pumps has *used* funds in 1984 in three main ways: (a) in paying tax and dividends out of profits before tax; (b) in building up stocks and debtors, the main components in working capital; and, most important, (c) investing in new fixed assets. The three main *sources* of funds were: (a) internally generated funds (profits plus depreciation); (b) bank overdraft; and (c) long-term loans. Perhaps this general overall view is given even better by the simple pie-charts in Fig. 9.6.

Sources of funds — Long-term loans, Profit before tax, Depreciation, Bank overdraft

Uses of funds — Tax, Dividends, Fixed assets, Working capital

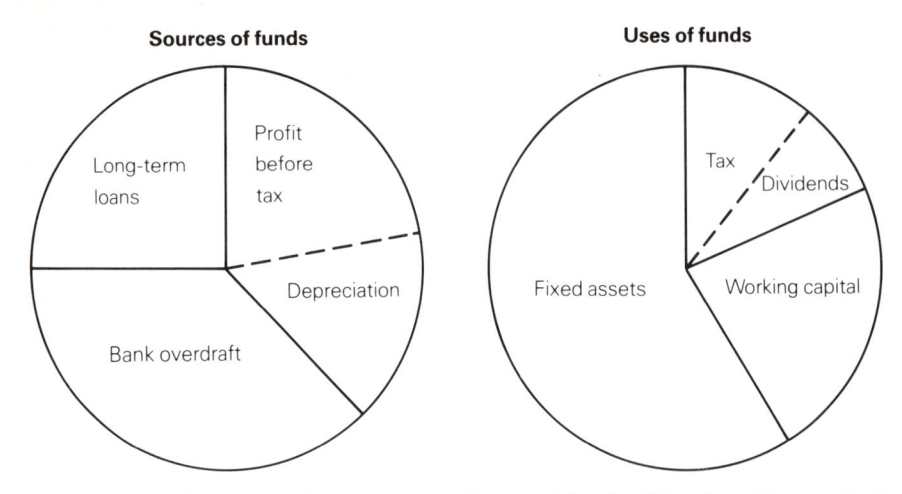

Fig. 9.6: Pie-charts showing sources and uses of funds, Hamilton Pumps Ltd, 1984.

In trying to predict the company's future need for funds, we must try to predict each of the main sources and uses of funds. We may assume no more long-term loans; and depreciation should be about £400,000. Working capital should be kept to a modest increase, say £100,000; and spending on fixed assets may now fall back to around £600,000 (50 per cent up on HC depreciation). On that basis we can calculate that unless the return on net assets reaches about 20 per cent (leaving, say, £650,000 profit before tax, after charging long-term interest, and perhaps £300,000 after tax and dividends), it will not be possible to make any reduction in the bank overdraft.

Obviously the assumptions above may be questioned; but they show the sort of approach to estimating future funds flows that can be taken. One of the keys is to make one's assumptions explicit; another is to quantify them. In the case of Hamilton Pumps, it seems that unless profits recover very sharply, or the investment in working capital can actually be cut, there is probably a need for more long-term capital to replace the bank overdraft and finance future expansion.

9.5 Views of Different Users

9.5.1 Shareholders

At the AGM David Jack, as Chairman, spoke about the results for the year 1984. He explained that the fall in profits was largely due to inflationary pressures, and the smaller dividend payments to a lack of liquidity because of the cash needed to expand capacity. He ended on an optimistic note, expecting a polite question or two. He was mistaken.

The investment manager of a large life assurance company, which had owned 100,000 shares in Hamilton Pumps Ltd for the past two years, spoke first. He was disturbed, he said, that the dividend had been cut (the final dividend had been halved from 2.50p to 1.25p, the same as the 1.25p interim dividend in both 1983 and 1984). He was also worried that the return on equity had virtually halved from 24 to 12½ per cent. No wonder the share price had dropped from 150p to 50p, with the PE ratio down from 11 to less than 7. Nearly half the net assets were now financed by borrowing; and the high rates of interest on this debt meant the interest cover was now dangerously low, at 4 times. Even apart from the question of financing, the operating performance had deteriorated badly. Return on net assets was down from 35 per cent to 20 per cent, partly due to the dramatic decline in profit margins from nearly 15 per cent to just over 10 per cent, and partly to a sharp decline in the rate of asset turnover, from 2.4 times to less than 2.0.

Other questioners, emboldened by this outspoken criticism, raised a number of other matters. How much of the increase in sales revenue was due to higher prices rather than increased volume? Was the rise in costs due to higher wages, increased materials prices, or what? To what extent could the expansion plans be postponed, or at least spread out over a longer period? Why were customers apparently now taking well over three months to pay, when the company's credit terms required payment within 30 days? Surely the charge for taxation was high, at nearly 50 per cent of profits before tax, in view of the capital allowances which should have been available on the new fixed asset expansion?

In attempting to reply, David Jack agreed that not enough thought had been given to the short-term liquidity needs of the company. There had been an unexpected increase in materials prices towards the end of 1984, which had partly caused the increase in year-end stocks. Although some of the borrowing needed to finance the expansion had been arranged on a medium-term (five-year) basis, the bank overdraft had risen faster, and higher, than had been anticipated. A major effort in the early months of 1985 to hold down working capital needs for funds (in respect of stocks and debtors) was now beginning to yield worthwhile results. There was no question of postponing the expansion: it was much too late for that. Indeed, the 1984 return on investment ratios gave somewhat too gloomy a picture, since the new fixed assets were included in the 'investment' although they had not yet started to contribute to 'returns'. The fall in profit margins was mainly due to fierce price competition in the overseas markets into which the company was expanding; and the signs were that it would be difficult to increase these margins much in the short term. He was cautiously optimistic about the future; but it would be premature to expect much improvement in profits in the current year, though he had every hope that the financial ratios would be looking stronger by the end of 1985.

9.5.2 Creditors

Three days after the AGM David Jack met Peter Hardman, the manager of one of the company's largest suppliers. Mr Hardman came straight to the point. His firm was most concerned at Hamilton Pumps taking three months to pay, instead of two months as previously. The deterioration in the company's liquidity position was indicated by the current ratio having fallen from 1.4 to 1.2, and the acid test ratio from 0.84 to 0.70; and these suggested that Hamilton Pumps was undercapitalised. He was worried that matters could get worse, especially if the bank should be unwilling to extend increased overdraft facilities. Mr Hardman felt he had no alternative but to insist that all his firm's accounts be settled within at most two months; failing which future orders would be supplied only against cash payment.

David Jack explained that Hamilton's practice had been to take about as long to pay suppliers as their own customers took to pay Hamilton. In 1984, partly as a result of increased competition, and partly because a larger proportion of business was now being done overseas where it was traditional to take longer to pay, they had been forced to allow customers a longer period of credit. This had in fact caused an increase of more than £150,000 in debtors at the year end. Hamilton would certainly be concentrating on close monitoring of their debtors' position over the rest of 1985, and he expected no net increase in the next few months.

Mr Hardman was not unsympathetic; but he reiterated that the overdue payment of accounts must be corrected. In order to avoid serious disruption to Hamilton's cash planning, he would accept this being done over the next three months.

9.5.3 Lenders

After lunch that same day, David Jack visited the bank, where he had arranged to discuss matters with the branch manager, Christopher Blackburn, who had recently taken over. He explained that the company was in the middle of a major expansion; and that at the same time higher prices were requiring a larger investment in trading stocks. In addition, it was now clear he would also have to reduce the amount of trade credit that Hamilton had been taking from suppliers. As a result, Hamilton would need to increase its bank overdraft from the present level – still around £1.0m, as in December 1984 – to closer to £1.5m.

Mr Blackburn expressed surprise, and remarked that he had asked for the meeting because his head office had instructed him to arrange for Hamilton's overdraft to be cut back to under £0.5 million by the end of 1985. From his viewpoint the signs for the immediate future were not encouraging, and even maintaining the present overdraft level, let alone increasing it as David Jack had just requested, could be justified only if clear plans to overcome the coompany's problems were agreed.

In particular, Mr Blackburn was concerned that a major expansion was being so largely financed by short-term borrowing; and he was critical of the level of both stocks and debtors. He felt these indicated some lack of management supervision in the past, which should be speedily corrected. It was also worrying that the expansion seemed to be into overseas areas where profit margins were lower and trade credit periods longer: the combination would continue to cause liquidity problems. With hindsight, it appeared that the long-term loans totalling £600,000, which had been arranged at the bank's insistence towards the end of 1984, had not been large enough to relieve the pressure on short-term overdraft facilities. Given the deteriorating profit record, however, and the high level of overall gearing, it seemed unlikely that more long-term borrowing could be arranged in the near future on acceptable terms. In the circumstances, given that the expansion programme was now almost completed, the only solution seemed to be a new issue of ordinary shares, though this would be difficult after the last 12 months' trading performance.

David Jack thanked Mr Blackburn for being so frank, but admitted that his refusal to permit any increase in the overdraft was rather a shock. He would consult his fellow-directors, and other members of the family, as a matter of urgency to see what proposals the company could make to satisfy the bank that matters were under control. He knew members of the family would be reluctant to see an equity issue which would dilute their own holdings; collectively the members of the family now held only just over half of the total issued capital, and it would be impossible for them personally to put up any significant amount of new capital.

9.5.4 Employees

Later that week, David Jack met three representatives of the employees to talk about wage levels.

The employees produced figures showing a 20 per cent increase in labour productivity in 1984.

	1983	1984
Total sales	£6,500,00	£6,750,000
Total employees	260	225
Sales per employee	£25,000	£30,000

They then put forward a claim for a wage increase of 20 per cent. This was made up of three parts: *(a) compensation for 5 per cent inflation in 1984, (b) compensation for anticipated inflation of 5 per cent in 1985, and (c) a half-share of the 20 per cent increase in labour productivity.*

David Jack was unable to negotiate without discussing the claim with his senior managers, but he felt he ought to point out some of the problems with a wage claim of such a size. Total wages, together with associated costs, had amounted to £2,250,000 in 1984. Thus a 20 per cent rise would cost nearly half a million pounds a year. This represented almost the entire 1984 profit before tax. The 1984 dividend had had to be cut; and the share price had already fallen by two thirds from its 1983 level. The effect of conceding the proposed wage increase would not only alarm the stock market, but probably cause the bank to call in the overdraft.

The employees' representatives felt there was room for increasing the selling prices of Hamilton's products, in order to provide for increased wages. They also believed that the fall in profits had been largely due to management's mistakes, for which they did not expect the employees to suffer.

Work Section

A. Revision Questions

A1 Give an example of a 'performance' ratio that might be useful for:
(a) a church; (b) an army; (c) a football team.

A2 Name one external standard for comparison.

A3 Name one internal standard for comparison.

A4 Name the three main groups of accounting ratios.

A5 What two different items in accounts do performance (efficiency) ratios compare profit to?

A6 Why does the return on net assets ratio use profit *before* interest?

A7 What is the relationship between asset turnover, profit margin, and return on net assets?

A8 Why is the stock turnover ratio not strictly a measure of the physical rate at which stocks are being 'turned over'?

A9 Define 'return on net assets'. Identify and define the two ratios into which it can be split.

A10 If a company had as much long-term borrowing as equity capital, what would its gearing ratio be?

A11 Identify and define one liquidity ratio. How does it differ from the other liquidity ratio?

A12 What are the possible consequences if the current ratio is:
(a) too high? (b) too low?

A13 Why does the acid test ratio leave out stocks?

A14 Could a company's dividend ratio ever be:
(a) exactly 1.0? (b) less than 1.0? (c) negative? Why, in each case?

A15 Why might a company with an issued ordinary share capital of £1.0m not have 1m ordinary shares in issue?

A16 What steps do you need to take to calculate the price/earnings ratio?

A17 Distinguish between 'return on net assets' and 'return on equity'.

A18 Identify and define separately the numerator (top line) and the denominator (bottom line) in the following ratios: (a) gearing ratio; (b) price/earnings ratio; (c) current ratio.

A19 What are three problems in making comparisons over time?

A20 What are three problems in making comparisons with other firms?

A21 Why is depreciation added to profit before tax, in order to calculate 'internally-generated funds'?

A22 Why does a funds flow statement begin listing internally-generated funds with profit before tax, rather than with sales revenue?

Analysing Accounts 157

A23 Name four sources of funds for a business firm.
A24 If the average number of days' credit taken by a firm's customers falls from 80 to 60, does that represent a source or a use of funds? Why?
A25 If a company regularly invests a smaller amount in new fixed assets than the amount of the annual HC depreciation expense, what is the implication?
A26 If a company owes more to its suppliers at the end of a period than at the beginning, is that a source or a use of funds? Why?
A27 What is the essential difference between a balance sheet and a funds flow statement?
A28 What use is funds flow analysis?
A29 Can a company have a positive generation of funds from operations if it makes a loss before tax? Why or why not?
A30 Why must sources of funds for a period always exactly equal uses of funds?
A31 Name four different potential users of published financial accounts.
A32 Why is management probably *not* a user of published financial accounts, to any significant extent?
A33 Which groups of users will be most interested in:
(a) gearing and liquidity measures? (b) shareholder measures?
A34 Which group of measures will *all* external users of accounts probably be concerned about? Why?
A35 If you were Mr Blackburn, the bank manager being asked to allow Hamilton Pumps Ltd to increase its bank overdraft, what information would you like to see in mid-1985, apart from the company's 1984 accounts?

B. Exercises and Case Studies

B1 Refer to The Rank Organisation plc's group profit and loss account for the year ended 31 October 1982, in Fig. 5.14 (p. 71). Calculate as many as possible of the 15 financial ratios listed in **9.3.4**.
B2 Refer to the Beecham Group plc's consolidated balance sheet at 31 March 1983, in Fig. 4.7 (p. 50). Calculate as many as possible of the 15 financial ratios listed in **9.3.4**.
B3 Refer to the Hamilton Pumps accounts (**9.2**) and financial ratios (**9.3**). If the net book value of the company's fixed assets were to be revalued upwards at 31 December, 1984, from £3.0m to £5.0m, which of the 15 accounting ratios would be affected? How?
B4 Refer to **3.2.3** (e) (p. 30).
Draw up a funds flow statement for Thompson Brothers Ltd for the year ended 31 December.
B5 Refer to College Printers Ltd's accounts for 1984 (p. 158). Comment on the company's performance and prospects.

College Printers Ltd Balance Sheet as at 30 June 1984

	1983 (£'000)		1984 (£'000)			1983 (£'000)		1984 (£'000)
Shareholders' funds					*Fixed assets*			
Issued share capital	10		10		Plant at cost		48		74
Reserves	14		20		Less: Accum. depn.		16		24
	24		30				32		50
Long-term loan	8		10		*Current assets*			
Current liabilities					Stocks		22		30
Bank overdraft	—		9		Debtors		56		60
Creditors	77		86		Cash		2		—
Taxation	3		5				80		90
	80		100						
	112		140				112		140

Profit and loss account for year to 30 June 1984

	1983 (£'000)	1984 (£'000)
Sales	160	200
Profit, before allowing for:	14	25
Depreciation	4	8
Interest paid	1	2
Taxation	3	5
	8	15
Net profit	6	10
Dividend paid	4	4
Profit retained	2	6

Analysing Accounts

B6 Super Traders Ltd's accounts for the calendar year 1983 contain the following information:
On 31 December 1983 there were:
  i. No current assets other than stocks, debtors and bank balance.
  ii. No liabilities other than shareholders' funds and current liabilities.
  iii. No assets other than fixed assets and current assets.
On 31 December 1983:

Current ratio (current assets: current liabilities)	1¾ :1
Acid test ratio (debtors and bank: current liabilities)	1¼ : 1
Net current assets	£75,000
Issued share capital in ordinary shares	£100,000
Fixed assets as a percentage of share capital	60 per cent
Stock turnover (based on year-end stock)	4.16 times
Debtor turnover based on a 52-week year	7 weeks

(a) Calculate the value of each of the current assets as at 31 December 1983.
(b) Ignoring taxation, construct in as much detail as possible the balance sheet of Super Traders Ltd as at 31 December 1983.

B7 The accounts of Hamilton Pumps Ltd for the year ended 31 December 1985 are set out in Fig. 9.7, and Fig. 9.8.
Calculate the following financial ratios for 1985:

a. Performance measures.
b. Gearing and liquidity measures.
c. Shareholder measures. (Share price at 31.12.85 = 100 p.)

B8 Refer to B7.

a. Prepare a funds flow statement for Hamilton Pumps for 1985.
b. Refer to **9.4.2**. The middle paragraph of this sub-section discusses a possible forecast of next year's (1985's) flow of funds for Hamilton Pumps Ltd. On the basis of the other assumptions made earlier in the paragraph, try to confirm the need for a return on net assets of about 20 per cent in 1985 in order to make a start in reducing the bank overdraft in that year.
c. Prepare your own estimate of possible funds flows in 1986 – making *and stating explicitly* what you think are reasonable assumptions.

B9 Refer to B7 and B8.
From your analysis of the 1985 results for Hamilton Pumps Ltd, what are the key comments you would make and the questions you would ask of the managing director:

a. as a shareholder?
b. as Mr Blackburn, his bank manager?
c. as a representative of the employees?

Hamilton Pumps Ltd: Balance Sheet at 31 December 1985.

		(£'000)
FIXED ASSETS		
Freehold property		800
Plant and equipment		2,400
		3,200
CURRENT ASSETS		
Stocks	1,250	
Debtors	1,750	
Liquid resources	200	
	3,200	
LESS: CURRENT LIABILITIES		
Creditors	1,600	
Bank overdraft	600	
Taxation	350	
Dividends payable	100	
	2,650	
NET WORKING CAPITAL		550
NET ASSETS		3,750
SHAREHOLDERS' FUNDS		
Issued ordinary 25p shares		1,000
Retained profits		1,650
		2,650
LONG-TERM LIABILITIES		
Mortgage debenture	500	
Other loans	600	
		1,100
CAPITAL EMPLOYED		3,750

Fig. 9.7: Hamilton Pumps Ltd: Balance Sheet at 31 December 1985.

Analysing Accounts

Hamilton Pumps Ltd: Profit and Loss Account for the year 1985.

		(£'000)
Sales		7,500
Operating profit *		925
Interest payable		175
Profit before tax		750
Taxation		350
Profit after tax		400
Ordinary dividends:		
Interim, 1.25p	50	
Final, 2.50p	100	
		150
Retained profit for the year		250

* After charging depreciation £400,000.

Fig. 9.8: Hamilton Pumps Ltd: Profit and Loss Account for the year ended 31 December 1985.

B10 Identify, with a brief explanation, how adjusting historical cost accounts to allow for inflation would affect:

  a. performance measures
  b. gearing and liquidity measures
  c. shareholder measures.

B11 Arrange to get the latest accounts of any public quoted company. Analyse them from the point of view of:

  a. a shareholder;
  b. the company's bank manager;
  c. an employee;
  d. a competitor;
  e. a student of accounting.

C. Essay Questions

C1 In analysing a company's business position, what information would you want to examine apart from the company's latest accounts? Why?

C2 Would statistics covering the last 50 years for a company be much more use than statistics covering only the last 10 years? Why or why not?

C3 What are the most serious problems likely to be met in trying to make comparisons (a) over time and (b) between companies?

C4 Refer to **9.5.1**. As a shareholder attending the AGM, to what extent do you think David Jack has convincingly answered the points made at the meeting?

C5 Refer to **9.5.3**. How has Hamilton Pumps Ltd arrived at its present financial position? How can it restore its once-strong balance sheet?

C6 Should employees be given access to more accounting information about their company? Consider the arguments for and against.

C7 Why can even a professional analysis of a company's published accounts so often produce misleading results?

C8 The Sandilands Committee on Inflation Accounting suggested that CCA ratios could be used to make comparisons over time, without any need to adjust the various money amounts to allow for the falling value of money (the B-adjustments in **8.3.3**). Discuss.

C9 A correspondent to the *Financial Times* once suggested that, to help readers of accounts, each company's annual report should print in bold type on its front cover the statement: 'The profit per cent on capital employed is x per cent.' Discuss this view.

C10 Comment on the following 1957 statement by a leading American accountant: 'Perhaps comparability among companies and industries is unattainable – perhaps it is not even desirable. Much of the demand for uniformity in accounting is based on a wish for unattainable certainty in man's financial affairs, and on a desire that the extremely complicated elements reflected in financial reports be made simple of understanding, even by the uninformed and ignorant.'

Part III Management Accounting

10 Costs and Budgets

10.1 Management Information
10.1.1 Introduction
10.1.2 Cost/Benefit Analysis
10.1.3 Information Requirements

10.2 Classifying Costs
10.2.1 Variable and Fixed Costs
10.2.2 Direct and Indirect Costs
10.2.3 Marginal and Average Costs
10.2.4 Short-run and Long-run Costs

10.3 Preparing Budgets
10.3.1 Budgetary Control
10.3.2 Objectives
10.3.3 Responsibility
10.3.4 Motivation

10.4 Using Budgets
10.4.1 Communication
10.4.2 Performance Appraisal
10.4.3 Management Action

10.5 Variance Analysis
10.5.1 Sales Variances
10.5.2 Expense Variances
10.5.3 Flexible Budgets

Objective: *To describe the main ways of classifying costs, and to explain how budgets are prepared and used.*

Synopsis: *Management accounting tries to help managers plan and control a business. There are four basic ways to classify costs in accounting: between (1) variable and fixed, (2) direct and indirect, (3) marginal and average, and (4) short-run and long-run.*

  Budgets are financial plans for a period, agreed in advance for (part of) a firm's operations. *They help set objectives and co-ordinate responsibilities. After the event, budgets communicate information, and help appraise the performance of managers and of business units.*

Variance analysis compares actual performance with budget. The technique of flexible budgets can be especially useful. The reasons *for variances should be investigated, and action taken, if necessary, to improve profits.*

10.1 Management Information

10.1.1 Introduction

So far this book has emphasised financial accounting. Chapter 1 described the differences between financial and management accounting; they were summarised in Fig. 1.3 (p. 5). We now conclude the book with two chapters on management accounting.

Management accounting relies on many of the same principles as financial accounting; it makes full use of internal balance sheets, profit and loss accounts, funds flow statements, and ratio analysis. These may apply only to certain parts of the firm, or for only fractions of a year. Management accounts use all the standards for comparison discussed in **9.1.2**: trends over time, internal budgets, and interfirm comparisons.

The management accountant aims to obtain and present information that will enable his firm's managers to make good decisions. Some decisions, like replacing a small item of equipment, may be routine; while others, like choosing whether to enter an export market or to make a new product line, may be vital to the firm's long-run overall success. Management accounting can help managers (not 'systems'!) to make better decisions.

Other books in this series look at specific business decisions: *Production Decisions; Marketing Decisions; Financial Decisions*. Such decisions may require the management accountant to produce special information from time to time. This chapter and the next concentrate on the process of regular budgeting within a firm, to see how planning, control and review interact. These three stages may be thought of respectively as looking to the future, managing the present, and learning from the past.

At the *planning* stage, management information is required to compare possible alternatives. For *control*, monthly management reports enable managers to see how events are turning out in practice, as compared with the plans made in advance. They also show how one area of the business continually interacts with others. (For example, if sales volume is less than planned, the production schedule may need to be cut back to avoid piling up unsold stocks. That will affect purchasing, finance, and industrial relations.) The same information may also be used to *review* the performance of business units, and of the managers in charge of them. Such feedback can often suggest how to manage part of the business more profitably in future.

Costs and Budgets 165

10.1.2 Cost/Benefit Analysis

The general notion underlying **cost/benefit analysis** is that something should be supplied as long as its value exceeds its cost. Unfortunately it is often hard to measure the cost of providing management information, and still more difficult to value the benefits. But there are likely to be diminishing returns. (A large retail firm may wish to reduce its losses from theft by employees and customers; but there will come a stage when hiring extra security staff would cost far more than the savings they would bring.)

Accounting departments usually have budgets themselves. Management accountants must produce as much useful information as they can within certain cost limits. This requires not only the skill (which most managers need) to keep costs down, but also the ability to see what extra information other managers might find useful. (Financial accountants have less need for imagination because many of the statements they furnish are required by law.)

It is possible for management accountants to supply *too much* data rather than too little. They should be concerned with quality (usefulness), not mere quantity. Modern data processing equipment is so powerful that some of the first companies to use computers for accounting found themselves in danger of being swamped with vast amounts of unusable data. Managers may not use the data provided, either because it isn't relevant, or because they don't know how to. To some extent, therefore, management accountants may have an educational role. They should take trouble to present reports in a way which recipients can understand, containing as much detail as necessary (but not *more*!).

10.1.3 Information Requirements

Management needs information to be up to date, frequently available, in sufficient detail, not too expensive, and communicated to the right people. Information is often more useful if it arrives quickly. Modern electronic data processing equipment is extremely fast compared to clerks using quill pens by the flicker of candlelight. Management accounts are usually produced monthly to allow frequent regular control of the firm's business. But some delay is inevitable, and holding meetings too soon after the end of the previous month may risk not all the financial results being ready in time.

Accounting records must include all transactions, and the arithmetic must be correct. Modern computers do not involve conventional 'books' of account, but each entry in the accounting records still needs to be supported by some kind of document. This may be an invoice for goods purchased, a copy invoice for goods sold, wages sheets and/or time cards for labour costs, and so on. These original ('primary') documents provide evidence that transactions were legitimate and properly authorised; and also enable auditors (whether internal or external) to check the accounting records if need be.

The amount of detail required affects the design of the business documents which first record transactions. One system can often be designed to satisfy both the financial accountant and the management accountant, which saves potential costly duplication. For instance, an invoice recording a sale will at least contain the customer's name and address, the date, and the value of the goods sold. This might be all the financial accountant needs to compute the annual value of the firm's sales and maintain the records of debtors. But the sales manager might find it useful to know details of the goods supplied, the sales area, and the salesman concerned. So the management accountant will see that such details are included on the document. Similar comments apply to records of wages, materials issued from stores to production departments, and so on.

10.2 Classifying Costs

The **cost** of something is what one must give up to get it. This is often money. But 'cost' is not the same as 'value'. Someone who buys a book for £5 is 'valuing' it, not at £5, *but at* more *than* £5. He might have been willing to pay as much as £12 for the book.

A business measures its costs:

a. to see whether a specific transaction is *profitable*, by comparing costs with revenues;
b. to help *control* operations, by comparing actual costs with pre-set standards.

A firm estimates **standard costs** *per unit* of production:
a. to compare actual costs against;
b. to value stock in hand at the end of a period (see Ch. 7);
c. to help set selling prices;
d. to establish **transfer prices** between different parts of a large business.

	Direct (£)	Indirect (£)	Total (£)
Variable costs			
Petrol (6.0p per mile)	720		960
Maintenance (2.0p per mile)	240		
Fixed costs			
Insurance	160		
Licence fee	80		1,740
Depreciation	1,000		
Garage rent		500	
Total costs	2,200	500	2,700

Fig. 10.1: Car operating costs for next year.

Costs and Budgets

One should beware of spurious accuracy! It is more important to get a rough idea of relevant costs than to make calculations to the nearest penny. Most costs can only be estimates. Indeed some accountants are unwilling to provide any cost figures at all unless they know for what *purpose* managers are likely to use them!

Example: *Gilbert Ltd keeps a four-year-old car in a garage with three other cars. The annual garage rent is £2,000, insurance costs £160 a year, and the annual licence fee is £80. The car does 30 miles to the gallon, petrol costs 180p per gallon, and maintenance is reckoned to cost 2p per mile. Depreciation is £1,000 per year, and the car is expected to travel 12,000 miles next year. Figure 10.1 classifies expected operating costs for next year between variable and fixed (**10.2.1**) and between direct and indirect (**10.2.2**).*

10.2.1 Variable and Fixed Costs

The expressions 'variable' and 'fixed' in relation to costs refer to the volume of activity or output. Thus a **variable cost** changes in proportion to output, while a **fixed cost** remains unchanged whatever the volume of output.

Example: *Gilbert's variable costs (petrol and maintenance) are 8.0p per mile; while fixed costs (licence fee, insurance, depreciation and garage rent) are £1,740 a year however many miles the car travels. Figure 10.2 charts the two kinds of costs against mileage.*

The distinction is not always clear-cut. Some expenses may be **semi-variable**: telephone costs and other utility bills often consist of a basic fixed charge plus an extra rate varying with usage (a 'two-part tariff'). And direct labour costs are often partly or wholly fixed, even though they are still commonly treated as if they were wholly variable.

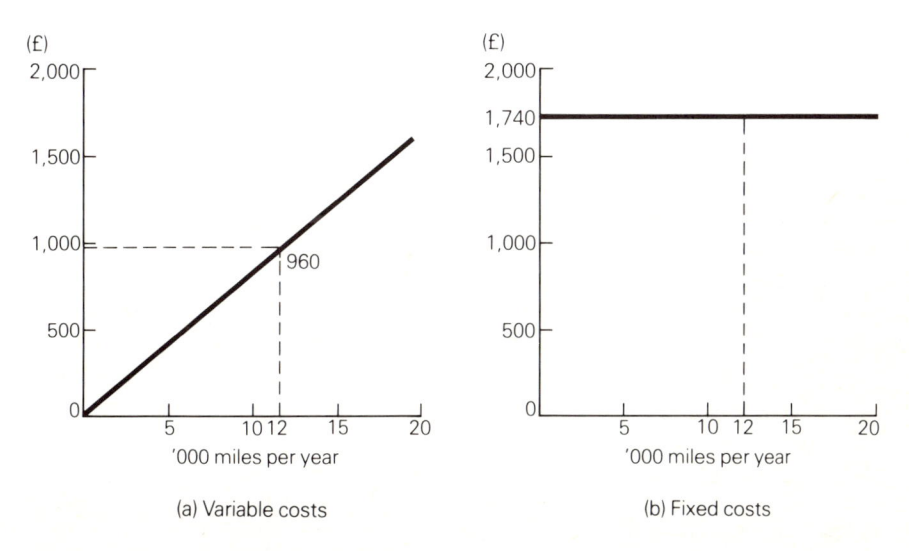

Fig. 10.2: Variable costs and fixed costs.

Fixed costs are fixed *over a given range of activity*. Outside that range they may alter as a result of changes in the scale of the business. Some firms also distinguish **non-variable costs**, such as advertising or research. These may change; but as a result of management's 'discretionary' decisions, rather than simply because of a change in volume. Outlays on advertising, for example, might well be *increased* if sales volume fell.

10.2.2 Direct and Indirect Costs

Most variable costs, and some fixed costs, are **direct costs** which can be directly *identified* with the unit or product whose costs are being measured. Gilbert's only **indirect cost** is garage rent, which cannot be directly identified with each car. If we want to estimate a garage rent cost for each car, we have to make an **allocation** on some reasonable basis. This might be (a) the relative floor space occupied; (b) the relative cost or net book value of each car; or (c) simply an equal amount per car. The basis for allocation may be arbitrary, not uniquely correct.

Some indirect ('overhead') costs may be regarded as *varying* more or less with output, even though they cannot be directly *identified* with particular units of production. On the other hand, it may be possible to identify certain fixed costs directly with products. Thus there are four possible combinations:

1. direct and variable, e.g. raw materials;
2. direct and fixed, e.g. depreciation;
3. indirect and variable, e.g. energy costs;
4. indirect and fixed, e.g. factory rent.

Whether a cost is direct or indirect may often be a matter of convenience. With enough effort it might be possible to identify nearly all costs with specific operations. But a management accountant must always ask: is the resulting 'accuracy' *worth* the cost of getting the information?

10.2.3 Marginal and Average Costs

The **marginal cost** is the extra cost incurred by producing one more unit of output. Gilbert's marginal cost of running a car is 8.0p. Where costs are being related to sales revenue, the difference between selling price and marginal cost is called the **contribution** per unit. Thus if Gilbert Ltd were hiring out its car at 25p per mile, the contribution would be 17p per mile.

The **average cost** is total costs divided by the total number of units of output. So Gilbert's average cost per mile, assuming the expected 12,000 miles are travelled in a year, is 22.5p per mile (= £2,700/12,000 miles). For many short-term business decisions it is marginal, not average, costs which are relevant.

> Example: *A nice example of the difference between average and marginal costs is given by the story of the office worker who went to have a haircut. When he returned, his boss asked him where he'd been.*
> *Worker: To have a haircut.*

Costs and Budgets

Boss: *In office hours?*
Worker: *Well it grew in office hours.*
Boss: *Not all of it, surely?*
Worker: *No; but then I didn't have it all cut off!*

Economists often regard marginal costs per unit of production as falling at first, due to **economies of scale**. Later marginal per-unit costs start to rise, due to diminishing returns, overtime premiums, etc. Average costs (AC) are higher than marginal costs (MC) to begin with, because the fixed costs have to be spread out over the number of units produced. When output is low, the fixed cost per unit (and hence the total average cost per unit) is obviously high. As long as marginal cost per unit is *lower* than average cost per unit, the average cost curve must be falling. (Each extra unit produced further reduces the average cost.) Similarly, as soon as the marginal cost per unit becomes higher than the average cost per unit, the average cost curve must be *rising*. (Each extra unit of output further increases the overall average cost.) Hence, as Fig. 10.3 shows, the marginal cost curve *crosses* the average cost curve when average costs per unit are at their lowest point.

Example: *Geoffrey Boycott's career average is 56.0, higher than any other batsman who has scored more than 30,000 runs. But finally the time has come for Boycott's Last Innings. You don't have to be an expert cost accountant to see that if he is out for less than 56, his average will fall (slightly); while if he scores more than 56, or is not out, his average will rise. Only if he scores exactly 56, or is not out 0 (a rare event!), will his average remain at 56.0.*

The point at which *marginal* costs are minimised may be taken to be roughly the minimum economic volume of output for any firm in an industry. It forms a sort of 'barrier to entry' for a new producer. But in practice different firms have widely different cost patterns. Unlike economists, accountants usually assume that marginal per-unit costs are *constant* (flat), at least throughout the 'relevant range' of output. And business firms are trying to *maximise profits*, not to produce at minimum cost.

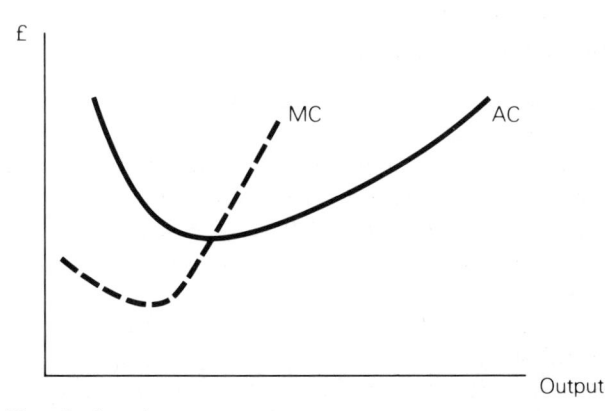

Fig. 10.3: Marginal and average cost curves.

10.2.4 Short-run and Long-run Costs

So far we have been discussing costs without much reference to *time*. But in the 'long run' a firm can change the *scale* of its operations. The **short run** is a period of time during which the inputs of some factors of production cannot be changed. The factor which is 'fixed' is often capital equipment, but it might be land or labour or materials. The calendar length of the short run may vary widely: it will be much shorter for a window cleaner than for a shipbuilder.

It follows that in the **long run** inputs of *all* factors of production can be varied. A producer can alter plant capacity, a distributor can increase warehouse size, and so on. Thus the 'long run' corresponds to the outlook facing a firm planning to *enter* an industry.

As we all know, another thing that takes time is *learning*. A firm's workers are likely to know more about how to make a product after they have been doing so for some months than on the first day. This may enable a firm to reduce its average costs per unit. The learning may relate more to the volume of output produced than to the lapse of time. If so, the firm with the largest market share, and therefore the largest output per unit of time, will be learning at a faster rate than its competitors. If this does result in lower costs, a firm which is 'further down the **learning curve**' can either reduce its selling price, or make a larger contribution margin on each unit sold.

10.3 Preparing Budgets

10.3.1 Budgetary Control

Budgets are formal business plans consisting of:

a. quantitative statements,
b. usually expressed in financial terms,
c. prepared and agreed in advance,
d. covering a specific period,
e. for (part of) a firm's operations.

A budget may cover revenue, expenses, output, profits, personnel, capital spending, cash, and so on.

The annual budget cycle in a business involves a number of steps:
1. stating basic assumptions and company objectives;
2. forecasting general economic and industry conditions;
3. preparing detailed sales budgets, suitably analysed (e.g. between products, regions, customers, time periods);
4. preparing suitably analysed budgets for: production, expenses, capital spending and cash;
5. co-ordinating the various subsidiary budgets into the **master budget** – the overall profit and loss account, funds flow, and balance sheet budgets.

Costs and Budgets

Budgets are not neutral forecasts of future events: managers accept a personal commitment to help *make* them happen. Nor are they merely ideal targets: budgets must be capable of achievement. Budgets should neither be *imposed* from on high ('top-down') nor simply emerge from below ('bottom-up'); managers normally discuss (or negotiate) the details with their superiors.

Preparing budgets forces managers to think ahead, especially to co-ordinate production and marketing; for example, to plan increases in capacity in good time to meet expected increases in sales. The budget process nearly always contains *feedback*; if the first draft reveals problems, certain changes may be needed. This may mean altering the *timing* of some planned events, to avoid bunching problems, especially in relation to **critical resources** (which may be money, manpower, raw materials, or physical facilities).

The one-year budget is normally split into months (or four-weekly periods). Many activities do not happen evenly throughout the year, so an amount in a monthly budget might not be exactly one-twelfth of the equivalent item in the annual budget. The annual budget itself may represent the first year of a longer (three- or five-year) planning period. Some companies prepare **rolling budgets**, adding an extra month's figures 12 months ahead as they drop the month just finished. Otherwise there is a danger of not looking far enough ahead.

In advance, budgetary control

a. sets objectives,
b. allocates responsibilities, and
c. motivates managers.

After the event, it

d. communicates information,
e. appraises performance, and
f. assists effective management action.

Each of these six functions is discussed separately over the next few pages.

10.3.2 Objectives

Many businesses do not think in terms of a single objective for the budget period, such as 'maximising profits'. This is partly because many business decisions have effects lasting well beyond the current budget period. For instance, the American General Electric Company identified the eight 'key result areas' listed in Fig. 10.4. Not all of these might suit other firms, and clearly some of them pose measurement problems. But most companies need to keep in mind their long-term objectives; otherwise short-term goals may absorb too much attention.

Budgetary control can also assist managers of 'non-profit' entities, such as schools, churches, the armed services. Organisations which do not sell their output on the market may find it useful to budget their output in physical rather than financial terms. Of course they need to pay attention to *quality* of output as well as quantity.

1. Profit
2. Market share
3. Productivity
4. Product leadership
5. Employee attitudes
6. Public responsibility
7. Staff development
8. Balance between short-term and long-term

Fig. 10.4: General Electric (US): Eight key result areas.

10.3.3 Responsibility

Someone must be in charge of each unit, and every manager needs to be clear exactly *what* he or she is responsible for. But a manager may not be able to control everything affecting his unit's results: it would be foolish to blame Mr MacGregor for all the huge losses of British Steel and the National Coal Board. Distinguishing in management reports between **controllable** and **non-controllable** items may not be easy.

Not all business units can measure their output in money terms. A research unit manager, for example, should be expected to keep to agreed levels of spending, neither much more *nor much less*. But it may be hard to measure the quantity and quality of his unit's output.

There are three different kinds of 'responsibility centre': (a) revenue centres, (b) cost centres, and (c) profit centres. A **revenue centre**, such as a sales department, generates revenue but doesn't spend much. More commonly, a **cost centre** is responsible for spending money, but not directly for earning revenue.

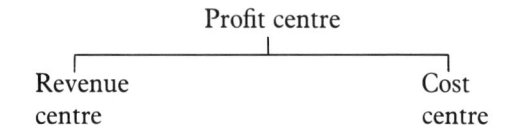

```
                  Profit centre
         ┌─────────────┴─────────────┐
      Revenue                       Cost
      centre                       centre
```

A **profit centre** sells its output, and controls both revenues and expenses. Its manager is responsible for *profit*, the excess of sales revenue over expenses. Thus he decides on 'trade-offs' between them, such as whether to spend more on promotion to boost sales. Where a profit centre sells some of its output to another part of the same firm, internal 'transfer prices' are required. If possible these should be based on the outside market price for similar goods.

10.3.4 Motivation

Most students work with more purpose if they know they are going to be tested. Business managers whose unit's performance is going to be compared with budget will not feel commitment to achieve results unless they think the

Costs and Budgets 173

standard is fair. Their detailed knowledge may make it desirable for managers to participate in setting their own budgets; but it is for top managers to judge whether a proposed budget represents an adequate performance. A budget that is either 'too easy' or 'too hard' to achieve will usually be a less effective motivator than one which is 'difficult but achievable'.

There is danger in judging a unit's performance entirely by *current* profits, if some decisions have longer-term effects. For example, a manager might be able to improve current profits by spending less on research; but it could be disastrous in the long run. In practice managers are normally judged on their 'track record' over a period of years. Business success has several aspects (see Fig. 10.4); and using several criteria is wiser than judging managers or business units by any single accounting figure, however cunningly devised.

10.4 Using Budgets

10.4.1 Communication

Budgets, which aim to communicate, should be simple and easy to read. Businessmen nearly always prefer rough figures soon to 'exact' ones later. Filling reports with trivial items, or with needlessly accurate detail, obscures what really matters.

Figure 10.5 shows an example of a monthly profit and loss summary (monthly balance sheets may also be useful). Attached schedules can give more details. In addition a brief report can summarise certain ratios (see Ch. 9) and point out

	Latest month October		Cumulative to date 10 months	
	Budget £'000 %	Actual £'000 %	Budget £'000 %	Actual £'000 %
Sales revenue				
Variable cost of sales:				
Materials				
Direct labour				
Production overheads				
Other variable expenses				
Contribution				
Fixed production expenses				
Other fixed expenses				
Operating profit (loss)				

Fig. 10.5: Monthly divisional profit and loss report.

key aspects of the results. And charts of past and projected future trends (adjusted for inflation) may be valuable.

Sending weekly reports is pointless if action is taken only once a month. A business school improved its financial reporting system by using suitably summarised figures once a quarter instead of absurdly detailed reports every month. On the other hand, timing *can* be important: small businesses, for example, may gain by being able to react *quickly* to changing events.

Signalling only important *exceptions* from an agreed standard can restrict needless detail, but requires judgement. If conditions have changed, deviation from budget may not be 'bad' (nor exactly attaining it 'good'). There can be perfectly sound *reasons* for a variance from budget.

If conditions change, the budget figures may not represent a good estimate of the current year's results. Monthly reports may then include a 'latest estimate for the current year', updated each month. This can help show whether a variance in one month is merely a *timing* difference, which will reverse itself next month, or the start of a trend resulting in large cumulative variances by the year-end. Clearly these could have different implications for management action.

10.4.2 Performance Appraisal

In appraising performance one needs a *standard* against which to judge actual results. If the budget is properly set, on most management reports there should be *no need to include last year's actual figures*. The budget should take them into account, together with expected changes, in setting the current year's standard. Their inclusion will clutter up the report and distract attention from what really matters: the budget and the current year's actual figures.

Various methods of **flexible budgeting** (see **10**.5.3) can often allow for changes in business conditions. *Major* changes may make it desirable to *revise* budgets, despite the time and effort involved. Otherwise managers may either become demoralised if actual results are compared with budgets which are now unattainable, or complacent if budgets are too easily achieved.

10.4.3 Management Action

Budgets should help managers manage: they are *not* rigid targets which must be exactly achieved at all costs, whatever has changed since they were agreed. There can be good reasons for actual results to differ from budget. Managers may not be able to control every item in their budgets, at least in the short run; but they are expected to react to changed conditions.

Budgetary control with monthly reporting may help managers to answer the following kinds of questions:

1. What has been happening recently? How does it differ from budget? Why?
2. How if at all will these events cause latest estimates of current year results to differ from budget *if no action is taken*?
3. What if anything can be done to counter unfavourable variances from

Costs and Budgets 175

budget, *or to increase favourable ones*? (Successful managers cash in on good luck!)
4. How soon will such action be effective? How much difference will it make?
5. After all proposed actions, what is now the latest estimate of current year results?

10.5 Variance Analysis

10.5.1 Sales Variances

It can be useful in internal reports to separate prices from the quantity of physical units. Suppose that actual sales revenue is £420, compared with a budget of £500. Figure 10.6 shows two different ways in which the **variance** of £80 could have arisen, with quite different implications for management action. In each case the overall variance between actual and budget sales revenue is analysed into a **volume variance** and a **price variance**.

	Units	×	Price	=	Revenue
Budget	50	×	£10	=	£500
Actual – A	60	×	£ 7	=	£420
Actual – B	35	×	£12	=	£420

Actual – A
| Volume variance | +10 | × | £10★ | = | +£100 |
| Price variance | 60 | × | –£ 3 | = | –£180 |

| Total variance | | | | = | –£ 80 |

Actual – B
| Volume variance | –15 | × | £10★ | = | –£150 |
| Price variance | 35 | × | +£ 2 | = | +£ 70 |

| Total variance | | | | = | –£ 80 |

Fig. 10.6: Analysis of sales variance

By convention, variance analysis multiplies the difference in volume by the *budget price* (£10★ here); and multiplies the difference in price per unit by the *actual volume*. Managers are thought more likely to be able to control volume than to control price; so the effect of a presumed controllable variance in volume is isolated by using budgeted price per unit.

10.5.2 Expense Variances

In looking at variance between actual and budgeted expenses, let us return to the Gilbert example. To keep it simple, we shall consider only the spending on petrol.

Example: *The 'budgeted' cost (see **10.2**) was 12,000 miles at 6.0p per mile = £720. Suppose that Gilbert's car actually travelled 15,000 miles in the year, and petrol actually cost 195p per gallon (at 30 miles per gallon = 6.5p per mile). Then the actual total cost of petrol in the year would be £975 (15,000 miles at 6.5p). How is this 'unfavourable' total variance of £255 on petrol to be split between volume and price?*

Clearly at least 3,000 miles at 6.0p per mile (= £180) is a volume *variance*, and at least 0.5p × 12,000 miles (= £60) is a price *variance*. But what should we call the balance of £15 (= 3,000 miles at 0.5p)?

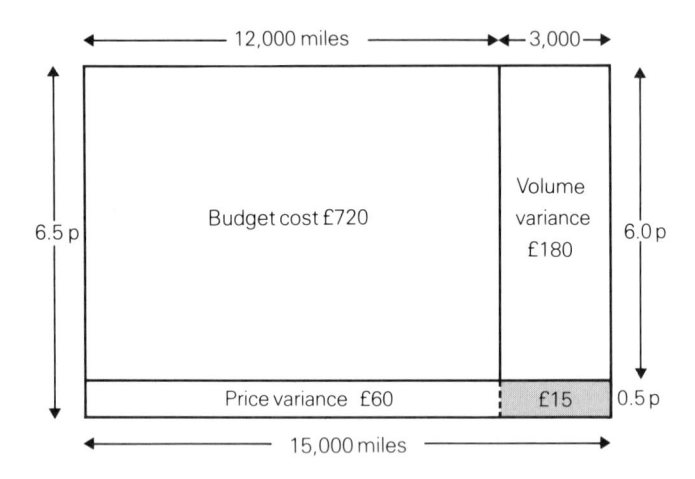

Fig. 10.7: Analysis of an expense variance.

Again we use the *budget* cost per mile to analyse the volume variance (giving 3,000 at 6.0p = £180; and again we use the *actual* volume to determine the *price* variance (giving 0.5p × 15,000 miles = £75). Thus the shaded area in the bottom right-hand corner of Fig. 10.7 is regarded as part of the *price* variance.

10.5.3 Flexible Budgets

When sales volume varies from budget, those expenses which are expected to change in line with sales volume ('variable expenses') are – *for that reason alone* – likely to differ from budget too. So it can be useful to tackle the review of actual profit versus budgeted profit in two stages:
1. Examine the change in contribution (sales revenue less variable expenses) due to changes in (a) sales volume and (b) selling prices.
2. Examine the change in (c) variable expenses and (d) fixed expenses compared with what would have been expected at *actual* sales volume. (c) Variable

Costs and Budgets

expenses will be different in the flexible budget from the original budget, if sales volume has changed; whereas (d) fixed expenses, of course, will not change merely because of a change in sales volume (by definition).

Example: *Suppose that budgeted sales revenue was £30,000 for a month (15,000 units at £2.00 each); variable expenses were budgeted at £1.20 per unit (60 per cent of sales revenue = £18,000); and fixed expenses were budgeted at £7,200 for the month. Actual sales revenue was £24,000 (12,000 units at £2.00); actual variable expenses were £16,000; and actual fixed expenses were £6,900. Figure 10.8 shows how to analyse the difference between budgeted profit of £4,800 and actual profit of £1,100 in two stages by using a flexible budget.*

	Original budget		Flexible budget		Actual	
	(£)	(%)	(£)	(%)	(£)	(%)
Sales revenue	30,000	100	24,000	100	24,000	100.0
Variable expenses	18,000	60	14,400	60	16,000	66.7
Contribution	12,000	40	9,600	40	8,000	33.3
Fixed expenses	7,200	24	7,200	24	6,900	28.7
Profit	4,800	16	2,400	16	1,100	4.6

Fig. 10.8: Flexing a budget for variance analysis.

The total profit variance of – £3,700 between the original budget profit (£4,800) and the actual profit (£1,100) is now split into two parts (–£2,400 and –£1,300) which can be analysed separately:

1. The variance of –£2,400 in contribution, between the original budget (£12,000) and the flexible budget (£9,600), due to the decline in sales:—
    a. sales volume is down by 3,000 units. This leads to a decline in:

sales revenue	–3,000	× £2.00	= –£6,000
variable expenses	–3,000	× £1.20	= +£3,600
contribution	–3,000	× £0.80	= –£2,400

    b. selling prices were unchanged, so in this case there is no sales price variance.
2. The total variance of –£1,300 in expenses, between the flexible budget and actual:

	Flexible budget	Actual	Variance
c. variable expenses	£14,400	£16,000	– £1,600
d. fixed expenses	£ 7,200	£ 6,900	+£ 300
			– £1,300

The convention is to use a + sign for a 'favourable' variance which increases actual profits over budget, and a − sign for an 'unfavourable' variance which reduces actual profits compared with budget. Thus if actual expenses are higher than budget, that is an unfavourable variance and has a − sign.

Thus we see that using a flexible budget is a convenient way to break down the analysis of variances step by step, in particular distinguishing between variances due to a change in sales volume, and those due to expenses being different from expected at the *actual* sales volume. In practice this is helpful because different managers are likely to be responsible. Clearly it is essential to split the apparent £2,000 *favourable* variance on variable expenses (between the original budget's £18,000 and the actual £16,000) into the £3,600 favourable variance due to the decline in sales volume and the £1,600 unfavourable variance due to spending more than 'should' have been spent at the actual sales volume.

Work Section

A. Revision Questions

A1 Name two respects in which management accounts may differ from financial accounts.
A2 How can the three stages of planning, control, and review be related to time?
A3 How is cost/benefit analysis relevant in providing management information?
A4 Why may management accountants in business to some extent have an educational role?
A5 Why do management accountants need imagination?
A6 What is the 'cost' of something?
A7 Why is someone who pays £20 for a pair of shoes not 'valuing' the shoes at £20?
A8 What are two main purposes of measuring business costs?
A9 Name three reasons for estimating costs per unit of production.
A10 Define (a) variable cost, (b) fixed cost. Give an example of each.
A11 Define (a) a semi-variable cost, (b) a non-variable cost. Give an example of each.
A12 Define (a) a direct cost (b) an indirect cost.
A13 Why is it sometimes a matter of *convenience* whether a particular cost is classified as direct or indirect?
A14 Define (a) marginal cost (b) average cost.
A15 Define 'contribution'.
A16 At a given scale of operation, why should marginal cost per unit fall at first as production volume increases, and then rise?
A17 If the marginal cost per unit is lower than average cost, is the average cost at that point falling or rising? Explain why.
A18 Explain precisely why the marginal cost curve *must* cross the average cost curve at the latter's lowest point.
A19 What assumption do accountants often make about marginal costs?
A20 Define the 'short run'.

A21 Name three characteristics of budgets.
A22 How does a budget differ from a neutral forecast?
A23 Why is discussion an important part of preparing budgets?
A24 Name three things a budget does in advance.
A25 Name three things a budget does after the event.
A26 What is a master budget?

A27 What is a rolling budget?
A28 Why may 'maximising the current year's profits' be unsatisfactory as a firm's sole objective?
A29 Why should a manager's performance be distinguished from that of the business unit for which he is responsible?
A30 Name three different kinds of 'responsibility centre'.
A31 What is a profit centre?
A32 Why may a manager who exactly meets his budget for research spending nevertheless be doing a poor job?
A33 Name two reasons why budgets should be simple.
A34 Name three possible useful supplements to monthly budget reports.
A35 How might reporting less often perhaps improve a budget system?
A36 Why may including a 'latest estimate for the current year' be helpful in monthly budget reports?
A37 Why should it be unnecessary to include last year's actual results in monthly management reports?
A38 Name one advantage and one disadvantage of revising annual budgets during the year.
A39 Why may a deviation from budget be acceptable?
A40 Name three kinds of question on which budgetary control may help to focus managers' attention.
A41 What is a variance?
A42 Into what two kinds of variance can an overall sales variance be analysed?
A43 Why are volume variances calculated by using budget prices (rather than actual prices)?
A44 What is a flexible budget? What is its purpose?
A45 Why is a minus sign used if actual expenses are higher than budget?

B. Exercises and Case Studies

B1 Shortfellows Ltd budget to sell 3,000 units in March, at an average price per unit of £2.40. Actual sales revenue in March, from 3,200 units, is £7,040.
    a. What is the total sales variance for March?
    b. Analyse the total variance between volume variance and price variance.

B2 Winslow and Terry Ltd budgeted total expenses in June at £14,400, on a sales volume of 1,400 units (of which fixed expenses represented £6,000). Actual expenses in June were £15,200 (variable £8,800 and fixed £6,400), on actual sales volume of 1,500 units.
Account in detail for the total difference of £800.

B3 Jason Escombe Ltd budgeted sales revenue in 1984 of £360,000, variable expenses of £240,000, and operating profit of £35,000. Actual sales revenue was £295,000, at selling prices 10 per cent higher than budgeted.
    a. Prepare the flexible budget figures for 1984.
    b. What could they be used for?

Costs and Budgets

B4 A public utility operates at 100 per cent of capacity for only four hours out of every 24 hours, at 50 per cent of capacity for a further four hours, and at only 25 per cent of capacity for the remaining 16 hours each day. Total operating costs are £96,000 per day. How should costs be allocated? (Capacity used is shown below.)

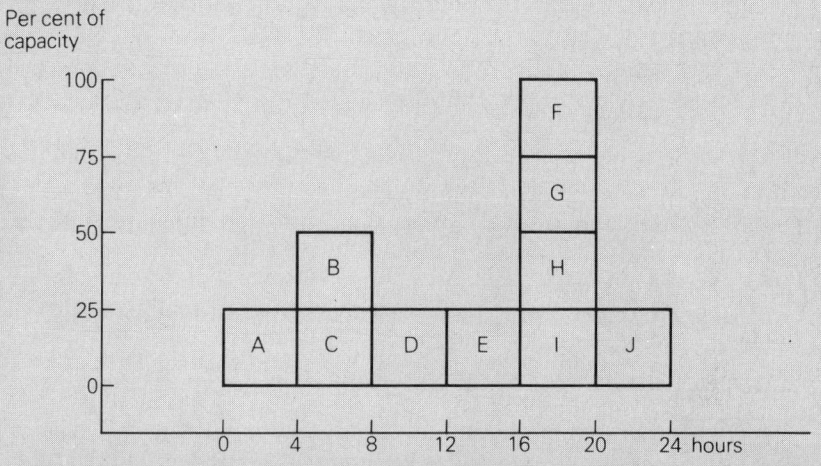

B5 Education Tapes Ltd imports taped lectures and sells them to schools and colleges. At the end of 1982 the company's balance sheet was as follows:

	(£'000)
Ordinary share capital (£1 shares)	50
Retained profits	40
Shareholders' Funds	90

Fixed Assets

Equipment and vehicles, at cost	100	
Less: Accumulated depreciation	25	
		75

Current Assets

Stocks	25	
Debtors	30	
Cash	10	
	65	

Less: Current Liabilities

Creditors	40	
Taxation	10	
	50	
		15
Net Assets		90

The accountant is given the following information to enable him to draw up budgets for 1983:

1. Sales. 7,000 tapes per month at £7 each (the price was £6 last year). Company policy is to keep one month's sales in stock. The price of imported tapes is expected to rise on 1.1.83 from £5 to £6, the first rise for over a year.

2. Expenditure.

Sales overheads	£20,000
Administrative overheads	£31,000
New equipment (to be bought on 1.1.83)	£15,000

3. Depreciation. At a rate of 10 per cent, using the straight-line method.

4. Tax and dividends. Tax is expected to amount to 50 per cent of net profit, and is payable in the following year. The intention is to pay a dividend of 10p per share during the year.

5. Credit. It is expected that the average collection period for debtors will be one and a half months instead of the current one month. On the other hand, the suppliers have decided to enforce strictly one month's credit to the company. All other transactions, except tax, are for cash.
   a. As accountant prepare: (1) a cash budget for 1983; (2) a profit and loss account budget for 1983; (3) an estimated balance sheet as at 31 December 1983.
   b. Use key ratios to comment on the figures you have prepared.

B6 Design an outline monthly management report for the financial results of a school. (Hint: remember it will have to be used by people who are *not* financial experts!)

B7 Mr Zebedee has a small workshop at the back of his house, where he employs three people making bedside cabinets. They each work for 40 hours a week, at a wage of £2.50 per hour. It takes four working hours to produce a cabinet, which sells for £20.00 and contains £4.00 worth of timber. Heating, rent, rates, etc. normally average £60.00 per week.

One Sunday one of the workers catches a cold and is away for the whole of the next week. He receives no pay for that week. The other two workers work six hours overtime each, for which they are paid at 'time and a half'. They manage to produce 25 cabinets between them, but due to haste they use 10 per cent more material than usual. Also the timber price has risen by 20 per cent. The weather is extremely cold that week, so the bill for overheads rises to £68.00 because of additional heating for longer hours.
   a. Calculate the budgeted profit for the week.
   b. Calculate the actual profit or loss for the week.
   c. Prepare a statement explaining the difference between the actual financial result for the week and the 'budget'. Distinguish between (i) quantity differences and (ii) price differences.

Costs and Budgets

B8 Alpine Novelties (Colorado) Inc produces two models of cuckoo clock. The company's budget for 1984 was as follows:

	Monster	Baby	TOTAL
Selling price each	$60	$25	
Sales quantities	2,000	8,000	
	$'000	$'000	$'000
Sales revenue	120	200	320
Variable cost of sales	60	160	220
Contribution	60	40	100

The actual figures for 1984 were as follows:

	Monster	Baby	TOTAL
Sales quantities	1,800	9,000	
	$'000	$'000	$'000
Sales revenue	90	240	330
Variable cost of sales	50	185	235
Contribution	40	55	95

Account for the drop in contribution between budget and actual.

B9 Household Industries Ltd make, amongst other products, a holder for toilet rolls. The manufacturing process is in three parts: (1) stamping out; (2) painting; (3) fitting with a centre rolling pin, and a bracket and screws for easy attachment to a door. The standard cost of a holder is £2.00, processing 90p, plus Materials £1.10, analysed as follows:

Processing 90p	Stamping	Painting	Fitting
	500 per hour	500 per hour	400 per hour
	Hourly cost	Hourly cost	Hourly cost
Wages	£160	£120	£60
Power	30	20	5
Depreciation	10	10	–
Overtime premium*	–	–	15
	£200	£150	£80

* Shortages of personnel force this department to work regular overtime, meaning higher wage rates for those hours.

Materials £1.10 consists of: Metal 65p; paint 15p; sundries 30p.

The management accountant makes a weekly comparison of actual with standard (or budgeted) costs and output. One week the actual performance figures were as follows:

Output of holders: 20,000.

Hours worked on holders, by departments: stamping 55; painting 49; fitting 40.

Expenses incurred in running departments:

	Stamping (£)	Painting (£)	Fitting (£)
Wages*	9,680	5,880	2,640
Power	1,650	980	200
Depreciation	550	490	–
Overtime premiums	–	–	720
	11,880	7,350	3,560

* A wage rise for some workers had caused some departments to experience increased costs.

Materials:	Metal	£13,800
	Paint	2,900
	Sundries	6,100
		£22,800

a. Calculate the actual cost per holder.
b. Analyse the difference between standard cost and actual cost.
c. Prepare a report setting out and discussing your main findings.

B10 Edison Ltd operates two small factories at Dudley and Walsall in the West Midlands, each employing 100 people in production of bicycle chains. All employees work for 150 hours a month, at a wage rate of £4.00 per hour, each producing on average 10 chains per hour. Material costs amount to 25p per chain, and Edison normally sells 300,000 chains a month, for £1.00 each, mainly to bicycle manufacturers. Fixed costs are budgeted at £80,000 a month.

A dispute about working conditions closes the Dudley factory for the month of October, and all 100 Dudley production workers are laid off and receive no pay for that month. Fixed costs, however, fall by only £8,000. The 100 Walsall workers are able to increase their productivity so that in October they actually produce 200,000 chains, all of which are sold at the usual price. They are rewarded by a productivity bonus amounting to 25 per cent of their normal wages. Thanks to a nearby metal manufacturer going bankrupt, Edison Ltd is able to buy materials for the month at a discount of 20 per cent off the normal cost.

a. Calculate Edison's actual profit or loss for October.
b. Prepare a table showing the difference between the actual result and the original budgeted contribution and profit for the month.
c. Compare the actual result with a flexed budget, showing what the expenses 'should have been' at the actual volume of sales.
d. Split the total labour cost variance for October between the difference due to efficiency (volume) and that due to rates of pay (price).
e. Summarise all the variances to explain the difference between the originally budgeted profit and actual profit or loss.

Costs and Budgets

C. Essay Questions

C1 Why does a manager need to know how a firm's costs vary with changes in output?

C2 Why is the concept of marginal cost important for managers?

C3 Explain the purpose of flexible budgeting.

C4 How does a budgeting system make use of feedback?

C5 If British Leyland is operating at a loss, shouldn't we be glad when there's a strike? Won't they *save* money? Explain fully.

C6 Do you agree that the use of budgetary control is essential if a firm is to meet its objectives?

C7 'Optimum use of accounting information can make more effective use of scarce management skills by allowing them to manage by exception.' Discuss.

C8 What would you expect an operating manager's main requirements to be in respect of a system of management reporting?

C9 'Our internal management accounting reports take far too long to tell me what I already knew.' How might a competent accountant respond to this (very common) criticism?

C10 'We prepare our annual budgets about 10 months through the previous year; but conditions change so fast in our industry that the budgets are already out of date before the budget year even begins.' What kind of solution, if any, might be appropriate; and what do you see as its main advantages and disadvantages?

11 Budgeting in Action

11.1 Introduction

11.2 Budgeting
11.2.1 Objectives
11.2.2 Profit Estimates
11.2.3 Detailed Budgets
11.2.4 Variance Analysis

11.3 Pyramid of Ratios
11.3.1 Return on Net Assets Analysed
11.3.2 Following the Woodcraft Trail
11.3.3 Interfirm Comparison
11.3.4 Management Action to Improve Performance

11.4 Conclusion

Objective: *To use a case example to show how management accounting makes use of ratio analysis and variance analysis.*

Synopsis: *Once budget objectives have been set, detailed profit estimates can be developed, forming the basis for comparing actual performance with budget. Variance analysis can then be used to determine to what extent plans have been met; and to help managers take appropriate action to improve profits.*

The division of the return on net assets ratio into a whole pyramid of ratios can be a powerful tool of management analysis. It emphasises the importance of managing assets as well as sales and costs. Interfirm comparison is another useful approach, which provides external standards to help managers improve performance.

11.1 Introduction

In the last chapter we looked at how costs can be classified, and at the preparation and use of budgets in management accounting. Some aspects of the budgeting process may be clarified if we now look in some detail at a case

Budgeting in Action

example of a business over the whole period of a budget cycle. This cycle lasts for more than 12 months, from the start of budget preparations for next year until after the end of that year.

In practice the processes of planning, controlling and reviewing business operations overlap with each other. Managers are in the middle of controlling the current year's operations at the same time as they are reviewing last year's performance, and starting to plan next year's. This overlap with the previous year will be omitted from our case example for the sake of clarity.

Example: *Woodcraft Ltd was established in the late 1970s to manufacture and sell three products (tables, cupboards and desks) for the medium-priced market. We begin to observe the company early in November 1982, when senior managers are meeting to consider, for the first time, the plans for the next financial year. It runs from 1 April 1983 to 31 March 1984.*

11.2 Budgeting

11.2.1 Objectives

The chairman, Mr Carstairs, began the meeting by reminding everyone that Woodcraft's main objective was to earn at least 10 per cent a year return on net assets, while avoiding undue risks. A second objective was controlled expansion.

The sales manager, Mr Sidney, then presented his estimates of £150,000 sales revenue for 1983/84 (Fig. 11.1), a 10 per cent increase over the current year. He thought the total market for their products would grow in volume by about 5 per cent. He also estimated £17,000 for the selling expenses: salaries £11,000; promotion £3,500; and commissions £2,500.

	Units	Price	Revenue
Tables	3,000	£15	£45,000
Cupboards	1,500	£20	£30,000
Desks	3,000	£25	£75,000
			£150,000

Fig. 11.1: Woodcraft: Sales estimates, 1983/84.

According to Mr Potter, the production manager, the existing plant and labour force could cope with this projected increase in sales, subject to more plant in the sanding department. Extra storage space would also be needed; but the labour force would be sufficient, given some overtime at peak periods. Mr Carstairs asked the accountant, Mr Addison, for a profit estimate and cash forecast at the next meeting at the end of November.

11.2.2 Profit Estimates

Mr Addison calculated the direct costs of producing the planned quantities of goods, using standard cost data for each product (Fig. 11.2). (The up-to-date figures were based partly on past results and partly on expected changes in conditions.)

	Units	Standard costs	Total costs
Tables	3,000	£ 9.10	£27,300
Cupboards	1,500	£13.20	£19,800
Desks	3,000	£14.30	£42,900

Fig. 11.2: Woodcraft: Estimated standard direct costs, 1983/84.

After estimating that administrative expenses would total £28,000, Mr Addison was able to prepare an overall estimate of net profit before tax for next year (Fig. 11.3).

	Tables (£'000)	Cupboards (£'000)	Desks (£'000)	Total (£'000)
Sales revenue	45.0	30.0	75.0	150.0
Cost of sales	27.3	19.8	42.9	90.0
Gross profit	17.7	10.2	32.1	60.0
Selling expenses			17.0	
Administrative expenses			28.0	
				45.0
Net profit before tax				15.0

Fig. 11.3: Woodcraft: Profit estimates, 1983/84.

For his cash budget, Mr Addison realised he needed more information. First he asked Mr Potter what the new plant would cost, and how much working capital would be needed for extra stocks of materials. Then he asked Mr Sidney what increase in the level of finished goods stocks was anticipated. After confirming that no change in trade credit terms was planned, he estimated the year-end debtors by using the past number of days sales in debtors. As a result he reckoned the company should plan on requiring £24,000 extra finance by March 1984.

At their next meeting the managers reviewed all these estimates carefully. The

Budgeting in Action

standard cost figures and expenses were acceptable, but a problem arose when the projected profit was related to the net assets. The estimates showed an increase in 1983/84 of £24,000 on the expected March 1983 net assets of £145,000. Thus the return on net assets in 1983/84 would be only 8.9 per cent, which was less than the 10 per cent required minimum.

$$\frac{\text{Profit}}{\text{Net assets}} = \frac{£\ 15{,}000}{£169{,}000} = 8.9 \text{ per cent.}$$

Mr Carstairs asked Mr Sidney whether higher prices could be charged without losing sales volume, or whether cutting prices might be a better policy. Mr Sidney suggested raising prices slightly, but with a larger budget for spending on promotion so as not to sacrifice volume. He thought prices for tables and desks could be increased by £1 each, and for cupboards by £2. Mr Addison then quickly worked out a revised profit estimate (Fig. 11.4) based on the new figures.

	Tables (£'000)	Cupboards (£'000)	Desks (£'000)	Total (£'000)
Sales revenue	48.0	33.0	78.0	159.0
Cost of sales	27.3	19.8	42.9	90.0
Gross profit	20.7	13.2	35.1	69.0
Selling expenses			23.0	
Administrative expenses			28.0	
				51.0
Net profit before tax				18.0

Fig. 11.4: Woodcraft: Revised profit estimates, 1983/84.

The return on net assets then worked out better, at 10.7 per cent.

$$\frac{\text{Profit}}{\text{Net assets}} = \frac{£\ 18{,}000}{£169{,}000} = 10.7 \text{ per cent}$$

The managers agreed to adopt the plan, and scheduled another meeting for the end of January to examine the detailed operating budget.

11.2.3 Detailed Budgets

Mr Addison left the meeting thinking of the hectic time ahead. He knew the problems of putting together a detailed operating budget. It was always hard to get the people responsible for each part to agree; yet without their agreement the plan would break down in practice. At last, however, all problems were overcome, and the budgets were prepared from the general plan. The cash budget showed that Woodcraft would have to raise much of the extra finance by April 1983 in order to carry out the plan. Mr Addison recognised that both profit budgets and cash budgets were vital for successful planning.

Figure 11.5 sets out the first monthly budget, for April 1983. There was more detail behind the selling and administrative expenses; but since no large variances were expected, they only appeared in total.

	Tables Units	£	Cupboards Units	£	Desks Units	£	TOTAL £
Sales revenue	300	4,800	200	4,400	250	6,500	15,700
Opening stocks	900	8,190	550	7,260	700	10,010	25,460
Made in month	400	3,640	300	3,960	350	5,005	12,605
Material	*5.10*	*2,040*	*6.00*	*1,800*	*9.10*	*3,185*	
Direct labour	*3.00*	*1,200*	*5.20*	*1,560*	*3.00*	*1,050*	
Overheads	*1.00*	*400*	*2.00*	*600*	*2.20*	*770*	
Closing stocks	(1,000)	9,100)	(650)	8,580)	(800)	11,440)	(29,120)
Cost of sales	300	2,730	200	2,640	250	3,575	8,945
Gross profit		2,070		1,760		2,925	6,755
Selling expenses							2,500
Admin. expenses							3,000
Profit before tax							1,255

Fig. 11.5: Woodcraft: Profit budget, April 1983.

The January meeting approved the operating details, after discussion; and then looked at the financing decision. Early in 1983/84 a large cash deficit was expected, but in later months the net cash inflow from sales would exceed costs and reduce the deficit. The managers decided to ask the bank to increase Woodcraft's overdraft to cover the short-term cash deficit. They also agreed on a new share issue later in the year, to finance the permanent increase in net assets which the company now

Budgeting in Action 191

planned. This decision was influenced by the need to maintain adequate liquidity ratios and low gearing, since a primary objective was to minimise risks.

Mr Addison was then left to produce detailed operating budgets for department heads to issue to each responsibility centre. Each salesman had to be given his sales target, along with the expenses he could incur; each machine operator had to be informed of the planned throughput and his allowed machine hours; and so on. Those chiefly responsible for that part of the plan would already have agreed to these figures.

11.2.4 Variance Analysis

As 1983/84 begins, the managers have to watch closely each stage of implementing the plan, to make sure that unforeseen snags do not interfere with its achievement. Once more accounting information is required. We look first at the month-by-month control procedure, using the budget figures, actual results, and variance analysis. (In some cases, control reports might be produced weekly, daily, or even more frequently.)

Mr Addison's information system recorded the key performance figures at the end of each month. He then arranged them into the same format as the detailed budget, to make it easy to compare the two. The differences between budget and actual were thus highlighted, allowing suitable corrective action to be taken on the basis of 'management by exception'.

Figures 11.6 and 11.7 show two examples of control tables for April 1983. These are only a sample of the many tables Mr Addison constructed. You can see how the 'variance' column highlights where there has been a deviation from plan. Figure 11.6 shows, for example, that one of the salesmen, Mr Duke, has fallen well short of his sales budget for both tables and cupboards.

	Budget			Actual			Variance		
	Duke	Earl	Total	Duke	Earl	Total	Duke	Earl	Total
Tables	140	160	300	120	161	281	−20	+1	−19
Cupboards	100	100	200	80	98	178	−20	−2	−22
Desks	110	140	250	110	142	252	0	+2	+2

Fig. 11.6: Woodcraft: Unit sales by salesmen, April 1983.

Figure 11.7 reveals problems in sanding tables, with actual machine hours being 15 higher than budget. On the other hand, the hourly running costs are less than budget because maintenance costs are down.

		Output (units)			Machine hours	
	Budget	Actual	Variance	Budget	Actual	Variance
Tables	400	400	0	70	85	+15
Cupboards	300	300	0	140	139	−1
Desks	350	350	0	154	153	−1
Total				364	377	+13

Costs/hour		Machine 1			Machine 2	
	Budget (£)	Actual (£)	Variance (£)	Budget (£)	Actual (£)	Variance (£)
Labour	2.00	2.00	0	2.00	2.00	0
Maintenance	0.60	0.42	−0.18	0.60	0.39	−0.21
Power	0.35	0.35	0	0.35	0.36	+0.01
Total	2.95	2.77	−0.18	2.95	2.75	−0.20

Fig. 11.7: Woodcraft: Sanding department variances, April 1983.

11.3 Pyramid of Ratios

11.3.1 Return on Net Assets Analysed

In planning, controlling and reviewing operations, internal managers use financial ratios to help them analyse performance, in the same way as we have already seen with external parties (see Ch. 9). The main difference is that managers can have any information they care to collect: in particular they can get information which is both (a) more detailed and (b) more frequent than in the annual published accounts for the whole company.

This additional information is especially useful with the performance ratios. They can be extended in a logical **pyramid** beyond the two ratios which we saw could be combined to form the 'return on net assets' ratio. Figure 11.8 shows how the pyramid can be built up. The results may be compared in detail:

a. with past periods,
b. with budgets,
c. with other firms.

The ratios can also be further analysed between (i) products, (ii) areas, and (iii) different types of costs within each heading.

Budgeting in Action

```
                        Profit
                       ────────
                      Net assets
                          │
            ┌─────────────┴─────────────┐
         Profit                       Sales
         ─────                       ──────────
         Sales                       Net assets
           │                             │
      ┌────┴────┐                 ┌──────┴──────┐
  Gross profit  Expenses        Sales          Sales
  ────────────  ────────       ────────────   ─────────────
     Sales       Sales         Fixed assets   Working capital
       │           │               │                │
   Materials   Selling exs.      Sales            Sales
   ─────────   ───────────     ───────────       ──────
     Sales        Sales        Land & bldgs.     Stocks

    Labour      Admin. exs.     Sales            Sales
   ───────     ───────────     ──────           ───────
    Sales        Sales         Plant            Debtors

   Overheads                                     Sales
   ─────────                                    ──────
     Sales                                       Cash
```

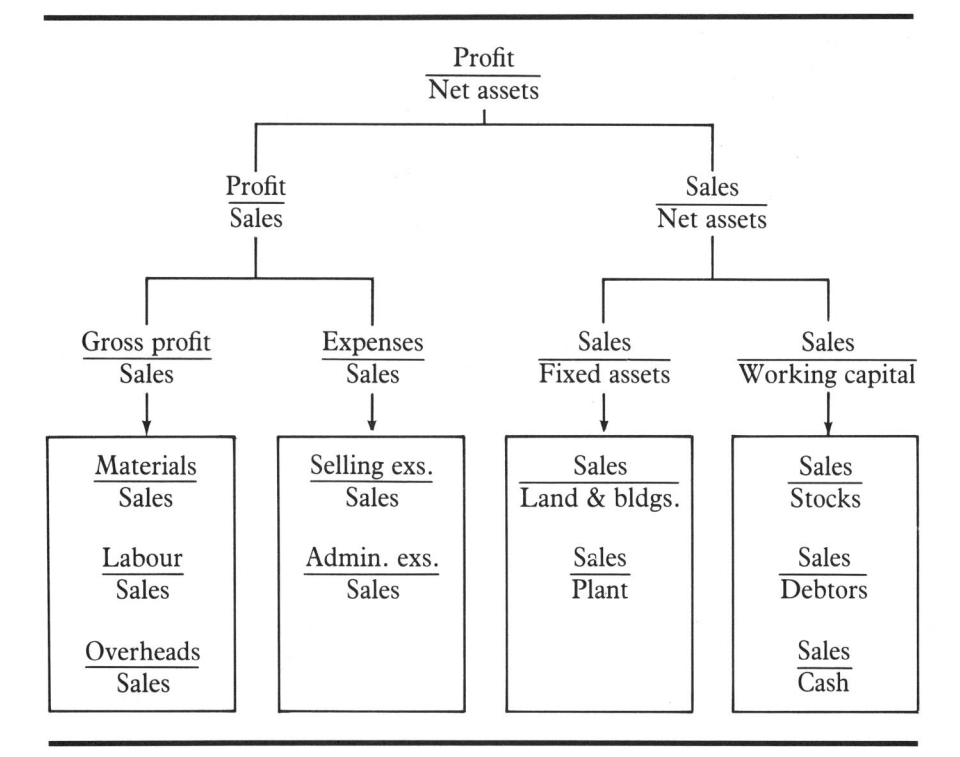

Fig. 11.8: Pyramid of ratios.

11.3.2 Following the Woodcraft Trail

When Mr Addison prepared Woodcraft's draft accounts for the year 1983/84, he drew up a pyramid of ratios and soon noticed certain disturbing features. He decided to look into them, and we shall follow his progress. You can see that the ratios he examines in turn are rather like a series of clues followed by a detective. In each case the ratio giving the clue is shown in **bold type**.

The starting point gives the first clue: the return on net assets ratio is only 8.3 per cent for the year, compared with the budget figure of 10.7 per cent. (All the ratios are comparing £'000: these are omitted for reasons of space.)

$$\text{Return on net assets:} \quad \frac{\text{Profit}}{\text{Net assets}} \quad \overset{Budget}{\frac{18}{169} = 10.7\%} \quad \overset{Actual}{\frac{14}{168} = \mathbf{8.3\%}}$$

When he analysed the return on net assets ratio between profit margin and asset turnover, Mr Addison found that it was the profit margins that was causing the shortfall.

	Budget	Actual
Profit margin: $\dfrac{\text{Profit}}{\text{Sales}}$	$\dfrac{18}{159} = 11.3\%$	$\dfrac{14}{155} = \mathbf{9.0\%}$
Asset turnover: $\dfrac{\text{Sales}}{\text{Net assets}}$	$\dfrac{159}{169} = 0.94$	$\dfrac{155}{168} = 0.92$

Now he had to discover why the profit margin was only 9.0 per cent instead of 11.3 per cent as budgeted. He looked at the main costs and saw that, while selling and administrative expenses were roughly in line with budget, higher direct costs were the main factor behind the fall in profit margin.

	Budget	Actual
Direct costs/sales	90/159 = 56.6%	91/155 = **58.7%**
Selling expenses/sales	23/159 = 14.5%	23/155 = 14.9%
Admin. expenses/sales	28/159 = 17.6%	27/155 = 17.4%
Total expenses/sales	141/159 = 88.7%	141/155 = 91.0%

Mr Addison's next move was to trace which of the three products was responsible for direct costs/sales being higher than budget. It was clearly the tables.

Direct costs/sales	Budget	Actual
Tables	56.9%	**62.9%**
Cupboards	60.0%	59.9%
Desks	55.0%	55.2%
Total	56.6%	58.7%

Further examination of direct costs/sales for tables showed that both materials and production overheads had cost more than planned.

Direct costs/sales for tables	Budget	Actual
Materials	31.9%	**35.3%**
Direct labour	18.8%	18.7%
Production overheads	6.2%	**8.9%**
Total	56.9%	62.9%

At last Mr Addison had managed to pin down the main cause of Woodcraft's return on net assets in 1983/84 being less than budget: it was due to the cost of materials and production overheads for tables. At this point we end our pursuit. If Mr Addison wished, he could go on to discover which materials and which production overheads had exceeded budget cost estimates.

Having identified what seems to have gone wrong, the management accountant can inform the manager(s) responsible. If they have not already done so, they can try to find out *why*. They can then take action to improve matters, or at least alter their estimates of likely future results.

Even if the overall ratios seem satisfactory, there may still be important variances at lower levels *which cancel each other out*. So analysis of the pyramid of ratios may be worthwhile even if the overall result seems to give no cause for alarm. And one should always remember that much drama may lie hidden behind a 'nil' variance.

For example, financial accountants have their own targets (in days) for how long it takes them after the end of the company's financial year to complete the preparation of the final accounts. Suppose in Woodcraft the allowed period is 45 days, so that the 1983/84 accounts should be ready by mid-May 1984. But in April 1984 the computer breaks down; one of Mr Addison's assistants is away ill, and another is getting married; a postal strike delays the receipt of certain information; the stocktaking turns out to be unusually complicated this year; and so on.

Despite all these obstacles, Mr Addison and his team work late into the evenings in order to meet their deadline. And when they do, after exceptional efforts, they may feel that simply to report a 'nil' variance is hardly a complete description of what has happened. Even humble authors have 'budgets' for the number of pages and deadlines for delivering manuscripts. Budgeting is part of general *management*; not merely a technical aspect of accounting in financial terms.

11.3.3 Interfirm Comparison

The comparison of actual against budget can suggest many areas which management might usefully examine. But alone they may fail to show up long-standing weaknesses of which nobody is aware. It is here that comparing a firm's ratios with those of other firms in the same industry can be so useful. The published accounts may not help much, because they contain too little detail, and different approaches to the many accounting conventions often make comparison unreliable.

Even in their management accounts different firms have different accounting methods and costing systems. So the Centre for Interfirm Comparison, which exchanges ratios anonymously between firms, standardises the results for all firms taking part in an industry scheme. In this way the comparisons are made much more useful.

Some examples of the type of questions which well-organised interfirm comparisons can help answer are:

a. Is our return on net assets high or low for the industry?
b. Are selling costs higher than for other firms of similar size?
c. Is stock turnover out of line with comparable firms?
d. Is working capital adequate by industry standards?

Trends over time for each set of ratios can add to their usefulness. But interfirm comparisons can never go into the same detail as that discussed earlier for Woodcraft Ltd. Only the more basic ratios are given, using fixed costs in total, or direct costs only in major categories. Similarly only the total sales figure is used, whereas internally this can be broken down into more detail.

Figure 11.9 shows the main ratios from Woodcraft Ltd's 1983/84 accounts alongside the equivalent ratios for four comparable firms in the same industry. These ratios suggest aspects of the company's operations which might be worth re-examining. It appears that there may be plenty of scope for Woodcraft to increase its efficiency and hence its profit.

		Woodcraft	A	B	C	D
1. Return on net assets	%	8.3	11.6	8.1	16.3	14.9
2. Profit margin	%	9.0	9.2	9.8	8.9	11.0
3. Asset turnover		0.92	1.26	0.83	1.83	1.35
4. Direct costs/sales	%	58.7	58.1	55.8	54.2	53.4
5. Selling exs./sales	%	14.5	14.8	16.4	19.1	18.4
6. Admin. exs./sales	%	17.6	17.9	18.0	17.8	17.2
7. Sales/fixed assets		2.1	2.4	2.1	2.3	2.5
8. Sales/current assets		1.4	2.0	1.3	3.4	3.1
9. Stock turnover		2.8	3.1	4.3	6.1	5.8
10. Days sales in debtors		60	45	43	41	42

Fig. 11.9: Woodcraft: Interfirm comparisons, 1983/84.

11.3.4 Management Action to Improve Performance

Figure 11.10 shows another approach to the pyramid of ratios. The diagram sets out how a company could increase its rate of return on net assets either by increasing profit or by reducing net assets employed for each £ of sales revenue (i.e. increasing asset turnover). When first estimates of profits for 1983/84 showed a return on net assets of only 8.9 per cent, Woodcraft Ltd followed the left-hand side of the pyramid: increasing profit, increasing sales revenue, increasing selling prices.

The management accountant is a member of the management team. Accounting information is vital in helping managers to take action to improve financial performance; but of course many other skills must be combined to earn maximum profits. In marketing (in addition to pricing policy), product design and quality, packaging delivery, advertising, and so on, may help to increase sales. In production, skilful purchasing, engineering, factory scheduling, industrial relations, stock management, and so on, may help to minimise expenses.

The same applies to trying to minimise net assets employed for any given level of profit. Fixed asset costs can be reduced by better plant layout, more intensive use, careful maintenance, efficient management of new capital projects, and so on. And working capital is important: good managers can often reduce the large amounts invested in stocks and debtors fairly quickly.

Budgeting in Action 197

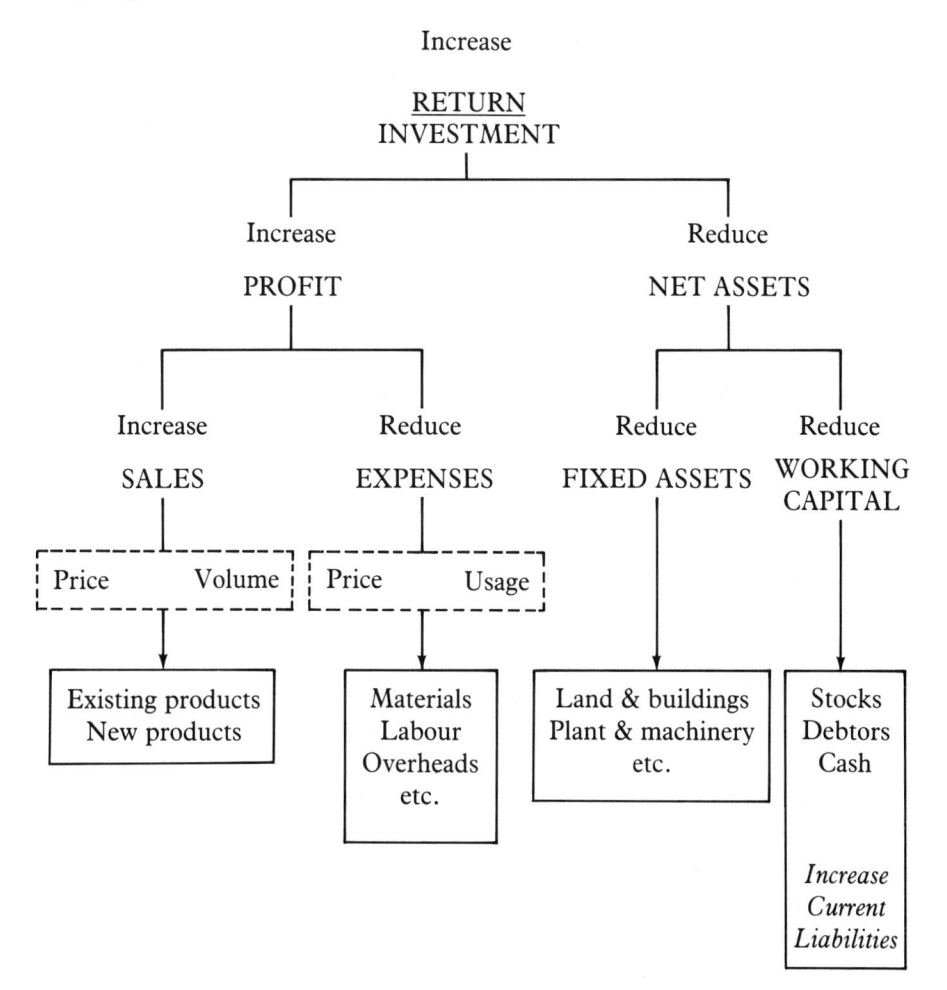

```
                         Increase
                         RETURN
                       INVESTMENT
              ┌─────────────┴─────────────┐
          Increase                      Reduce
           PROFIT                     NET ASSETS
      ┌───────┴───────┐          ┌───────┴───────┐
   Increase        Reduce      Reduce          Reduce
    SALES        EXPENSES    FIXED ASSETS     WORKING
                                               CAPITAL
```

| Price Volume | | Price Usage |

Existing products		Materials		Land & buildings		Stocks
New products		Labour		Plant & machinery		Debtors
		Overheads		etc.		Cash
		etc.				
						Increase
						Current
						Liabilities

Fig. 11.10: Management action to improve performance.

11.4 Conclusion

We have now completed our discussion of accounting and decision-making. Some of the detailed aspects of financial accounting have taken much of the space; but we have also tried to relate the text to the making of decisions, whether by external users of published financial accounts or by internal users of management accounts.

Chapter 1 outlined various types of users and their needs, and described the differences between financial and management accounting.

Chapter 2 covered the documents comprising a company's 'accounts'. Chapter 3 listed the 'accounting guidelines' (fundamental concepts and accounting conventions) which underlie financial accounts (Fig. 3.1, p. 22);

and also outlined the double-entry approach to accounts. Chapters 4 and 5 discussed the items in, and format of, the balance sheet and profit and loss account; and Chapter 5 also discussed the matching principle, and its use in deciding whether to treat expenditures as expenses or as assets (Fig. 5.8, p. 67).

Then followed three more detailed chapters. Chapter 6 on fixed assets emphasised the two main factors needed to calculate depreciation expense (economic life and method). Chapter 7 noted the 'lower of cost or market value' rule in valuing stock, and the impact of stock valuation on the amount of profit for a period (Figs 7.1 and 7.2, p. 99 and 100). Chapter 8 discussed the two different approaches to accounting for inflation: constant purchasing power (CPP) accounting challenging the use of money as the unit of account, and current cost accounting (CCA) challenging the use of historical cost (rather than current value). We also stressed the importance of allowing for inflation in looking at trends over time.

Chapter 9 analysed accounts in the context of external financial accounts; but we saw later that the same ratios (listed in Fig. 9.4, p. 149) can also be used to analyse management accounts. Chapter 10 discussed the nature of costs, and outlined how to prepare and use budgets in planning, controlling and reviewing business affairs. Finally Chapter 11 applied these ideas to a specific example, and developed the 'pyramid of ratios' and interfirm comparison.

Accounting will no doubt continue to evolve in adapting to ever-changing business conditions; but the principles and approaches used in this book should help you to keep up with the latest practice. The basic aim of financial accounts, to present a 'true and fair view' of a company's affairs, will probably not change; even though accounting information alone cannot fully cover *all* important aspects of a business. And management accounting, which is less fettered by conventions, will surely continue to aim to help business managers make better, more profitable, decisions.

Work Section

A. Revision Questions

A1 What was Woodcraft's main financial objective for 1983/84?

A2 What did Mr Sidney, Woodcraft's sales manager, expect to happen to the company's market share in 1983/84?

A3 What three aspects of production did Mr Potter, the production manager, expect the projected increase in sales volume to affect?

A4 From which two sources did Mr Addison, the accountant, derive the figures for standard direct cost of production?

A5 What four aspects of investment in assets did Mr Addison investigate in order to prepare the cash budget for 1983/84?

A6 What problem arose when Woodcraft's managers reviewed the overall consequences of the original budget figures for 1983/84?

A7 What two adjustments were proposed to raise the budgeted return on net assets from 8.9 per cent to 10.7 per cent in 1983/84?

A8 Why did Mr Addison expect problems in putting together a detailed operating budget?

A9 Which two sorts of budgets did Mr Addison recognise were both vital for successful planning?

A10 Why were selling and administrative expenses shown only in total on the monthly profit budget?

A11 How did Woodcraft's managers plan to finance the company's short-term need for cash at the beginning of 1983/84?

A12 How did they plan to finance the permanent need for funds arising out of the company's expansion?

A13 What ratios were the managers concerned about from the point of view of minimising risk?

A14 Why might control reports be needed more often than once a month?

A15 What do you understand by 'management by exception'?

A16 In what respects may internal management accounts be of more help to managers than external financial accounts?

A17 What are three basic standards of comparison for a firm's ratios?

A18 Into what four main sets of ratios can a firm's return on net assets ratio be sub-divided by the 'pyramid of ratios'?

A19 Name in order the ratios by which Mr Addison was able to pin down the main reasons for Woodcraft's shortfall in return on net assets.

A20 What two actions should the Woodcraft managers responsible take after *what* has apparently gone wrong has been identified?

A21 Why may it be useful to study the pyramid of ratios even if the return on net assets ratio appears to be satisfactory?

A22 In what two respects was it suggested that authors have 'budgets'?

A23 Suggest two respects each in which the following may, in effect, have 'budgets': (a) doctors; (b) airline pilots; (c) cooks.

A24 Why is interfirm comparison useful?

A25 Give three examples of questions which interfirm comparison may help to answer.

A26 Name three potential difficulties with interfirm comparisons.

A27 Name two basic ways in which a firm could try to increase its return on net assets.

A28 Name three aspects of marketing which may help to increase sales.

A29 Name three aspects of production management which may help to reduce expenses.

A30 Name two reasons why management of working capital may be important.

B. Exercises and Case Studies

B1 Assume that Woodcraft Ltd's net assets at 31 March, 1982 amounted to £130,000, and that 1982/83 profit was £15,000.
   a. Calculate and compare the 1983/84 budget with the 1982/83 actual return on net assets ratio, using 'average' not 'end-of-year' net assets.
   b. Do you regard the change brought about by this different method of calculation as significant? Why or why not?

B2 Refer to Figs 11.1 to 11.4.
   a. Calculate what revised profit estimate would have resulted if Mr Sidney had proposed to reduce selling prices by 10 per cent and expected as a result to increase sales volume by one third for all three product lines (with no change in selling expenses).
   b. Comment on your answer, with special reference to the distinction between total sales revenue and total contribution.

B3 The adjustment to selling policy as a result of Mr Sidney's suggestions for 1983/84 affected the budgeted profit but not the budgeted net assets. In what respects, if any, might you have expected net assets to be affected by the change? Try to quantify your answer.

Budgeting in Action

B4 Refer to the interfirm comparison in Fig. 11.9 (p. 196).
  a. Which aspects of Woodcraft Ltd's operations seem to call for special further examination? Why?
  b. What accounts for firm C's high return on net assets?
  c. Why do you suppose that firm B's asset turnover ratio is lower than Woodcraft's? (Hint: look at ratios 9 and 10.)
  d. If you could obtain *two* further pieces of information about the five companies whose ratios are listed, what would you ask for? Why?

B5 *Spot the industry*. Set out below are 'balance sheet percentages' for business enterprises in five different industries. Only the assets part of the current cost balance sheet is shown, and any intangible assets (such as goodwill) have been omitted. The items have been expressed as a percentage of the total 'net assets' in each case; and to provide an (important) extra clue, the sales revenue (also expressed as a percentage of net assets) is given as well. The five industries concerned are (in alphabetical order): 1. Distillers; 2. Electricity generation; 3. Engineering; 4. Motor vehicle manufacture; 5. Retail store.

The problem, of course, is to identify each of the above industries with one of the five lettered columns of balance sheet percentages. In attempting this, please write down your main reasons for your suggested answers.

	A	B	C	D	E
Tangible fixed assets:					
Current cost	109	212	53	170	127
Accum. depreciation	7	129	22	77	64
Net book value	102	83	31	93	63
Trade investments	4	1	6	—	9
Working capital:	(6)	16	63	7	28
Stocks	18	57	58	7	40
Debtors	6	29	10	5	33
Liquid resources	(1)	(13)	6	—	(6)
Current liabilities	(29)	(57)	(11)	(5)	(39)
Total net assets	100	100	100	100	100
Sales revenue	278	202	36	25	172

B6 A, B and C are small producers of plastic containers who take part in an interfirm comparison scheme. You are a member of firm A's management. In the light of the information given, suggest, with reasons, areas where your firm might usefully examine its affairs. (Hint: Employ a few key ratios where necessary.)

End of year balance sheets (£'000)

	A		B		C	
Fixed assets						
Freehold property	178		146		166	
Plant and machinery	110		206		167	
Motor vehicles	210		96		83	
		498		448		416
Current assets						
Stocks†	517		313		244	
Debtors	232		185		128	
Cash at bank	378		74		62	
		1,127		572		434
		1,625		1,020		850
Shareholders' funds						
Ordinary issued shares		700		500		500
Reserves		112		225		110
		812		725		610
Debentures		300		20		10
Current liabilities						
Bank overdraft	250		—		—	
Trade creditors	170		160		140	
Tax	33		75		50	
Dividends	60		40		40	
		513		275		230
		1,625		1,020		850

* Including work-in-progress: A £100,000; B £95,000; C £82,000.

Profit and loss accounts

	A		B		C	
	(£'000)	(%)	(£'000)	(%)	(£'000)	(%)
Sales revenue	1,052	100	1,373	100	1,040	100
Cost of goods sold:						
Direct labour	200	19	192	14	156	15
Direct materials	210	20	333	24	208	20
Variable overheads	126	12	164	12	125	12
Fixed factory overheads	179	17	164	12	145	14
Marketing expenses	95	9	163	12	156	15
Admin. expenses*	158	15	165	12	125	12
	968	92	1,181	86	915	88
Net profit before tax	84	8	192	14	125	12
	1,052	100	1,373	100	1,040	100

* Including interest charges: A £27,000; B £2,000; C £1,000.

C. Essay Questions

C1 Why does business planning require attention to both cash and profit?
C2 Discuss the advantages and disadvantages of using 'rolling budgets'.
C3 Explain to someone who knows nothing about accounting what 'variance analysis' means.
C4 Explain how changing the sales budget may affect the cash budget.
C5 What are the benefits of variance analysis?
C6 How can the 'pyramid of ratios' approach be used as a tool of management control?
C7 What problems would you expect to find in preparing and using a budget for a research and development department?
C8 Write a brief memo to persuade your firm's managing director that participating in an interfirm comparison scheme would be worthwhile.
C9 Discuss the main potential difficulties in interfirm comparisons.
C10 How can the budgeting process allow for unknown future rates of general inflation?

Appendices

Appendix 1.

Retail Price Index since 1970 (January 1974 = 100)

	March	June	Sept.	Dec.	Average for year ending March	Dec.
1970	71	73	74	76	70	73
1971	78	80	81	82	75	80
1972	84	85	87	89	82	86
1973	90	93	95	98	87	94
1974	103	109	111	117	96	109
1975	124	137	141	146	114	135
1976	151	156	161	168	142	157
1977	176	184	186	188	163	182
1978	192	197	200	204	186	197
1979	211	220	233	239	202	224
1980	252	266	270	276	234	264
1981	284	296	301	309	272	295
1982	313	323	323	326	303	320
1983	328	335	339	343	324	335

Appendix 2.

Professional Bodies and Qualifications

ACA	Associate of ICAEW (English Chartered Accountants)
ACCA	Associate of the Association of Certified Accountants
ACertA	Association of Certified Accountants
ACMA	Associate of the Institute of Cost and Management Accountants
CA	Chartered Accountant (Scotland)
CCAB	Council of Combined Accountancy Bodies
CIPFA	Chartered Institute of Public Finance and Accountancy
FCA	Fellow of ICAEW (English Chartered Accountants)
FCCA	Fellow of the Association of Certified Accountants
FCMA	Fellow of the Institute of Cost and Management Accountants
ICAEW	Institute of Chartered Accountants in England and Wales
ICMA	Institute of Cost and Management Accountants
ICAS	Institute of Chartered Accountants in Scotland

Appendix 3.

Accounting Abbreviations and Acronyms

BS	Balance Sheet
BV	Book Value
CA	Current Assets
CCA	Current Cost Accounting
CL	Current Liabilities
COGS	Cost of Goods Sold
COSA	Cost of Sales Adjustment
CPP	Constant Purchasing Power
DPS	Dividends Per Share
EBIT	Earnings Before Interest and Taxes
ED	Exposure Draft
EPS	Earnings Per Share
FA	Fixed Assets
FG	Finished Goods
FIFO	First In First Out
HC	Historical Cost
LIFO	Last In First Out
Ltd	Limited
MI	Minority Interests
MV	Market Value
NBV	Net Book Value
NRV	Net Realisable Value
P&L	Profit and Loss
PAT	Profit After Tax
PBT	Profit Before Tax
P/E	Price/Earnings (ratio)
plc	public limited company
RC	Replacement Cost
RE	Retained Earnings
RM	Raw Materials
ROCE	Return On Capital Employed
ROI	Return On Investment
RONA	Return On Net Assets
ROTA	Return On Total Assets
RPI	Retail Price Index
SL	Straight Line (depreciation)
SSAP	Statement of Standard Accounting Practice
SYD	Sum of the Years' Digits (depreciation)
VAT	Value Added Tax
WC	Working Capital
WIP	Work-In-Progress

Glossary

*An asterisk * refers to another item described in the Glossary.*

A-Adjustments: Inflation accounting * adjustments (either CPP or CCA to the accounts of a single period; as opposed to adjustments needed to make inflation-adjusted accounts comparable between years (B-adjustments*).

Accounts: Profit and loss account* for a period, balance sheet* as at the end of that period, and notes to the accounts*, together with the auditors' report*. (For larger companies, also a funds flow statement*.)

Accounts Payable: = creditors. Amounts due to suppliers for goods or services purchased on credit.

Accounts Receivable: = debtors. Amounts due from customers for goods or services sold on credit.

Accruals Concept: The principle in accounting of recording transactions in the period to which they relate, rather than when cash is paid or received in respect of them.

Accrued Charge: Liability* not yet invoiced*, often relating to period costs*.

Accumulated Depreciation: The total part of fixed asset* cost (or valuation) cumulatively charged as depreciation* expense since acquisition.

Acid Test: Ratio of quick assets* (debtors* plus liquid resources*) to current liabilities*. Rule of thumb: should normally be 1.0 or more.

Allocation: Allotment of cost* to a cost centre*.

Amortisation: Depreciation*, usually of an intangible fixed asset* such as patent rights, leases or goodwill*, or of a 'wasting asset' such as a mine.

Appropriation Account: Final part of the overall profit and loss account*, disclosing how the profit* for a period has been 'appropriated' between dividends*, transfers to special reserves*, and retained profits*.

Asset: Valuable resource owned by a business, acquired at a measurable money cost.

Asset Turnover: Ratio of sales revenue* divided by net assets*. Asset turnover × profit margin* = return on net assets*.

Associated Company: Company in which another company (i) owns at least 20 per cent of the ordinary shares*, but not enough (more than 50 per cent) to make it a subsidiary*; and (ii) participates in management.

Audit: External examination of financial accounts* (and records and systems) by independent professional accountants, to report whether accounts give a true and fair view*. See also: internal auditor*.

Glossary

Auditor: Independent professional accountant appointed by shareholders* to check company's financial accounts*.

Authorised Share Capital: Amount of share capital (both ordinary* and preference*) authorised (by shareholders*) to be issued. Any excess of authorised over issued share capital* is unissued share capital.

Average Cost: (a) Total cost* of a product or process divided by the number of units produced. (b) Method of stock valuation (see 7.2.2).

Bad Debt: Debt reckoned to be uncollectible.

B-Adjustments: Inflation accounting* adjustments needed to make financial figures comparable between years. They may apply to many financial figures, including A-adjusted* accounts (either CPP* or CCA*).

Balance Sheet: Classified statement of financial position of a business, showing assets*, liabilities*, and shareholders' funds* at a particular date. In UK now normally in vertical* rather than horizontal* format.

Bank Overdraft: Amount due to bank on current account, legally payable on demand, and included in current liabilities*.

Bankruptcy: Legal process occurring when person is unable to pay liabilities* due. Equivalent process for companies is called liquidation* or winding-up*

Below the Line: The part of the profit and loss account* below the line showing profit after tax* for a period; containing extraordinary items* as well as the appropriation account*. See Fig. 5.14 (p. 71).

Book-keeping: That part of accounting which deals with recording actual transactions in financial terms, in books or maybe on cards, tape or disc.

Book Value: Balance sheet* amount shown for asset*. Under historical cost* accounting usually represents not 'value', but 'costs less any amounts written off*'.

Budget: Financial or quantitative statement, prepared and agreed prior to the budget period by those responsible, reflecting the policies to be pursued during that period to attain agreed objectives.

Capital: (a) Issued ordinary share capital*. (b) = capital employed*. (c) Contrasted with revenue*.

Capital Allowance: Tax equivalent of depreciation* of fixed assets*, calculated according to Inland Revenue rules.

Capital Employed: Shareholders' funds* plus long-term liabilities*. = net assets*, since balance sheets* balance.

Capital Expenditure: Expenditure* treated as an asset* on balance sheet*, because it is being matched* with expected future benefit; in contrast to revenue expenditure*, which is treated as an expense* in the profit and loss account*.

Capitalise: To record expenditure* as an asset*, in contrast to writing it off* as an expense*.

Cash: Legal tender banknotes and coins. In accounting, 'cash' on balance sheet* usually includes amounts 'owed' to firms by banks. See liquid resources*.

Cash Discount: Reduction in price of goods sold offered in return for prompt settlement by debtor.

Cash Flow: Usually defined as 'retained profits* plus depreciation*' for a period, which is 'internally-generated' cash flow.

Certified Accountant: Member of Association of Certified Accountants.

Chartered Accountant: Member of Institute of Chartered Accountants (of England and Wales, Scotland, or Ireland).

Consistency: Principle in accounting, and other statistics, of treating similar items in the same way, to produce meaningful results and to allow comparisons over time.

Consolidated Accounts: Accounts for a group of companies, 'consolidated' by combining the separate assets* and liabilities* of all subsidiaries* with those of the 'holding' ('parent') company.

Constant Purchasing Power (CPP) Accounting: Method of inflation accounting* which treats money of different dates as 'foreign currencies', using the Retail Price Index* as the exchange rate*.

Contribution: Sales revenue* less variable costs*, perhaps on a per-unit basis. Also called 'variable profit'.

Control: Process of managing the present and immediate future. Often consists of comparing actual performance with budget*; investigating *reasons* for any variance*; and taking *action* to improve matters.

Controllable: Cost* reckoned to be under control of responsible manager, the extent perhaps depending on time period involved.

Conventions: Accounting practices found useful by experience: e.g. double entry, separate entity, money terms, historical cost. See **3.1.2**.

Convertible Loan: Loan convertible at holder's option into ordinary shares* on pre-arranged terms. Shown in balance sheet* as long-term liability* up to date of conversion actually occurring (after which it is split between ordinary share capital* and share premium*).

Corporation Tax: Tax payable by companies on taxable profits*, either at 45 per cent (for 1984/85), or at reduced 30 per cent rate for smaller companies.

Cost: Amount given up in exchange for goods or services received. May be treated in accounts either as an asset* or as an expense*. Usually what is given up is either cash* or a promise to pay cash in future; but see also opportunity cost*. Not normally employed without some further explanatory qualifying adjective, e.g. variable cost, historical cost, marginal cost, etc.

Cost and Management Accountant: Member of the Institute of Cost and Management Accountants.

Cost/Benefit Analysis: Process of trying to assess 'profitability' of something where either costs or benefits or both are hard to measure in financial terms. Often applied to social costs or benefits.

Cost Centre: Unit or operation in respect of which costs* are determined.

Cost Of Goods Sold (COGS): Costs* identifiable with stocks*, e.g. raw materials and components, direct labour, production overheads; but excluding selling expenses and administrative expenses.

Glossary

Cost Of Sales Adjustment (COSA): In current cost accounting*, difference between the current cost of goods sold in period and their historical cost*. Usually represents an extra deduction from profit in current cost accounting*; but if specific prices are falling it might *increase* HC profit*.

Cost-Push Inflation: Type of inflation held to be caused by firms 'passing on' increases in costs* (e.g. from wages, imports, taxes). Depends partly on absence of competition, and requires an 'accommodating' increase in money supply.

Credit Note: An invoice* crediting instead of charging customer, often to correct or reduce an amount invoiced earlier.

Creditors: = Accounts payable. Amounts due to suppliers for goods or services purchased on credit. In balance sheet* may also include accrued charges*.

Critical Resource: Sometimes called 'limiting factor'. Factor of production which, at a particular time, may limit activity, often due to shortage of supply in the short term.

Cumulative: Means that any past unpaid preference* dividends must be made good before any ordinary* dividend may be paid.

Currency Debasement: Process of reducing purchasing power* of currency, originally by fraudulently adding base metal to precious metal, now by more sophisticated methods.

Current Asset: Cash* or any asset* expected to be converted into cash, or consumed in the normal course of business, within 12 months from the date of the balance sheet*. Examples: stocks, debtors.

Current Cost Accounting (CCA): System of current value* accounting recommended by government committee in 1975. Main features: continues to use money as unit of account* (hence not strictly a method of accounting for general inflation*, though usually so described), and shows assets* and expenses* at current replacement cost* instead of historical cost*.

Current Liabilities: Amounts owing to others, expected to be paid within 12 months from date of balance sheet*, e.g. creditors*, bank overdraft*, tax, dividends*.

Current Ratio: Measure of liquidity*, current assets* divided by current liabilities*. Rule of thumb: should normally be between 1½ and 2.

Current Value: Usually means current replacement cost* of asset*, but may refer to net realisable value*. Unlike historical cost*, which is usually a definite known fact, current value is usually only a hypothetical estimate.

Days' Sales in Debtors: Debtors* divided by daily sales (i.e. by annual sales revenue* divided by 365). Ratio indicating how much trade credit customers are taking.

Debenture: Long-term liability*. (Latin: 'They are owed.')

Debtors: = Accounts receivable. Amounts due from customers for goods or services sold on credit. In balance sheet* often includes prepayments*.

Declining Balance Depreciation: Method of writing off* cost* of fixed asset* as expense* over its economic life by charging constant percentage of (declining) net book value* each year.

Demand-Pull Inflation: Type of inflation* held to be caused by excessive aggregate money demand in relation to output. 'Too much money chasing too few goods.'

Depreciation: Process of writing off* as expense* the cost* (or valuation) of fixed asset* to spread total cost over its economic life.

Direct Cost: Cost that is directly *identifiable* with particular process or product.

Directors' Report: Report required with annual accounts*, containing certain information if not published elsewhere. See 2.4.2.

Dividend: Cash payable to ordinary* (or preference*) shareholders* out of profits*, if declared by a company's directors.

Dividend Cover: Profits* divided by dividends* for a year (maybe on a 'per share' basis).

Dividends Per Share: Ordinary dividends* divided by number of ordinary shares in issue.

Dividend Yield: Dividends per share* for a year divided by market price per share.

Double-Entry Accounting: System of recording business transactions based on the idea that there are two aspects to all transactions: a 'source' of funds and a 'use' of funds.

Earnings Per Share (EPS): Profit after tax divided by number of ordinary shares in issue.

Economies of Scale: Reductions in average costs* per unit arising from increase in scale of operation, e.g. due to greater technical efficiency of larger plant sizes, spreading of fixed costs* over more units, etc.

Equity: Owners' equity*, shareholders' funds*. Usually refers only to ordinary* (not to preference*) shareholders*. Residual financial interest in a firm's assets.

Exceptional Items: Items in profit and loss account* which are unusual on account of their size, deducted in calculating operating profit, in contrast to extraordinary items*, which are unusual on account of their nature, and are charged below the line*. See 5.4.6 (c).

Exchange Rate: Price of currency unit in terms of a foreign currency.

Expenditure: Amount spent, = cost*. May be either revenue* (expense*), or capital* (asset*).

Expense: Amount written off against profit* in an accounting period in respect of goods or services consumed.

Exposure Draft (ED): Proposed SSAP*, published for criticism and comment before final version appears.

Extraordinary Items: Profit and loss account* items which appear below the line* on account of being: (a) material, (b) of a type expected not to recur frequently, and (c) derived from events or transactions outside the ordinary activities of the business. See 5.4.6 (c).

Feedback: Link between planning* and control*; modification of an activity as a result of comparing actual result with budget*.

Glossary

Final Dividend: Second dividend for a year, unpaid at year-end; when added to interim dividend★ for the year (normally paid in that year), makes up total dividends★ for the year.

Financial Accounting: External accounting, leading to published accounts★ for shareholders★ and other outsiders.

Financial Year: The 12-month period for which a firm chooses to prepare its financial accounts★.

Finished Goods: Stocks★ of completed manufactured products, held for sale.

First In First Out (FIFO): Method of valuing stock★, assuming most recent purchases remain in stock at the end of an accounting period.

Fixed Asset: Resource, either tangible or intangible★, with relatively long life, intended to be held for use in producing goods or services, not for sale in the ordinary course of business.

Fixed Cost: = Period cost★. Cost which, within the 'relevant range' of output, is fixed for a given period whatever the level of output.

Flexible Budget: System of 'flexing' budget when actual sales volume differs from original budget★, so that variable costs★ in flexed budget represent expected amount at *actual* sales volume. See **10.5.3**.

Full Costing: Costing method which allocates indirect (overhead) costs★ to products or cost centres★, in addition to direct costs★. Required for valuing stocks★ in financial accounts. Contrast marginal costing★.

Funds Flow Statement: Accounting statement required for larger companies, showing sources and uses ('applications') of funds for a period.

Gearing: Proportion of long-term liabilities★ in capital structure (possibly including bank overdraft★) represents *financial* gearing. Proportion of fixed costs★ to total operating expenses represents operating (or 'business') gearing.

Gearing Ratio: Long-term liabilities★ (perhaps plus bank overdrafts★) divided by capital employed★ (long-term liabilities plus shareholders' funds★).

Going Concern: Assumption that a business entity will continue in operation for the foreseeable future (as opposed to being wound up★).

Goodwill: Excess of purchase price paid on acquisition of another firm over net book value★ of its tangible net assets.

Group Accounts: = consolidated accounts★.

Historical Cost (HC): Traditional accounting convention of showing assets★ and expenses★ at actual past money cost, rather than (a) at hypothetical current value★ (as in current cost accounting★) or (b) at re-stated past cost in terms of constant purchasing power units (as in CPP accounting★).

Horizontal Format: Old form of balance sheet★, showing net assets★ (on the right) and capital employed★ (on the left) side by side, rather than underneath each other, as in the modern vertical format★.

Indexation: Process of linking money amounts (either actual payments or accounting entries) to the rate of inflation★ as measured by the Retail Price Index★; as in government securities, tax thresholds, pensions, constant purchasing power★ accounting.

Indirect Cost: Cost* not directly identifiable with product or cost centre*; may be allocated* on some reasonable basis, in full costing*, or not allocated at all, in marginal costing*.

Inflation: Rise in the 'general' (weighted average) level of money prices, usually measured by the (annual) rate of increase in the Retail Price Index*. See Appendix 1 on p. 204.

Inflation Accounting: Constant Purchasing Power* accounting. (Current Cost Accounting* is *not* a method of adjusting accounts* for general inflation*.)

Intangible Asset: Valuable, relatively long-life non-tangible asset* owned by a business, acquired at a measurable money cost*, and not yet written off* (either against reserves* or against profit*). Examples: leases, patents, goodwill*.

Interest: Compensation for borrowing or lending money for a period of time, comprising (a) pure time-preference, (b) risk premium, and (c) inflation premium.

Interest Cover: Measure of financial gearing*; profit before interest and tax divided by interest expense (usually only on long-term liabilities*, but perhaps including bank overdraft* interest).

Interim Accounts: Financial accounts prepared for publication to shareholders, covering a period shorter than 12 months, and not subject to audit. Required, in abbreviated form, for larger companies.

Interim Dividend: First (of two) dividends* payable in respect of a year's profits*, the second being the final dividend*.

Internal Auditor: Employee responsible for reviewing the internal accounting system, preferably independent of the firm's accountants. Not to be confused with the external auditor.

Inventory: = stock*.

Invoice: Document showing details of goods sold, used as the basis for accounting records both by buyer and (a copy) by seller.

Issued Share Capital: Legal capital of a company, arising from issue of shares* (ordinary and preference) to shareholders*.

Last In First Out (LIFO): Method of valuing stock*, not used in UK, which assumes that most recent purchases have been used up in the current accounting period, leaving earlier purchases in stock at the end of the period.

Learning Curve: Phenomenon where production costs based on time may fall as producers learn.

Liability: Amount owing to a creditor*; often in respect of goods or services purchased, but also applies to tax, proposed dividends, or long-term loans.

Limited Company: Form of business organisation in which liability of owners (shareholders*) for the company's liabilities* is *limited* to the nominal amount* (fully paid) of their shares*. Abbreviated to 'Ltd'; in larger companies to 'plc' (= public limited company).

Liquidation: = winding-up*. Legal process of ending a company's life, by selling all its assets* for cash*, paying off the creditors*; and distributing any residual amount to the shareholders*.

Glossary

Liquidity: Extent to which liquid resources* are available to meet liabilities as they become due. Time is the crucial element here.

Liquid Resources: Cash in hand and at bank, plus short-term marketable securities.

Long Run: Period of time in which all fixed costs* are reckoned to be variable.

Long-Term Liability: Liability due for settlement more than 12 months after the date of the balance sheet*.

Loss: Negative profit*, where expenses* exceed sales revenue*. Though not the aim, often the result of business.

Management Accounting: Accounting internally for management's own use, as opposed to external financial accounting* for shareholders* and other outsiders.

Marginal Costing: Costing method which allocates only variable costs*, not fixed costs*, to products. (Also sometimes called 'direct costing', but this may mislead, since a 'direct' cost can be fixed, or an indirect cost variable.)

Master Budget: Overall aggregation of various budgets for parts of a business, perhaps for part of a year, into a single profit and loss account budget, balance sheet budget, and cash budget for the whole company.

Matching Principle: The accounting principle according to which expenditures* are carried forward as assets on the balance sheet* only if there are expected to be sales revenues* in future periods against which they can be matched. Expenditures which cannot be matched against sales revenues, or which can be matched against sales in the current period, are written off* as expenses* in the current period's profit and loss account*.

Minority Interests: Equity* interests of minority shareholders* in subsidiary companies* which are less than wholly-owned, shown in the holding company's group accounts* (a) as a long-term 'liability' on the balance sheet*; (b) as a deduction from profit after tax in the profit and loss account*.

Monetary Asset/Liability: Asset receivable or liability payable in money (as distinct from real* assets, such as stocks* or tangible fixed assets*).

Monetary Gain/Loss: In Constant Purchasing Power* accounting the profit arising in terms of constant purchasing power from owing money amounts (or the *loss* arising from being owed money amounts or holding cash*).

Net Assets: = capital employed*. Total assets less current liabilities*, i.e. fixed assets* plus working capital*.

Net Book Value (NBV): Cost (or valuation) of fixed assets*, less accumulated depreciation*.

Net Current Assets: = working capital*. Current assets* less current liabilities*.

Net Realisable Value (NRV): Net amount for which asset* could currently be sold; if less than cost*, used for valuing stocks*.

Nominal Value: = 'par value'. Face value of security or share, unrelated to current market value. Usually refers either to ordinary shares*, with nominal value often of £1 or 25p each, or to government securities, with nominal value of £100.

Non-Controllable: Applied to a cost*, means not easily controllable by a manager, especially in the short run, e.g. local rates.

Non-Variable Cost: Cost which is neither fixed* nor variable*: it may change (not stay the same), but not necessarily in proportion to output, e.g. advertising, research. = 'discretionary' cost.

Notes to the Accounts: Detailed notes forming part of the financial statements, explaining many items in more detail than on the face of the accounts.

Opportunity Cost: The hypothetical revenue or other benefit that might have been obtained by the 'next best' alternative course of action, which was forgone in favour of the course actually taken.

Ordinary Share Capital: Capital of a company, consisting of issued ordinary shares*. See also authorised share capital*.

Overhead Cost: = indirect cost*. A cost not directly identifiable with a product or cost centre*.

Owners' Equity: = shareholders' funds.

Partnership: Form of enterprise with two or more partners (owners), each with unlimited personal liability to meet the firm's debts in full.

Period Cost: = fixed cost*, incurred in a period regardless of volume of output.

Petty Cash: Notes and coins. 'Cash' in accounts also includes amounts due from banks on current and deposit accounts. See also liquid resources*.

Planning: Establishing objectives and formulating policies to achieve them. Budgets* are short-term plans, often for one year ahead, expressed in financial terms.

Preference Share Capital: Form of share capital entitled to fixed rate of dividend* (usually cumulative*) if declared, and to repayment of a stated amount of money on liquidation*, with priority over ordinary shares.

Prepayment: Expense* paid in advance of the period to which it relates, shown as a current asset* on balance sheet*, often combined with debtors*.

Price/Earnings (P/E) Ratio: Market price per ordinary share* divided by the most recent annual earnings per share*.

Price Variance: Variance* due to difference between budget* price and actual price, calculated using *actual* volume. See also volume variance*.

Product Cost: Cost attributed to product, maybe equivalent to direct cost*.

Profit: Surplus of sales revenue* over expenses* for a period.

Profit and Loss (P&L) Account: Accounting statement showing result (profit or loss) of business operations for a period.

Profit Centre: Business unit with manager responsible for sales revenue* as well as for costs*.

Profit Margin: Operating profit before interest and tax, as a percentage of sales revenue*. Profit margin × asset turnover* = return on net assets*.

Prudence: = conservatism. An accounting concept sometimes clashing with the convention of consistency*. Inclination of accountants to recognise sales revenue* (and therefore profit*) only when reasonable certainty exists, but to make provision for all known liabilities (losses and expenses) whether their amount is known with certainty or is a best estimate.

Public Limited Company (plc): Name given to public limited company, in place of former 'Limited company' (abbreviated to 'Ltd').

Published Accounts: Accounts★, usually for a year, of a public company.

Purchasing Power: = value of money. What money will buy in real★ terms, usually measured by the 'basket of goods and services' comprising the constituent items in the Retail Price Index★.

Pyramid of Ratios: Related network of financial and accounting ratios, stemming from analysis of return on net assets★ ratio.

Qualified (Accountant): Professional accountant, member of one of the six main accountancy bodies.

Qualified (Audit Report): Audit report including a 'qualification', i.e. an explanation of, or expression of disagreement with, some aspect of the financial accounts★ (for which the company's directors are responsible). See 2.4.6.

Quick Assets: Assets★ which can quickly be turned into cash, e.g. cash itself, marketable securities, and debtors. Hence the acid test★ ratio is sometimes called the 'quick ratio'.

Ratio Analysis: Expressing one amount (often financial) in terms of another, and using the result as a basis for comparison, either over time, with budget, or with other firms.

Raw Materials: Input to manufacturing process, held for a time as stocks★.

Realisation: The concept in accounting that sales revenue★ (and therefore profit★) is recognised only when it is 'realised' in cash or in other assets the ultimate cash realisation of which can be assessed with reasonable certainty.

'Real' Terms: Amounts expressed after adjustments to allow for inflation★ (either CCA★ or CPP★), as opposed to HC★ money amounts. 'Real' assets are those not consisting of *money* amounts (e.g. stocks★ and fixed assets★).

Replacement Cost: Amount for which it is estimated that an asset held could currently be replaced. Basis for CCA★. *Not* the expected ultimate cost when the asset is actually replaced in the future.

Reserves: Shareholders' funds other than issued share capital, including: share premium★, revaluation reserve★, cumulative retained profits★.

Residual Value: Net realisable value★ of fixed asset★ at the end of its economic life (to the present owner), needing to be estimated in advance for purposes of calculating depreciation expense★. Often, for convenience, assumed to be zero.

Retail Price Index (RPI): Monthly government statistic measuring the weighted average of money prices of representative 'basket of goods'. Based on January 1974 = 100. See Appendix 1 on p. 204. The year-on-year rate of increase in the RPI is usually regarded as 'the' rate of (general) inflation★.

Retained Profits: = retained earnings. Amount of profits★ earned by company (either for current period or cumulatively) and not yet paid out in dividends★ to shareholders★.

Return on Equity: Profit after tax divided by shareholders' funds*.

Return on Net Assets: Operating profit before interest and tax divided by net assets* (= by capital employed*). Apex of pyramid of ratios*. = profit margin* × asset turnover*. Also called 'primary efficiency ratio'.

Revaluation: Process of including asset* in accounts* at estimated current value* when higher than historical cost*. (Not to be confused with revaluation of a currency.)

Revaluation Reserve: Increase in shareholders' funds* needed to 'balance' increase in net book value* of assets* due to revaluation*.

Revenue: (a) = sales revenue*. (b) = Inland Revenue, the tax authorities. (c) = as contrasted to capital*, relating to the profit and loss account* rather than to the balance sheet*.

Revenue Centre: Business unit whose manager is responsible for sales revenue*.

Revenue Expenditure: Expense*, charged in profit and loss account*, as opposed to capital expenditure* which relates to assets*.

Rolling Budget: Budget* which is continually updated by a new period being added at the end as the most recent past period is dropped.

Sales Revenue: = turnover*. A firm's trading income for a period from selling its products.

Secured Loan: Liability* 'secured' on asset, with lender having legal right to proceeds from sale of that asset on liquidation*, up to amount of the liability. Any balance of liability is 'unsecured'; while any balance of proceeds swells pool of funds available for unsecured creditors.

Semi-Variable Cost: Cost* which is partly fixed* and partly variable*.

Shareholders: Usually refers to ordinary shareholders, who own company in proportion to number of shares held; but legally may also refer to preference shareholders.

Shareholders' Funds: = owners' equity. Amount shown in company balance sheet* as attributable to ordinary (and sometimes preference) shareholders.

Share Premium: Excess of issue price over nominal value* of shares.

Shares: see ordinary share capital*, preference share capital*.

Short Run: Period within which not all factors of production are variable.

Standard Cost: Predetermined cost, maybe per unit, that 'should' be attained.

Statements of Standard Accounting Practice (SSAPs): Mandatory requirements issued by accountancy bodies regarding accounting treatment of certain items, e.g. SSAP 9 on stock valuation, SSAP 12 on depreciation.

Stewardship: Original basis for financial accounting*, to account regularly to dispersed shareholders*. Partly intended for protection of steward.

Stocks: = inventories*. Holdings of goods, either as raw materials and components, work-in-progress*, or finished goods*, with a view to sale (perhaps after further processing) in the ordinary course of business.

Stock Appreciation: Part of apparent HC* accounting profit on stocks* due solely to an increase in their price, not to a 'real' increase (in volume).

Stock Exchange: Market for buying and selling securities.

Glossary

Stock Relief: Tax allowance intended to prevent corporation tax* being charged on stock appreciation*; abolished in 1984 Finance Act.

Stock Turnover: Annual sales revenue* divided by value of stocks* held; ideally calculated using cost of goods sold.

Straight-Line Depreciation: Method of writing off* cost* of fixed asset* in equal instalments over its estimated economic life. If life is n years, annual depreciation expense* will be $1/n \times$ (cost − residual value*).

Subsidiary: Company most or all of whose equity* shares are owned by another (its 'holding' or 'parent' company).

Sum-of-the-Years' Digits (SYD): Method of accelerated depreciation* of fixed assets*. If life is 4 years, sum of years' digits is 10 (= 1 + 2 + 3 + 4); so first year depreciation is 4/10 of cost, second year depreciation is 3/10 of cost, and so on.

Taxable Profit: Differs from 'profit before tax' in financial accounts* (a) by deducting tax capital allowances* instead of (book) depreciation, and (b) by deducting any special allowances, such as stock relief*. Also takes account of any accounting expenses 'disallowed' by tax authorities, and of any timing differences.

Taxation: In company accounts, means UK corporation tax on taxable profits, plus any foreign tax on profits earned abroad. Excludes other taxes, such as local rates, employers' national insurance, etc., which are included in operating expenses.

Trade Investment: Investment (usually long-term) in another company connected with the business. If more than 20 per cent of that company's equity*, would normally count as associated company*; and if more than 50 per cent, as subsidiary*.

Trading Account: Name sometimes given to part of the profit and loss account* ending with gross profit (or loss) before interest and tax.

Transfer Price: Internal price at which goods or services are transferred from one part of a firm to another. Can be important in evaluating performance of profit centres*.

Trend: Underlying pattern of a series of figures over a significant period of time. Does not necessarily imply continuing momentum: 'trends go on until they stop'.

True and Fair View: Aim of financial accounting, implying that generally accepted accounting concepts and conventions have been followed.

Turnover: = sales revenue*, the 'turnover' of the products being sold.

Unit of Account: Numeraire in accounting. Traditionally the monetary unit (as in HC, and, interestingly, in CCA*); but in times of inflation* an alternative − the constant purchasing power unit − has been suggested (as in constant purchasing power* accounting).

Usage Method: Method of depreciating fixed assets*, based on total number of 'units' produced in a period divided by the total number expected to be produced over its economic life. Depreciation expense, on this basis, becomes variable* instead of fixed*.

Value Added: Difference between sales revenue★ and cost of bought-in materials and services. Roughly = profit plus wages.

Variable Cost: Cost which varies directly in proportion to output.

Variance: Difference between budget★ and actual amount. (Not to be confused with a statistical variance, which is a dispersion around the mean (average) value of a group of data.)

Variance Analysis: Quantitative comparison between budgeted and actual results for a period. Basic components usually refer to quantity (or volume or usage) and price (or rate or cost).

Vertical Format: Modern form of balance sheet★, showing net assets★ and capital employed★ underneath each other (in either order), rather than side by side (as in horizontal format★).

Volume Variance: Variance★ between budget★ and actual attributable to difference between budget and actual volume (both priced at *budget* price).

Winding-up: = liquidation★. Legal process of ending a company's life.

Working Capital: = net current assets★. Excess of current assets★ over current liabilities★.

Work-In-Progress (WIP): Partly-completed stocks★ in manufacturing process; valued at lower of cost or net realisable value★ (but see 7.3.3 for long-term contracts).

Write off: To charge an expenditure★ as an expense★ in the profit and loss account★, as opposed to capitalising★ it, i.e. recording it as an asset★ at cost★ on the balance sheet★.

Yield: Rate of return on investment (usually security). Interest★ or dividend★ for a year, divided by current market price.

Index

See also list of Abbreviations on page 205.

G *refers to an entry in the Glossary (pages 206 to 218).*

A-Adjustments G 124, 128, 140
Abbreviations (acronyms) 205
Accelerated depreciation 84
Accountants, characteristics of 7
Accounting 1
  as a profession 5
  Constant Purchasing Power (CPP) 119
  Conventions G 23
  Current Cost (CCA) 125
  Double-entry G 24, 63
  Financial G 3
  foundations of 21
  guidelines 22
  Inflation G 116
  Management G 4,163
  purpose of 22
Accounts G 7, 13
  Payable G 43
  Receivable G 47
Accruals Concept G 23
Accrued Charge G 43
Accumulated Depreciation G 44, 81, 88
Accuracy 5
Acid Test Ratio G 147
Acronyms (Abbreviations) 205
Action, management 174, 194
Additional statements 14
Alison Robbins example 10
Allocation (of cost) G 168
Amortisation G 45, 81
Analysing accounts 15, 68, 138
Annual General Meeting 39, 44
Appendix 1: Retail Price Index 204
Appendix 2: Professional bodies 204

Appendix 3: Abbreviations 205
Appropriation Account G 69
Asset G 13, 44
  Turnover G 146
  valuation 13
Associated Company G 46, 72
Associated Dairies (ASDA) 141
'Attributable profit' 107
Audit G 16, 24, 72
Auditor G 6, 165
Auditors' Report G 16
Authorised Share Capital G 39
Authors and budgets 195
Average Cost G 102, 168

Bad Debt G 64
B-Adjustments G 124, 128,140,150
Balance Sheet G 13, 36
  changes 26
  comparative figures 50
  format 13, 37
  and profit and loss account 60, 69
Bank Overdraft G 43
Bankers 3, 150
Bankruptcy G 23, 39, 42, 207
Beecham Group 50
Below the Line G 72
BOC International 41
Book-keeping G 7
Book Value G 45, 82
Borrowing: *see* Liability
Boycott's Last Innings 169
British Leyland 185
British Steel 17, 172

Budget   G 170
  cycle   170, 186
  periods   171, 174, 191
  using   141, 173
Budgetary control   171
Budgeting in action   186
Business transactions, recording   28

Capital   G 207
  Allowance   G 89
  Employed   G 48
  Expenditure   G 66
  gain   40, 60, 148
  maintenance   130
  and revenue   66
  Share: see Share Capital   G
  transactions   14, 28
Capitalise   G 82
Cash   G 47
  Discount   G 43
  Flow   G 89
  and liquid resources   47
  and profit   14, 88
  and reserves   41
Centre for Interfirm Comparison   195
Chairman's statement   15
Characteristics of accountants   7
Chopping up into short periods   4
Classifying costs   166
Combination of CCA and CPP   129
Communication   173
Companies' Acts   6, 16, 24
Company accounts   13, 16
Comparative figures   49
Comparisons   88, 140, 162
  over time   124, 127, 140, 150
Competitors   3
Computer accounting   165
Conservatism   23, 46, 61, 82, 97, 107
Consistency   G 23, 102
Consolidated Accounts   G 72
Constant Purchasing Power (CPP)   119
  Accounting   G 119
  basic rules   119
Consultative Committee of Accountancy Bodies (CCAB)   6
Contribution   G 168, 176
Control   G 164
  Budgetary   171
  Controllable   G 172
  Controlling   4, 187
  Conventions   G 23
  Convertible Loan   G 43
  Copyrights   45

Corporation Tax   G 44, 69
Cost   G 208
  Average   G 102, 168
  Benefit Analysis   G 165
  Centre   G 172
  classifying   166
  Controllable   G 172
  Direct   G 168
  discretionary   168
  Fixed   G 167
  of Goods Sold (COGS)   G 62, 98, 104
  Historical   G 24
  Indirect   G 168
  Marginal   G 105, 168
  and market value   97
  and net realisable value   97
  Non-controllable   G 172
  Non-variable   G 168
  Opportunity   G 43
  Overhead   G 66, 105
  Period   G 66
  Product   G 66
  -push Inflation   G 117
  Replacement   G 126
  of Sales Adjustment   G 126
  Semi-variable   G 167
  Standard   G 166
  Variable   G 167
Costs and budgets   163
Courtaulds   44
Credit Note   G 64
  sale   46
Creditors   G 42, 43
  views of   154
Critical Resource   G 171
Cumulative   G 41, 117, 174
Currency Debasement   G 117
Current Asset   G 46
  Cost Accounting (CCA)   G 119, 125
  Liabilities   G 43
  purchasing power accounting see: Constant Purchasing Power
  Ratio   G 147
  Value   G 13, 24, 119
Customers   3

Days' Sales in Debtors   G 146
Debenture   G 42
Debt ratio   147
Debtors   G 46, 146
Declining Balance Depreciation   G 84
  arguments for   85
Demand-pull Inflation   G 117
De minimis non curat lex   49

Index

Depreciation   G 66, 72, 80, 121
  accelerated   84
  Accumulated   G 44, 81, 88
  Declining Balance   G 84
  information required for   81
  Straight Line   G 83
  and tax   89
  Usage Method   G 87
Direct Cost   G 168
Directors' remuneration   72
  Report   G 15, 72
Disagreement and audit report   16
Disclosure   17, 25
  required   72
Discount, Cash   G 43
'Discretionary' costs   168
Disposal of fixed assets   87
Distribution of profit   40, 60
Dividend   G 39, 69
  Cover   G 148
  Final   G 44
  Interim   G 44
  payout ratio   148
  Per Share   G 148
  preference   41
  Yield   G 148
Divisional profit and loss report   173
Documents, design of   165
Donations   72
Double-entry Accounting   G 24, 25

Earnings Before Interest and Tax (EBIT)   146
Earnings Per Share (EPS)   G 148
Eastman Kodak   135
EBIT   146
Economic life of fixed asset   82, 88
Economies of Scale   G 169
Efficiency measures   146
Employees, needs of   3
  views of   155
Equity   G 13, 43, 142
European Economic Community   25
Exceptional Items   G 72, 87
Exchange Rate   G 42
Exchanging assets and liabilities   25
Expenditure   G 65
  Capital   G 66
  Revenue   G 66
Expense   G 210
  or asset?   65
  variances   176
Exposure Draft   G 25
External auditor: *see* Auditor   G

Extraordinary Items   G 72

Feedback   G 171
Final Dividend   G 44
Financial Accounting   G 3
  and management accounting   5, 105
  qualities needed   7
Financial
  fixed assets   46
  gearing   147
  statements   9
  Year   G 13, 150
Finished Goods   G 46, 103
First In First Out (FIFO)   G 100
Fixed Asset   G 14, 44
  Amortisation   G 81
  Depreciation   G 66, 80, 121
  disposal of   87
  valuation   40
Fixed Cost   G 167
Flexibility   174
Flexible Budget   G 174, 176
Flows and stocks   10
Following the Woodcraft trail   193
Foreign currency borrowing   42
  concept   120
'Foreseeable losses'   107
Format, Horizontal   G 13, 26, 37
  Vertical   G 38, 48
Formula for declining balance depreciation   85
Foundations of accounting   21
Francs: Belgian, French and Swiss   120
Full Costing   G 105
Fundamental accounting concepts   22
Funds analysis   151
  Flow Statement   G 16, 151

Gearing   G 211
  adjustment   126
  and liquidity measures   142, 147
  Ratio   G 147
General Electric Company   135
General Electric (US)   171
General Motors   49
German hyper-inflation   119
Gilbert Ltd. example   167
GKN 139,   150
Glossary   206–18
Goethe   24
Going Concern   G 23
Goods returned   64
Goodwill   G 45
Government   3, 23

Index

Gregorian calendar change 13
Group Accounts G 72
Guidelines, accounting 22

Haircut example 168
'Half-life' of the pound 118
Hamilton Pumps example 143
Hampton CPP example 121
Hayek, Professor F. A. 118
Historical Cost (HC) G 13, 24
Horizontal Format G 13, 26, 37
Hotel full of different guests 48
Hyper-inflation, German 119

Imperial Chemical Industries 88, 128
Indexation G 130
Indirect Cost G 168
Inflation G 117, 204
   Accounting G 40, 116, 150
Information management 164
Inland Revenue
   and accounts 122
   and depreciation 89
   and LIFO stock valuation 101
Insider questions 2
Institute of Chartered Accountants 6, 131
Intangible Asset G 81
   fixed asset 45
Interest G 68
   Cover G 147
   rates 42
Inter-firm comparisons 140, 150, 195
Interim Accounts G 7
   Dividend G 44
Internal Auditor G 7
Internally-generated cash flow 151
Inventory G 46
Investment income 46, 72
Invoice G 64, 165
Issued Share Capital G 39, 148

Judgement 22, 150

'Key result' areas 172

Laker Airways 43
Last In First Out (LIFO) G 100, 121
Learning Curve G 170
Legal and other requirements 24
Lenders, needs of 3
   views of 154
Liabilities G 13, 42
LIBOR 42
Life of fixed asset 82, 88

Limited Company G 3
   liability 39
Limiting factor 171
Liquidation G 23, 39, 42
Liquidity G 37, 142, 147, 153
Liquid Resources G 47
Listed companies 25, 39
Lives of fixed assets 82, 88
Local community 3
Long Run G 170
Long-term contracts 106
   Liability G 14
Loss G 14, 60
Lower of cost and market value 97
Luck 175

MacGregor, Mr. Ian 172
Machine-hour method of depreciation 87
Maintaining control 155
Management accountant 196
   characteristics of 7
   qualities needed 7
Management Accounting G 4, 163
   details included 4, 68
   and financial accounting 5, 105
Management action 174, 194
   information 164, 192
   needs 173
Managing director's liver 24
Manufacturing stocks 103
Marginal Costing G 105, 168
Margin of error 24, 139, 150
Market trader example 10
   value 39, 97, 148
Mary Mullins example 65
Master Budget G 170
Matching Principle G 46, 65, 81, 106
Measuring inflation 117
Methods of depreciation 83
   identifying stock 100
Minority Interests G 72
Monetary Asset/Liability G 121
   Gain/Loss G 123
   Working Capital Adjustment 126
Money as common denominator 10, 119
Monthly accounts 171
Motivation and budgets 172

National Coal Board 172
   government 3
Negative profit 14, 60
   retained profits 40, 69
Net Assets G 48
Net Book Value G 82, 85

Index

Net Current Assets   G 48
Net Realisable Value   G 97
Nil variance drama   195
Nominal Value   G 39, 213
Non-controllable   G 172
Non-operating income   46, 72
Non-profit entities   23, 171
Non-variable Cost   G 168
Notes to the Accounts   G 14, 48

Objectives of budgets   171, 187
Obsolescence   82, 88
Old Mistresses example   111
Operating expenses   65, 67
Opportunity Cost   G 43, 214
Ordinary Share Capital   G 39
Outsider questions   2
Overdraft, Bank   G 43
Overhead Cost   G 66, 105
Owners' Equity   G 13

Partnership   G 39
Part-years   88
Patents, copyrights and trade marks   45
Performance appraisal   174
 measures   142, 146
Period Cost   G 66, 106
Petty Cash   G 47
Physical stock   97, 146
Planning   4, 164, 187
Plant and equipment   45
Practical training   7
'Practice'   6
Preference Share Capital   G 41
Preparing budgets   170
Prepayment   G 47
Presentation   47, 67
Previous year figures   50
Price/Earnings (P/E) Ratio   G 148
Price Variance   G 175
Primary efficiency ratio   146, 216
Problems in measuring sales   63
 in using ratios   150
Problem-solving   4
Product Cost   G 66, 106
Production overheads   66, 105
Professional bodies   5, 204
 qualifications   204
Profit   G 4
 and assets employed   139
 and cash flow   14, 88
 Centre   G 172
 on disposal of fixed assets   87
 estimates   174, 188

Margin   G 141, 146
 Retained   G 40, 60, 69, 121, 148
 and stock valuation   98
Profit and Loss Account   G 14, 59, 68
 and balance sheet   60, 69
 format   67, 70
Property   45
Prudence   G 23, 46, 61, 82, 97, 107
Public Limited Company (plc) G 39
Published Accounts   G 7, 49, 161
Purchasing Power   G 117
Purpose of accounting   22
Pyramid of Ratios   G 192

Qualified Accountant   G 5, 204
 Audit Report   G 16
Qualities needed for accounting   7
Quick Assets   G 147
Quoted companies   25, 39

Racal Electronics   40
Rank Organisation   71
Ratio Analysis   G 139
Ratios, Pyramid of   G 192
 summarised   149
Raw Materials   G 46, 103
Realisable value   97
Realisation   G 23, 61
'Real' terms   G 120
'Recognising' a sale in accounts   61
Recording business transactions   28
Replacement Cost   G 126
Research and development costs   45
Reserves   G 40
 and cash   41
Residual Value   G 82
Responsibility for budgets   172
 centres   172
Retail Price Index (RPI)   G 117, 204
Retained Profits (earnings)   G 40, 60, 69, 121, 148
Return on Equity   G 148
 on Investment (ROI)   121, 139, 153, 189
 on Net Assets   G 139, 146, 162, 192
Revaluation   G 40, 87
 Reserve   G 40, 87
Revaluing fixed assets   40, 87
Revenue   G 216
 and capital   66
 Centre   G 172
 Expenditure   G 66
 Sales   G 14, 60
 transactions   28
Revising asset lives   88

Index

Rip Van Winkle   123
Risk   142, 147
Rolling Budget   G 171
Rouding numbers   49

Sainsbury   141
Sales Revenue   G 14, 60, 150
   variances   175
Sandilands Committee   130
Scale, Economies of   G 169
Score-keeping   4
'Second-hand' market for shares   39
Secured Loan   G 42
Selling costs   66
Semi-variable Cost   G 167
Separate entity convention   23
Seven Days in May example   34
Share Capital   39
Shareholders   G 2, 27
   measures   142, 148
   return   40, 60, 148
   views of   148, 153
Shareholders' Funds   G 13, 39, 120
   changes in   27
Share Premium   G 40
Shares   G 27
Short Run   G 170
Spot the Industry example   201
Spurious accuracy   49, 166, 173
SSAPs   G 5, 17, 25
SSAP 16: Current Cost Accounting   131
Standards for comparison   49, 140, 164, 174, 192
Standard Cost   G 166, 168
Statements of Standard Accounting Practice (SSAPs)   G 5, 17, 25
Statistical tables   15, 49
Stewardship   G 3
Stock Appreciation   G 102, 216
   Exchange   G 25, 148
   Relief   G 102, 217
   Turnover   G 146
   valuation   96, 102
Stocks   G 46
   and flows   10
Straight Line Depreciation   G 83
Subsidiary   G 46, 72
Sum-of-the-years Digits   G 87, 217
Suppliers, needs of   3
   views of   154
Survival   4

Tangible fixed assets   45
Taxable Profit   G 69, 101, 217
Taxation   G 44, 69, 122

Tax year end   13
Tesco   141
Thompson Brothers example   28
Trade Investment   G 46, 72
   marks   45
Trading Account   G 67
Transactions, recording   26, 28
Transfer Price   G 166
Trend   G 16, 140, 174
Trendy Footwear example   98
True and Fair View   G 7, 16, 22, 24, 198
'True worth'   37
Turnover   G 60, 217

Uncertainty and audit report   16
Uniformity   162
Unilever   24
Unit of Account   G 5, 10, 24, 119
University study and accounting   7
Unlimited liability   39
Usage Method of Depreciation   G 87
Users of accounts   1
Using budgets   141, 173
   ratios   139

Value Added   G 61, 107, 218
Value Added Tax (VAT)   63
Valuing stock   96
Variable Cost   G 167
Variable-rate loans   42
Variance   G 174
   Analysis   G 141, 175, 191
'Venture accounting'   3
Vertical Format   G 38, 48
Video-taping market trader   10
Volume Variance   G 175
Vosper   17, 139

Wear and tear   82
Winding-up   G 4
Woodcraft example   187, 193
Workers, needs of   3
   views of   155
Working Capital   G 48, 153
   cycle   47
Work-in-Progress (WIP)   G 46, 103, 107
Write Off   G 66

Yield   G 218
   Dividend   G 148

Zero book value   82, 86, 88